RUSSIAN LITERATURE, 1995–2002:
ON THE THRESHOLD OF THE NEW MILLENNIUM

Writers have a difficult time making a living in contemporary Russia. Market-driven publishing companies have pushed serious domestic prose to the fringes of their output and few people have money to buy books. The disintegration of the Soviet Union in 1991 led Russian society to become polarized between an increasingly prosperous minority and a very poor majority. This divide is mirrored in the writing community, with some writers supporting conservative, nationalist pro-Soviet thinking, and others, liberal, democratic, pro-Western thought.

N.N. Shneidman, in the tradition of his previous volumes – *Soviet Literature in the 1970s, Soviet Literature in the 1980s,* and *Russian Literature, 1988–1994* – investigates the Russian literary scene with special emphasis on the relationship between thematic substance and the artistic quality of recently published prose. Shneidman argues convincingly that, despite the many challenges besetting it, literary activity in Russia continues to be dynamic and vibrant. The future development of Russian literature may depend on general economic, political, and social factors, but a new generation of talented writers is fast moving past older forms of ideology and embracing new ways of thinking about Russia.

N.N. SHNEIDMAN is a professor emeritus in the Department of Slavic Languages and Literatures at the University of Toronto.

N.N. Shneidman

Russian Literature, 1995–2002:

On the Threshold of the New Millennium

UNIVERSITY OF TORONTO PRESS
Toronto   Buffalo   London

ISBN 0-8020-8724-8 (cloth)
ISBN 0-8020-8670-5 (paper)

Printed on acid-free paper

National Library of Canada Cataloguing in Publication

Shneidman, N.N.
Russian literature, 1995–2002 : on the threshold of the new
millennium / N.N. Shneidman.

Includes bibliographical references and index.
ISBN 0-8020-8724-8 (bound). – ISBN 0-8020-8670-5 (pbk.)

1. Russian fiction – 20th century – History and criticism.   I. Title.

PG3098.4.S553 2004   891.73'509   C2004-901461-7

University of Toronto Press acknowledges the financial assistance to its
publishing program of the Canada Council for the Arts and the Ontario
Arts Council.

This book has been published with the help of a grant from the Canadian
Federation for the Humanities and Social Sciences, through the Aid to
Scholarly Publications Programme, using funds provided by the Social
Sciences and Humanities Research Council of Canada.

University of Toronto Press acknowledges the financial support for its publishing activities of the Government of Canada through the Book Publishing
Industry Development Program (BPIDP).

Contents

Preface   vii

1 Russian Literature and Society on the Threshold of
   the New Millennium   3

2 The Seniors' Prose   29

3 The Mature Generation   52

4 The New Writers of the *Perestroika* Era   80

5 Women Writers   111

6 The Writers of the Conservative 'Patriotic' Camp   133

7 The Mystery Novel Writers   154

8 The New Names of 1995–2002   165

Conclusion   182

Notes   185
Bibliography   193
Index   201

Preface

The end of the twentieth century was marked by the change of political leadership in Russia, and a certain stabilization of the political and economic situation in the country. Literature, culture, and the press have been affected by these changes in many different ways. The privatization of most means of literary production and distribution have made possible the appearance of works by many new aspiring writers and poets. The glut of new works on the market, however, has hardly improved the artistic quality of the prose published. Moreover, business interests rather than creative accomplishment have determined, in most instances, publication policy.

The purpose of this study, which is intended as a sequel to my *Russian Literature, 1988–1994: The End of an Era* (Toronto 1995), is to investigate the current Russian literary scene and to provide a general survey of Russian prose published between 1995 and 2002. This study is limited in scope and it is impossible to discuss here the works of all Russian authors active today. My selection of narratives has been determined by the artistic and social relevance of the works analysed, and it is representative of contemporary Russian literature in general. I discuss only works of prose written in the Russian language and published in Russia proper, by authors currently residing in the country. The only exceptions are the novels of Chingiz Aitmatov, who is presently a Kirghiz diplomat in Belgium, and of Mikhail Shishkin, who was awarded the 2000 Booker Russian Novel Prize and is currently residing in Switzerland.

The political contention between former Soviet official writers and those exiled and residing in the West has been, with the collapse of the Soviet state, muffled. All the same, the creative process is undeniably influenced by one's place of residence and life experience. Thus, the works of many former émigré writers, such as Aleksandr Solzhenitsyn, Georgii Vladimov, or Eduard Limonov, who have recently returned and settled in Russia, still bear the mark of emigration. Similarly, works by writers such as Leonid Girshovich and Dina Rubin, who live abroad, or even the novels of Vasilii Aksenov and Vladimir Voinovich, who divide their time between the West and Russia, do not tend to reflect the constantly changing situation in Russia today.

It is difficult to categorize contemporary Russian literature. In addition to the split between the liberal writers and those belonging to the conservative 'patriotic' camp, there is an overlapping of themes, styles, and genres in most contemporary works. Moreover, different generations of contemporary Russian writers have been influenced by diverse and changing political, ideological, and educational conditions. It is clear that life experience and education have affected the creative output of various authors in different ways. Hence, I have for the most part employed a generational approach to this study of contemporary literature, which in current circumstances appears to be the most appropriate.

Chapter 1 provides a general overview of the political, economic, and social atmosphere in the country, with particular reference to its impact on literary production. It discusses, among other things, the book publishing business, the strife in the writers' community, and the current Russian literary scene more generally. Chapter 2 examines the prose of senior authors, veterans of Soviet and Russian literature, who are presently over seventy, as well as of those who have died in the last few years. This list includes Aleksandr Solzhenitsyn, Viktor Astaf'ev, Anatolii Azol'skii, and a few others. Chapter 3 focuses on the prose of members of the mature generation, those who are today mainly in their late fifties and sixties. Detailed attention is paid to the works of Vladimir Makanin, Anatolii Kim, Boris Ekimov, and Eduard Limonov, among others. Chapter 4 investigates the literary development of writers such as Iurii Buida, Mikhail Butov, Valentin Pelevin, Vladimir Sorokin, and others whose works first appeared in print in Russia in the days of *perestroika*. Chapter 5 explores the works of women writers, including Tat'iana Tolstaia, Irina Polianskaia, and Liudmila Ulitskaia. Chapter 6 deals with the prose of writers belonging to the conservative 'patriotic' camp. Chapter 7 discusses the works of contemporary mystery novel authors, and chapter 8 investigates those writers who published their first significant works between 1995 and 2002: Oleg Pavlov, Andrei Dmitriev, Andrei Volos, Dmitrii Lipskerov, Anton Utkin, and Sergei Gandlevskii, among others.

This study is expository in nature, investigating artistic and social issues in an integrated manner. Some of the works discussed might have been written prior to 1995, but most were published in Russia between 1995 and 2002. All translations from Russian, unless quoted from English sources, are my own, and I have adopted here, with minor exceptions, the widely used transliteration system of the Library of Congress. At first mention, titles are given in Russian, with an English translation in parentheses; in subsequent references, they are given only in Russian.

I would like to acknowledge my debt, and express my gratitude, to all those who helped me in the course of my work on this study, but I accept sole responsibility for any inaccuracies and mistakes that may persist. Special thanks are due to the Department of Slavic Languages and Literatures, University of Toronto, for the generous support of my research.

N.N. SHNEIDMAN
June 2003
Toronto, Canada

RUSSIAN LITERATURE, 1995–2002:
ON THE THRESHOLD OF THE NEW MILLENNIUM

1

Russian Literature and Society on the Threshold of the New Millennium

The 1980s were a decade of turbulence and transition in Soviet domestic life and foreign policy. The ascent of Mikhail Gorbachev to power in 1985, and the introduction of the policies of *glasnost'* and *perestroika*, undermined the ideological and political control of the Communist Party and destabilized the Soviet system of government and its planned economy. The upheavals that followed, including the failed anti-Gorbachev coup d'état in August 1991, led to the disintegration of the Soviet Union and the creation of a Commonwealth of Independent States, composed of most of the former Soviet Union republics. The year 1992 marked the beginning of a new era in Russia. Still a multicultural state comprising many autonomous national regions, but without the former Soviet Union republics, the Russian Federation began its painful transition from a planned socialist to a market economy, and from totalitarianism to democracy.

The road from communism to democracy, however, is full of seemingly insurmountable obstacles. Most Russian citizens have no former experience of life in a society with a market economy. Moreover, they have little tolerance for the newly created allegedly democratic institutions, and no respect for the new government and the state bureaucracy, which is inefficient, abusive, and corrupt. Russia is currently one of the most corrupt nations in the world.[1] The privatization of state property in the early 1990s, under the leadership of President Boris Yeltsin, led to social polarization. The rapid economic reforms created two classes of 'new Russians,' the rich and the poor. Today, close to half of the national wealth in Russia is controlled by no more than 10 per cent of Russia's citizens, and the living standard of close to half of the population is below the poverty line.

Early in 2000 Vladimir Putin became president of the Russian Federation, selected to this position by Yeltsin and his close associates. Since he was appointed heir to Yeltsin by the very people who founded the current economic system, and were interested in preserving it, Putin could do little to invigorate the Russian economy. Instead, he concentrated on strengthening his domination over political life in the country, and on the consolidation of power and control in the hands of the Kremlin. Thus, Putin's government assumed control of most independent television stations and much of the print media, and introduced new laws which restricted considerably freedom of expression.

Today, at the beginning of the new millennium, the situation in Russia continues to be volatile. Some positive legislative achievements have been made in the economic field, but the independence and stability of most political parties and social institutions, including the judiciary, may still be questioned. Crime, alcoholism, and narcotic addiction are on the rise. The black market accounts for 25 per cent of the total Russian economic output, and only close to half of all taxes are collected. Furthermore, the Russian criminal underground has infiltrated all levels of economic and state activity, and has become an integral part of the developing Russian 'democratic' system. In addition, the war in Chechnia, to which there is yet no end in sight, places a great strain on government resources and makes political and economic reforms even more difficult.

Capitalism in Russia currently takes the form of a sharply distorted economy in which commodities export and the import of consumer goods prevail. While this situation may appear dire, there is no well-developed political movement to take advantage of it. Most Russians are apathetic, tired of political bickering, and continue to believe that a strong leader may find a solution to Russia's problems. In any event, only 5 per cent of respondents to a poll conducted by the Russian Public Opinion Centre chose European society as a model for the development of Russia. Twenty per cent favoured a return to communism, and 60 per cent said that the country should follow its own unique path.[2]

The transition to a market economy and full-fledged democracy in Russia is clearly still in its early stages, and the process is slow and agonizing. In all likelihood it will take years, if not generations, before Russia's political and social institutions, as well as most citizens of the Russian Federation, will be ready and able to adapt to the requirements of life in this new social environment. The possibility of change will be determined not by economic development alone; it will also be conditioned by a shift in the mentality of the populace, and by the acceptance of a new set of social, moral, and ethical democratic values. Along with economic growth, culture, literature, the arts, and the media have an important role to play in this social and intellectual transformation.

Literary Politics and the Writers' Unions

Literature as a form of art always reflects, to some degree, the social, political, and economic reality in which it is created. An artist in a free society can use his or her creative imagination to venture beyond the immediate realm of personal experience, yet even one's subconscious and imaginative faculties are rooted in the real world and nurtured by past experiences or experimental knowledge. In the Soviet days many writers and poets refused to succumb to the pressures of the Soviet regime and preferred to go into hiding underground. Even they, however, could not avoid the effects of their life experience, and their Soviet background, because that was the only reality they knew. Most contemporary Russian writers are likewise the product of Soviet upbringing and education, and the current changes in their mentality, brought about under the influence of the new social environment in which they work, are still in the early stages of development.

A decade after the collapse of the Soviet state, the life of most individual Russians has changed drastically, and members of the creative intelligentsia in general, and of the writers' community in particular, struggle to survive in the new social and economic conditions. Thus, the creative output of most contemporary writers reflects not only their artistic approach to literature, but their ideological, political, and social attitudes to the new Russian state as well. In the late Soviet era there were two distinct streams of literature: official Soviet literature and underground, anti-Soviet *samizdat* and *tamizdat* literature. In the USSR Soviet underground literature was taboo, but it was published, recognized, and studied in the West, regardless of its artistic merit.

Today, there are similarly two divergent ideological literary streams in Russia. One includes all liberal writers, regardless of their artistic inclinations; the other incorporates all Russian conservative, 'patriotic' writers. Since there is no censorship in Russia, and the country currently has a multi-party political system, the literature of both streams is published without interference from, or censorship by, state authorities. The literature of each stream has its own readership, and representatives of the two groups criticize and attack each other on political and ideological grounds. Most western Slavists and literary scholars ignore the literature of Russian 'patriotic' writers, despite the fact that this literature represents an important social and cultural, albeit not artistic, phenomenon.

The ideological split between the conservatives and liberals is reflected in the organizational framework of the writers' community, and in the establishment of two antagonistic writers' unions. In the Soviet days the Writers' Union was a professional organization, and an arm of the Communist Party. It was in control of the creative output of its members and in charge of literary production in the USSR. The disintegration of the Soviet Union brought into the open ideological dissent in the writers' community and led to the break-up of the former Writers' Union. In January 1992, two new bodies were formed to replace it, the International Commonwealth of Unions of Writers and the International Association of Writers' Unions. These allegedly international organizations were composed of writers' unions from the former Soviet union republics, currently independent states.

The former RSFSR Writers' Union likewise split into two independent antagonistic organizations: the Russian Union of Writers and the Union of Russian Writers. The Moscow, St Petersburg, and provincial writers' unions split in the same manner as well. The break-up of the RSFSR Writers' Union was caused by deep ideological discord, and by the extreme views of some of its members. The new Union of Writers of the Russian Federation is conservative, nationalistic, pro-Slavic, anti-Western, and claims affinity to the Russian historical heritage and the Russian Orthodox Church. Vasilii Belov, Iurii Bondarev, Vladimir Krupin, Vladimir Lichutin, Aleksandr Prokhanov, and Valentin Rasputin, as well as a number of young writers, primarily from the provinces, belong to this conservative union.

The newly formed Union of Russian Writers, by contrast, while it adheres to old Russian cultural values, is also liberal, democratic, pro-Western, and supports freedom of expression, human rights, and political reform. Andrei Bitov, Viktor Erofeev, Evgenii Evtushenko, and Vladmir Makanin, among others, and again, many writers of the younger generation, belong to this liberal union. The conservative and liberal unions have separate offices and publish distinct periodicals and newspapers. Thus, the monthlies *Nash sovremennik* (Our Contemporary) and *Molodaia gvardiia* (Young Guard), and the weekly *Literaturnaia Rossiia* (Literary Russia) are edited and published by members of the conservative Russian Writers' Union. The periodical newspaper *Den' literatury* (The Day of Literature), edited by Vladimir Bondarenko, also supports the agenda of the conservative 'patriotic' camp. The journal *Moskva* (Moscow), edited by Leonid Borodin, promotes a Christian Orthodox program. Most other mainstream periodicals are controlled by liberals or independent editors uninterested in political wrangling. Up until May 2001 *Literaturnaia gazeta* (Literary Gazette) mainly expressed views in support of the liberal camp. After the appointment of Iurii Poliakov as editor-in-chief, however, the weekly paper began to advocate the reunification of the two writers' unions, and opened its pages to conservative nationalistic writers as well.

In the Soviet era being a member of the Writers' Union was a privilege which provided with prestige and many material and social benefits. Today, membership in a union may provide professional status, but no employment or pension benefits. Many writers are annoyed by this situation. Thus the well-known writer Oleg Pavlov asserts that 'not one of the writers' unions is a union of toilers. The present unions are branches of political movements. All they dream about is a return to power and reinstating their former privileges. In the meantime literary work in Russia is equal to slave labour. There is no protection for the author's copyrights ... and no way to keep in check the publishing monopoly which brought down the writers' pay to a level below the poverty line.'[3]

Despite the difficult economic situations of most individual Russian writers, the ideological squabbles and hostility between the two writers' unions continue. Moreover, there is internal strife and disagreement within each union. In the old tradition the Tenth Congress of the Russian Writers' Union took place in Moscow in 1999. The speeches at the Congress were mostly concerned with ideological and nationalistic issues. According to Vasilii Belov, foreign influence now poses the greatest danger to Russia, because it is similar to that which destroyed Yugoslavia. 'Foreign influence' refers primarily to the infiltration of the Latin script in advertisements and television programs. Valentin Rasputin, on the other hand, declares in a tone of alarm that 'before our eyes a second revolution is taking place in Russia, one which is more terrifying and destructive than the first one.'[4]

Despite the ideological rift in the Russian literary community, efforts have recently been made to patch up the differences between the various unions and to form a joint writers' organization with a common platform. This is essential in order to gain access to the Russian state administration, to reclaim the property of the former Soviet Writers' Union, and to wage battle for the improvement of the economic conditions and political rights of Russian writers. It appears, however, that the ideological schism is so deep, and the animosity and mutual hate so intense, that no rapprochement is currently possible. In view of the above it has been suggested that for purely economic reasons an All-Russian Writers' Union, in the form of an association composed of the separate writers' unions, be created. This new organization would become the sole inheritor of all the property which previously belonged to the former USSR Writers' Union. The liberal Union of Russian Writers sent an open letter to the Tenth Congress of the Conservative Russian Writers' Union, proposing to establish such an association. Unfortunately, no relevant decision has been adopted at the Congress, and no reunification is imminent.[5] Early in May 1999 the Second Congress of the liberal Union of Russian Writers took place in Moscow. Delegates from sixty regions, representing a total membership of 3,500, participated in the gathering. The tone of the speeches at the Congress was measured, and the subject of presentations was mostly professional.

Two years later, when much of the USSR Writers' Union property had already been squandered, a new open letter calling for the unification of the diverse unions appeared in the press. It was signed by Sergei Mikhalkov, the chairman of the International Commonwealth of Writers' Unions; the editors of *Literaturnaia gazeta*, *Literaturnaia Rossiia*, and *Roman-gazeta* (Novel-Newspaper); and the director of the '*Sovetskii pisatel*' (Soviet Writer) publishing house.[6] Reaction to the proposed merger by most members of both unions was negative. Everyone agreed that it would be feasible to form an association which would give writers a unified voice in their struggle for better living, working, and publication conditions without infringing on the political and ideological activities of the various unions. In answer to the question of whether the unification of the two writers' unions is essential, Rasputin stated bluntly that he could not imagine himself as a member of a creative union to which Evtushenko and Iurii Chernichenko belonged.[7]

The internal strife in the Russian litterary community, and the extreme ideological views expressed in various literary journals, are a reflection of the current political and intellectual situation in Russia. In the late 1980s and early 1990s ideological dissension within the writers' community assumed political form and many writers became directly involved in political activity. One of Russia's better-known writers, former émigré Eduard Limonov, even became the organizer and leader of the anti-government National-Bolshevik Party, and was put in jail for allegedly buying and illegally storing arms.

Most conservative writers limit their anti-government activities to public appearances, journalism, and biased fiction. They express extreme chauvinistic, nationalistic, even fascist views. Moreover, they call for the formulation of a new Russian national 'idea' to replace the communist ideology of the Soviet era. This 'idea' would have to express, of course, the messianic role of Russia and its unique path of development. In the nineteenth century the 'messianic component' of the Russian 'idea' produced the two extremes of Bolshevism and pan-Slavism. Both preached national unity with no room for dissent. Today, those advocating the renewal of the old ideals are mainly nativist, xenophobic, and militant isolationists. They form new alliances in which neo-Stalinist communists, crude xenophobes, and sophisticated nationalists join hands with religious conservatives in the struggle for power, as well as for the hearts and minds of the Russian people.[8]

Among the anti-democratic writers of the conservative 'patriotic' camp stand out authors formerly identified with Soviet 'village prose.' Rooted in the Russian native soil movement and Slavophilism, these writers defended the patriarchal character of the Russian village and opposed the intrusion of city culture and technological progress into the Russian countryside. Today writers such as Belov and Rasputin are particularly active in preaching their adherence to the Russian Ortho-dox Church, and they claim that Russian Orthodoxy should be part of the new national ideal. In a lengthy article in which the 'patriotic' principles of contemporary Russian culture are expressed, Kapitolina Koksheneva writes that 'the conservatives have always asserted that the essence of Russianness was determined by faith – Russian Ortho-dox faith ... The creative work of Russian writers always expressed the national relation to life ... Conservative writers believe in personality, liberal writers believe in individualism.'[9]

It is well known that in tsarist Russia religious practice was in most instances an expression of faith. Today, on the other hand, it is rather an expression of adherence to old traditions, and of a need to fill a vac-uum created by the dissolution of the Soviet state and the abolition of Marxist atheistic ideology. Some join the church in Russia for religious reasons, but many are impelled by social and educational consider-ations. Indeed, many of the current religious nationalists were, just a decade ago, card-carrying members of the Communist Party, and one may suspect that there is a pinch of hypocrisy in the rapid transformation of their *Weltanschauung*. Systems of government, even social structures, may change over night, but the nature of people, their mentality and psychological make-up, change very slowly, if at all.

At the time of Yeltsin's rule the ideological leaders of the conservative right and the writers of the 'patriotic' camp were regularly ignored by the government establishment. With the ascent of Vladimir Putin, however, there have been visible attempts of a rapprochement between the far right and Putin's administration. On 10 August 2000 Putin received in his office the writer and editor of the rabidly anti-Western and anti-government weekly *Zavtra* (Tomorrow), Aleksandr Prokhanov, and the editor of the pro-communist newspaper *Sovetskaia Rossiia* (Soviet Russia), Valentin Chikin. After the meeting both editors endorsed the leadership of Putin in their newspapers.

The Literary Scene

In general terms, the current Russian literary scene is paradoxical. The number of writers and titles published increases regularly, but the number of readers of serious prose, and the artistic quality of most narratives published, are in decline. A number of interrelated causes shape the current complex state of affairs in Russian literature. First, the difficult economic situation affects both readers and writers. The reader who has little money to buy books turns away from serious prose and spends his or her cash on pulp literature which is entertaining and easy to follow. The writer who is unable to sell the product of his or her labour often stops writing serious fiction and starts producing detective novels.

The pressure of the market, however, affects even those writers who stick to their old trade. Since publication honorariums are small, and royalties are low, very few authors can survive and support their families on the income generated from writing serious prose. Hence, most writers are forced to supplement their income by working as journalists, translators, or editors and have little time to perfect their artistic craft. Much of the literature currently on the market is thus hastily produced and superficial, especially the works of authors lacking a vivid imagination and of members of the younger generation with inadequate life experience.

The decline in the artistic quality of the literature published in the second half of the 1990s can also be attributed to other causes. In the days of *perestroika*, and in the immediate post-Soviet years, a number of new names appeared on the literary scene. Some of these new authors perfected their works in the underground for years before they could publish them officially. Still others mastered one theme, which has recently exhausted itself, and are currently unable to diversify their creative range. Many of these writers continue to publish, but they produce mediocre texts which fail to satisfy the high expectations of either readers or critics. The early works by authors such as Viacheslav P'etsukh, Anatolii Gavrilov, Valeriia Narbikova, Andrei Korolev, or Aleksandr Lavrin, for example, were much better than their recent publications. There are also authors of well-known narratives, writers of the mature and older generation, who currently rest on their laurels and produce little of any significance. They are satisfied with reputations established many years ago. Andrei Bitov, Ruslan Kireev, and Mikhail Kuraev, among others, belong to this group. The current quality of Russian literature is also influenced by the conscious decision of a number of writers to become involved in practical endeavours not directly related to literature or the arts. Thus, for example, Belov and Rasputin have turned their main attention to political activity, Krupin has become a Russian Orthodox educator, and Anatolii Pristavkin is now an important government bureaucrat.

The current Russian literary scene has also been affected, perhaps more than at any other time, by the shift of generations. The past few years have witnessed the passing of a number of well-known, prolific Russian prose writers whose names and works are closely connected with the Soviet era. Most prominent among them are the former editor of *Novyi mir* (New World), Sergei Zalygin (1913–2000); the editor of *Oktiabr'* (October), Anatolii Anan'ev (1925–2001); Viktor Astaf'ev (1924–2001); I. Grekova (1907–2002); Iurii Davydov (1924–2002); Evgenii Nosov (1924–2002); Petr Proskurin (1928–2001); Vladimir Kornilov (1928–2002); Fridrikh Gorenshtein (1932–2002); and Andrei Sergeev (1933–98), among others.

In addition, many writers of the older generation, as well as those connected with the spirit of the so-called *shestidesiatniki*, or those who have matured in the period of post-Stalin thaws, are now in their late sixties and seventies, and produce little work of literary merit. Representatives of former Soviet war prose Grigorii Baklanov and Iurii Bondarev belong to this group. The former so-called *sorokaletnie*, which include writers such as Anatolii Kim, Anatolii Kurchatkin, and Bitov, are in their late fifties and sixties. They are torn between old values and a new reality, and their slowly diminishing output is in most instances below the level of their earlier works in substance and spirit. Hence, most literature published in Russia today is written by those who are in their thirties, forties, and early fifties and who entered the literary scene during the years of *perestroika* and in the post-Soviet era. Mikhail Butov, Oleg Ermakov, Aleksandr Ivanchenko, Aleksandr Kabakov, Sergei Kaledin, Valeriia Narbikova, Marina Palei, Viktor Pelevin, Viacheslav P'etsukh, Irina Polianskaia, Nina Sadur, Mikhail Shishkin, Aleksei Slapovskii, Vladimir Sorokin, Aleksandr Terekhov, Tat'iana Tolstaia, Liudmila Ulitskaia, among others, emerged on the scene in the decade between 1985 and 1995. Most of these writers continue to be active and publish regularly. Some, however, like Ivanchenko, Terekhov, or Narbikova, published little of literary substance in the second half of the 1990s. Among the new names of the late 1990s it is necessary to single out Andrei Dmitriev, Sergei Gandlevskii, Dmitrii Lipskerov, Nikolai Kononov, Oleg Pavlov, Ol'ga Slavnikova, Andrei Utkin, and Marina Vishnevetskaia. The writers who made their debut in print in the second half of the 1990s are thematically and artistically diverse. This diversity ranges from Slavnikova's traditional realism, to Lipskerov's narratives steeped in fantasy, to Kononov's poetic prose and emphasis on the psychological investigation of his characters.

The appearance of a great number of new authors whose creative personalities began to take shape in the post-Soviet era has had both a positive and a negative effect on the quality of contemporary Russian prose. The new authors have widened the thematic and artistic range of contemporary Russian literature, but lack of training and professional guidance adversely affects the language and style of many of them. Moreover, it curtails their ability to utilize a variety of artistic devices, stripping their texts of poignancy and depth. It appears that in current Russian conditions, when creative freedom knows no bounds and editorial guidance is at a premium, talent, and especially self-discipline, which many young writers are lacking, become of utmost importance.

The 1990s was, perhaps, the first decade in Russian literary history that did not produce either a single great new writer or a work of prose which could be placed among the recognized classics. The novel in Russia is no longer a carefully constructed artistic edifice, but rather a haphazard collage, written, in most instances, in poor literary Russian and littered with slang and foreign words. The structure of this novel is loose, and there is seldom psychological exploration of the reasons which motivate human action. Characterization in the novel is shunned, and direct speech and Aesopian language are replaced with the play of words and experimentation with various styles. The modern hero is often characterized by a sick imagination and morbid fantasy. Moreover, most novels lack depth. Thus, while popular narratives by authors such as V. Pelevin, for example, may be innovative, topical, and possess some dramatic intensity, they lack atmosphere, sincerity, and depth.

Contemporary Russian prose defies classification. Neither the thematic, generic, artistic, or generational approaches could cover the range of literature under discussion in an acceptable manner. In the Soviet days there was a clear divide between different thematic literary streams – city prose, youth prose, village prose, war prose, and the labour and historical themes – and the writers' community was divided along similar lines. Today, authors write on similar subjects, but the demarcation lines are no longer there, and a thematic and stylistic overlapping prevails in many contemporary novels. Moreover, when one compares the current prose with that of the Soviet period it becomes clear that, despite thematic similarity, the recent political, economic, and social changes have affected the essence of the subjects discussed. Thus, while the old themes remain, the methods and substance of portrayal have evolved to reflect the new reality. For example, the former Second World War theme in Soviet literature initially evolved into novels and stories about the war in Afghanistan, by writers such as Ermakov and Prokhanov. Recently, the war theme has shifted to portrayal of the Russian military debacle in Chechnia.

Russian 'village prose,' as it was defined in the Brezhnev era, likewise no longer exists. Belov and Rasputin still occasionally write about life in the Russian countryside, but the Russian village described in their works of the 1960s and 1970s has changed beyond recognition. Mass migration, transformation of the means and methods of agricultural production, and the natural demise of the generation of the Darias and Matrenas have created a new reality. Hence, the emphasis in most works by former 'village prose' writers is no longer on the psychology, the habits, and way of life of the peasant, but rather on the negative ramifications of the political and economic changes which have taken place in Russia in the last two decades. These writers are critical of the current situation and nostalgic for the Soviet past. They criticize and idealize Soviet reality at the same time. They forget, however, the horrors of collectivization and the famines, and suggest that the communists of today are capable of governing Russia better than their Soviet predecessors. In any event, the reader who wants to obtain a more truthful and objective picture of Russian agricultural communities is advised to become familiar with the prose of Boris Ekimov, in particular his novella 'Pinochet' (Pinochet).[10]

Soviet youth prose, the main objective of which was ideological education and indoctrination, ceased to exist with the disappearance of its main sponsors, the Soviet government and the Young Communist League, and the substance of the historical novel has changed. Uniformity in the interpretation of the historical past has given way to a variety of interpretations of the same events, and current assessments often tell the reader more about the convictions of the author than about the actual historical state of affairs. The Soviet labour and production theme faded away with the privatization of state property and changes in the means and methods of production. The Soviet worker, the hero of socialist labour, has been replaced by the successful entrepreneur, businessman, or bureaucrat who knows how to manipulate the system and become rich by exploiting and abusing simple folk.

The Russian city did not vanish, and city life remains an important subject of contemporary prose, but the emphasis in this prose has changed as well. City prose once concentrated on the portrayal of the so-called city *byt*, or daily life of the urban middle class, and the investigation of the intricate family relationships of the city intelligentsia. But the composition of the middle class has changed drastically, and so have its interests and problems. Contemporary prose set in Russian urban centres concentrates primarily on investigation of the effects of the recent political, economic, and social changes on the lives of the city inhabitants, and, along with personal and family problems, it discusses issues such as corruption, crime, housing, and living standards. Thus, for example, in the novel *Nedvizhimost'* (Real Estate; 2001), Andrei Volos explores the complicated procedures of real estate transactions in the privatized housing market in Moscow and the new accommodation problems faced by the residents of the capital. Ol'ga Slavnikova, on the other hand, delves in her novel *Odin v zerkale* (Alone in the Mirror; 1999) into the eternal problems of love, marriage, and infidelity, which become extremely complicated in the new conditions of post-Soviet city and business life.

Prose fiction is often nurtured by autobiographical and confessional material, but in the last decade memoirs have made a special mark.

Many authors publish in loosely arranged narratives their notes, diaries, observations, and reminiscences, without any chronological sequence, and without trying to disguise their past. Many such works by Sergei Gandlevskii, Evgenii Evtushenko, Nina Gorlanova, and Andrei Sergeev elicit public interest, and one such narrative, *Al'bom dlia marok* (Stamp Album; 1995), by Sergeev, was awarded the 1996 Booker Russian Novel Prize.

Great nineteenth-century Russian novels are remembered not only for their style, structure, and imagery, but also for the depth of the ideas expressed and explored in them, and the sincerity and commitment of their authors. Today, most authors are indifferent, if not heartless, observers of the difficult life in contemporary Russia. Modern Russian literature informs and may even entertain the reader, but as opposed to classical Russian literature, it does not teach, inspire, or heal. This is particularly true of the liberal authors; those belonging to the 'patriotic' camp are committed to their conservative cause, and they defend their dogmatic right-wing positions and attack their opponents with frantic determination. As in the Soviet days, ideology continues to be the main prerogative in their art. Their prose may be thematically distinct, but their criticism of the current Russian system of government is unequivocal. Most writers of the conservative camp follow in the traditions of Russian conventional realism and seldom innovate or experiment with genre, style, or language. This literature is boring, because it is repetitious and offers nothing new. The prose of liberal writers may be of low artistic quality, but it is more interesting. Thematically and stylistically innovative, it may surprise, astound, and puzzle the reader.

Historically, Russian literature has reflected social processes more than any other foreign literature. That does not mean, of course, that this literature necessarily mirrors reality. While it may reflect the author's interpretation of events, it can also be augmented by his or her imagination. Good literature usually explores feelings and passions and reveals human emotions. Now that literature is no longer a tool of ideology, it is free to explore and reflect the human psyche, and the emotions and passions of the individuals portrayed. Unfortunately, this is not happening in contemporary Russian literature, and public taste is no longer determined by the reading public. Instead, in order to make up for the artistic shortcomings in current prose, public taste is manipulated by publishers and booksellers. With the help of advertisements and promotions they dictate, up to a point, the public need, and writers are often forced to comply. For a manuscript to be accepted for publication a liberal writer is required to produce a gripping story in which there is an inventive and fascinating plot, and a mixture of politics, sex, scandal, insolence, and some mystery. Most contemporary novels and novellas rarely appeal to the reader's emotions, and many writers are merely skilled professional scribblers rather than creators of works of art. That is not to say that there are no talented authors in Russia today. Indeed, writers such as Mikhail Butov, Andrei Dmitriev, and Anton Utkin exhibit much promise, but it remains to be seen whether they too will succumb to the pressures of the market, as many others have already done.

In the first half of the 1990s the writers of the liberal camp could be subdivided into three distinct groups. To one group belonged those who followed in the traditions of Russian conventional realism. Another group was composed of those who identified with Russian postmodernism. To the third group belonged those who combined traditional realistic narrative modes with a variety of elements of postmodernism. Some literary scholars attempt to analyse contemporary Russian literature within the context of the evolution of different literary genres and artistic trends.[11] The theoretical substantiation of most literary terms, however, in particular Russian postmodernism, is so vague and contradictory that it is often difficult to determine whether a writer is a realist, a postmodernist, an adherent of the avant-garde, or of conceptualism, or of all of the above mixed together.

It is well known that in postmodern art there is always a fusion of form and a confusion of realms – a combination of fact and fiction, with emphasis on improvisation, play, and abstraction. Form is not conjunctive but disjunctive, and the world described is not hierarchical but fragmented, and in a state of anarchy. Postmodernism does not aspire towards accuracy of knowledge. It denies the very ideas of reality and truth, and it elevates relativism into an end in itself. This literature destroys affinities, and it aims at the marginal and the impersonal. It is characterized by a high degree of reflexivity, intertextuality, scepticism, irony, and parody, which often evolves into straight plagiarism. In view of the multitude of traits ascribed to postmodernism, one may wonder how many postmodern characteristics are required for a work of art to be included in this category.

For example, I.S. Skoropanova[12] includes Andrei Bitov, Evgenii Popov, Vladimir Sorokin, Liudmila Petrushevskaia, Dmitrii Galkovskii, Iurii Buida, Viktor Pelevin, and Viacheslav P'etsukh, as well as

Anton Utkin, for his novel *Khorovod* (The Round-Dance; 1996),[13] in her list of important postmodern prose writers. N.L. Leiderman and M.N. Lipovetskii, on the other hand, exclude Petrushevskaia. Instead, she is classified together with Vladimir Makanin as a 'post-realist,' a new designation intended to unite those who allegedly combine determinism with the irrational, and the study of the socio-philosophical essence of humans with the metaphysical elements in their nature.[14] As if to replace Petrushevskaia in their list of postmodern writers, Leiderman and Lipovetskii include, without much justification, Tat'iana Tolstaia. Another scholar, Roza Glintershchik, even includes Vladimir Makanin in her list of postmodernists.[15] Since there is no uniformity in the practical application of theoretical literary terms, it is difficult not only to classify contemporary Russian authors according to genre, style, or artistic inclination, but also to analyse and compare their recent creative output in a meaningful fashion. At this point it is also worth noting that by the late 1990s many Russian writers and critics had abandoned their initial post-Soviet fascination with postmodernism and returned to conventional realism.

The 1990s were marked by the emergence on the literary scene of a significant number of new women writers. In addition to the appearance in the late 1980s of Tolstaia and Petrushevskaia, the early 1990s brought to the fore the names of Gorlanova, Narbikova, Polianskaia, Ulitskaia, and Svetlana Vasilenko. In the second half of the decade Vishnevetskaia and Slavnikova made their appearance in print, the latter both as a writer and a critic. There are also a few young female writers, like Ekaterina Sadur[16] and Rogneda Smirnova,[17] who published their first books in 1998. Their prose is still weak, but they demonstrate narrative skills and there is hope for the future.

Thematically, the prose of contemporary Russian women writers differs little from that of their male counterparts. It is, however, more introspective, emotional, and occasionally sentimental. It also provides a female view of how recent changes in Russia have affected women's fate, and a glimpse into the predicament and social status of Russian women on the threshold of the new millennium. The better-known Russian women writers are rarely involved with issues which preoccupy representatives of Western ideological feminism. Instead, they concentrate on investigation of the female character, and on the problems which Russian women face in their daily lives. Single motherhood, sexuality, infidelity, and loneliness, as well as the difficult economic conditions of post-Soviet Russia, are at the heart of their works.

It is also worthwhile to note that the second half of the 1990s was the period of the rapid development of the Russian mystery and detective novel, and writers such as Boris Akunin, Aleksandra Marinina, Polina Dashkova, and Dar'ia Dontsova have become household names in contemporary Russian society. Most authors of detective novels combine mystery and contemporary Russian *byt*, while Akunin sets his novels in the Russian historical past.

In normal circumstances literary criticism has an important role to play in fostering the development of literature. It is called upon to serve the reading public, and shape, up to a point, its artistic tastes. In Soviet conditions the critic was a servant of the omnipotent state and his or her role was determined by the ideological requirements imposed by the communist regime. Today, in a free society, the role and responsibility of the critic has changed drastically, and he or she is no longer subject to the pressures of state authorities. The above notwithstanding, the critic's position is currently replete with a number of new complications which may hamper his or her work, defile taste, and compromise his or her moral values.

Most newspapers and periodicals today exist on money provided by sponsors and are accordingly required to promote the political, social, and cultural interests of their benefactors. Hence, literary critics, whether in the daily press or literary journals, are obliged to follow suit and their first responsibility is to the commercial concerns of literary production, rather than the artistic quality of the books reviewed. The selection of a book for critical review is determined primarily by its commercial value, and literature is seldom analysed solely as a work of art. Instead, it is usually approached as a product to be sold to the consumer. Consequently, critics are often forced to review work not according to their personal artistic standards and tastes, but rather against the criteria established by the market, and in many instances criticism can even become a form of advertisement.

Much of contemporary literary criticism is hastily produced, subjective, superficial, and couched in generalities. Most critics address only the contents of the books under consideration. They discuss only *what* the author of a novel writes about. Seldom do they deal with the issue of *how* the author writes, and rarely do they pose the question *why*, or examine the author's approach to his or her subject. Moreover, many critics use their platform not to analyse serious prose but to attack their opponents, promote their own ideas, exhibit their erudition, and elevate themselves above other writers. Nevertheless, most literary journals try to expand the space allotted to book reviews and provide information about the appearance of new publications, which may be of use to the inquisitive reader.

Most established critics of the older generation, such as Lev Anninskii, Irina Rodnianskaia, or Alla Latynina, and some of those who spend most of their time working in literary journals, such as Sergei Chuprinin or Natal'ia Ivanova, seldom review books, but they often write serious survey articles on the current state of Russian literature. More active are the members of the intermediate generation of critics, which includes, among others, Aleksandr Ageev, Pavel Basinskii, Dmitrii Bavil'skii, Dmitrii Bykov, Sergei Kostyrko, Viacheslav Kuritsyn, Andrei Nemzer, Vl. Novikov, Mariia Remizova, and Karen Stepanian. Many critics are on the staff of newspapers or journals, and in addition to literary criticism have other administrative and editorial duties. Thus, for example, the well-known critic Aleksandr Arkhangel'skii is deputy editor-in-chief of the equally well-known Moscow newspaper *Izvestiia* (News). There are also a number of writers from the younger generation, like Aleksei Varlamov, Oleg Pavlov, and Ol'ga Slavnikova, who, apart from writing prose, regularly produce critical articles. In addition, there is a widely developed system of amateur literary criticism, as well as an exchange of opinions about books, authors, genres, and styles on the Internet. It is premature to speculate on the influence of the Internet on the development of artistic quality and critical thought, but some of the opinions expressed on the net will certainly find their way into the printed media.

Serious literary criticism is also affected by another reality. Liberal and conservative critics ignore both each other and the works of authors from the opposing camp. Svetlana Vasilenko decries the fact that Russian 'aesthetic criticism does not exist any longer. It is divided into two camps, and it is under the influence of ideology.'[18]

Literary Prizes

The evolution of the literary process in Russia in the second half of the 1990s can be characterized by the growth of literary sites on the Internet and the appearance of a number of literary clubs and salons in which groups of writers, poets, and critics assemble, from time to time, to read their works and exchange opinions on a variety of literary and cultural subjects. This period was also marked by the proliferation of literary prizes established and sponsored by various banks, financial institutions, organizations, and individuals. In general terms, since most professional authors have a hard time making ends meet, the many generous prizes awarded to contemporary Russian writers are of great financial significance. Publication royalties are low, and many private publishers refuse to pay them at all, claiming, rightly or not, that the sale of a given book has not covered the original publication costs incurred.

The award of literary prizes does not, however, reflect in any way the current state and artistic quality of Russian literature. In the Soviet days literary prizes were awarded on the basis of the ideological reliability of a work of art. Today, most members of juries are guided by personal biases, as well as by the requirements of commercial, ideological, or political considerations established by the sponsors. Thus, the standards for most prizes are seldom determined by artistic quality, and an award can often surprise the reading public and even baffle the author himself. The establishment of so many literary prizes has influenced, to a degree, the formation of literary tastes, and even fostered a new phenomenon whereby many authors write with the apparent objective of satisfying the expectations of sponsors and jurors, hoping thus to be nominated for, and perhaps awarded, the coveted prize.

The most prestigious award is the Booker Russian Novel Prize, which is worth US$12,500. Established in 1992, it is awarded annually for the best novel of the year. A new jury is appointed each year. It accepts nominations, selects a short list, and finally chooses the winner. In Britain the award of the Man Booker Prize in English literature is an important sign of recognition and a guaranteed ticket to financial success. Unfortunately, in Russia few can remember the names of the early Booker Prize winners.

Initially, the Russian Booker Prize was intended for the best novel published in a given year. In reality, however, in the early 1990s it was most often granted in recognition of the literary merit of a writer's general creative output, rather than for a single work of art. Thus, for example, Vladimir Makanin received the Booker Prize in 1993 for one of his minor works, the novella 'Stol pokrytyi suknom i s grafinom poseredine' (Cloth-Covered Table with Carafe in the Middle; 1993), while Bulat Okudzhava received the 1994 Booker not for a novel, but for his autobiographical narrative *Uprazdnennyi teatr* (The Closed-Down Theatre; 1993).

The situation changed somewhat after 1994, when at least some prizes were awarded for full-length novels. In 1995 Georgii Vladimov received the Booker for his novel *General i ego armiia* (The General and His Army; 1994), a narrative about the experience of the Soviet Army in the Second World War. The 1996 Prize was awarded to Andrei Sergeev for his *Al'bom dlia marok* (Stamp Album; 1995), a seemingly casual collection of personal notes, diaries, observations, documents, and scraps of poetry. In 1997 the prize was given to Anatolii Azol'skii, a writer of the older generation, for his novel *Kletka* (Cage; 1996), a convoluted narrative about life on the run in Stalinist Russia. In 1998 the award was presented to Aleksandr Morozov, an administrator and editor of a Russian theological journal, for his novella 'Chuzhie pis'ma' (Someone Else's Letters; 1997), written thirty years ago, but only recently published in *Znamia* (Banner). In 1999 the Booker Prize was awarded to Mikhail Butov for his novel *Svoboda* (Freedom; 1999). The title of the novel reflects both its style and content. It is the first time since its inception that the prize was awarded to a member of the younger generation of Russian writers. In 2000 Mikhail Shishkin, a current resident of Zurich, received the prize for his novel *Vziatie Izmaila* (The Conquest of Izmail; 1999). In 2001 Liudmila Ulitskaia received the Booker Prize for her novel *Kazus Kukotskogo* (The Kukotskii Case; 2000), originally published in *Novyi mir* (New World) under the title *Puteshestvie v sed'muiu storonu sveta* (Travel to the Seventh Side of the World; 2000). And in 2002 the prize was awarded to Oleg Pavlov, for his narrative *Karagandinskie deviatiny, ili Povest' poslednikh dnei* (Karaganda Commemorations, or a Tale of the Last Days; 2001). Pavlov's main competitor was Sergei Gandlevskii's *NRZB* (NRZB; 2002). Despite its official designation as a novel, *NRZB* is rather an extended novella. Pavlov's narrative is a compilation of episodes from army life, written in the spirit of Astaf'ev's prose. *NRZB*, in turn, deals with intellectual subjects, and the personal problems addressed are reminiscent of Iurii Trifonov's Soviet city prose. Both narratives, however, are short in length and limited in scope, and they lack the dramatic intensity one should expect from an award-winning novel.

In addition to the Booker Prize there is a parallel, smaller award, the so-called Little Booker awarded annually for different literary accomplishments. In 1995 the periodicals *Rodnik* (Spring – Riga) and *Idiot* (Idiot – Witebsk) shared the prize for the best Russian language journal in the former Soviet Union republics. In 1996 the poet Gandlevskii received the prize for the best debut in prose for his autobiographical sketch 'Trepanatsiia cherepa' (Trepanation of the Skull; 1995). In 1997 Mikhail Gasparov and Aleksandr Gol'dshtein shared the prize for their books on the historical-philosophical essence of Russian literature. In 1998 Emma Gershtein and Mikhail Bezrodnyi shared the prize for studies of memoir and autobiographical prose dedicated to literary life in Russia. In 1999 Vladimir Bibikhin received the award for *Novyi Renessans* (The New Renaissance; 1998) a book devoted to the study of the development of the essay as a literary form. In 2000 the 'Little Booker' acquired a new sponsor and it was awarded to the Cultural Development Fund 'Iuratin' in the city of Perm; in 2001 the 'Little Booker' was presented to V.P. Golyshev for the best translation of an English novel into the Russian language.

In the old Soviet tradition the Russian Federation continues to award annual State Prizes for Literature. Viktor Astaf'ev received the prize in 1995, and Andrei Bitov and the poet Evgenii Rein were awarded it in 1996. In 1997 prizes were presented to Grigorii Baklanov, Boris Ekimov, and Mikhail Kuraev. In 1998 Inna Lisnianskaia and Aleksandr Revich won the prizes. Vladimir Makanin received the prize in 1999, and in 2000 Vladimir Voinovich and Andrei Volos were presented with the prizes. In 2001 the St Petersburg writer Daniil Granin was awarded the State Prize for prose fiction. It is interesting to note that members of the State Prize jury are allowed to submit their own works for competition, and consequently some of them are awarded prizes. Thus, in 2001 Granin, a member of the jury, was awarded the prize, and 36.3 per cent of all State Prizes in literature were awarded to jury members.[19]

In addition to the awards outlined above, the Academy of Russian Literature presents an annual prize for short fiction, named after Apollon Grigor'ev, which is worth US$25,000. There is also a prize named after Andrei Belyi; an anti-establishment prize, the so-called anti-Booker; a prize for the National Best-seller in the amount of US$10,000, divided between the author, publisher, and the nominator; a 'Triumph' prize established by a Russian independent charity foundation; and a prize for the best literary debut, as well as prizes sponsored by the conservative 'patriotic' writers' community, such as the International Prize named after Mikhail Sholokhov, a prize named after Aleksandr Nevskii, and several other prizes. It is interesting to note that early in 2002 the Sholokhov prize was awarded to Slobodan Milosovic, presently on trial in The Hague for alleged war crimes, for 'his irreconcilable position in the struggle for the human rights and freedom of the Serbian and Balkan people.'[20]

There is also an annual Solzhenitsyn prize, worth US$25,000. The money comes from the Russian Social Foundation, established by Solzhenitsyn, and is supported by the income from royalties for his book *Arkhipelag GULag* (The Gulag Archipelago; 1973–4). The Solzhenitsyn prize aspires to be non-political and objective and may be awarded to authors belonging to either the conservative or the liberal writers' organization. It is expected, however, that a nominated author would be dedicated to the Russian literary tradition; that he or she would search for new means of national self-expression; and that he or she would conduct an exemplary personal life. Leonid Borodin and Valentin Rasputin, among others, have been awarded, at different times, the Solzhenitsyn Russian Literature Prize. Finally, prizes are awarded annually by literary journals for the best contributions published in a given year, as well as by some regional governments, including the administrations of the Ekaterinburg and Volgograd regions.

It is possible to conclude that the abundance of literary prizes provides writers with publicity and financial support, but it also confuses the reading public and erodes the criteria established for good literature.

Publishing and the Reading Public

The transition to a market economy in post-Soviet Russia has for the most part affected negatively the former Soviet intelligentsia, the disappearing Soviet middle class, and the former prestige elite. These were the social strata most interested in the development of culture, literature, and the arts. Members of the intelligentsia bought the multivolume editions of the collected works of Russian and Soviet classics, as well as the new titles of contemporary Soviet literature. They were chiefly serious readers, interested in narratives of deep psycho-philosophical, historical, and artistic significance, and the main subscribers to Soviet literary journals.

In the Soviet days the political power elite was made up primarily of members of the *nomenklatura*, and the prestige elite was primarily composed of members of the creative intelligentsia. In general terms, the intelligentsia consisted of members of the educated middle class, including teachers, scientists, engineers, physicians, and bureaucrats. Today, the power elite consists of important political figures, those in high government positions, and business leaders. The composition of the creative intelligentsia has also changed. It is now mostly composed of political analysts, consultants, image makers, and public relation advisers. Writers, poets, artists, and leading actors are also part of the current intelligentsia, but their role has altered. In the Soviet era, their duty was to serve the regime and educate and influence the masses in the necessary spirit. Today, their objective is to entertain the elite and those who can still afford their contribution and services.

Changes in the social composition of society, the abolition of censorship, and the changing tastes of the reading public have greatly affected the media, the periodical press, and the book publishing business. Moreover, the technology of the advertisement business, and the modes and methods of public opinion creation, have perverted the fine balance between artistry and popular mass culture, and between the quality and quantity of literary production. In addition, publication and mailing costs have continued to rise, increasing the price of books and making selling novels more difficult. For example, in 2001 paper was five times more expensive than it was in 1998, and the production cost of periodicals has also risen considerably. Furthermore, beginning on 1 January 2002, a new tax on the sale of books was introduced, raising the retail price of books by 30 to 40 per cent.

Since most members of the former intelligentsia, the avid readers of literary texts, are now impoverished and have no money to buy books or subscribe to expensive periodicals, it is essential that they have access to public libraries. There are close to 100,000 public and academic libraries in Russia, but only 6 to 7 per cent have the financial resources to acquire newly published books.[21] For a number of years the Institute 'Open Society' (The Soros Fund) paid for 1,700 library subscriptions of leading Russian literary journals to be delivered to public and academic libraries in provincial Russia, a practice which is currently being discontinued.

There are also other factors which determine the popularity of artistic fiction and the fact that today more than a third of all Russians read no books at all. In Soviet times, when the daily and periodical press was tightly controlled by the government and the Soviet reader was hungry for information unavailable in the media, he or she would turn to fiction in search of the truth. A good writer could often delude the vigilant eye of the censor and express, between the lines, views contrary to those officially required. Today there is a glut of publications, but fewer readers than a decade ago. There is an over-abundance of information in the daily press, weekly magazines, and television, and literature has turned from an educational and inspirational artistic medium into a source of excitement, hype, and entertainment, as well as a means of psychological escapism from the dreary conditions of life in contemporary Russia.

Accordingly, in the second half of the 1990s, the circulation of the most important literary journals in Russia continued to decline. In October 1994 48,750 copies of *Znamia* appeared in print; in December 2001 only 8,300 copies were published. The circulation of *Novyi mir* declined from 29,000 in November 1994 to 12,350 in December 2001, and the circulation of *Oktiabr'* dropped from 38,200 in November 1994 to 5,920 in December 2001. The circulation of *Literaturnaia gazeta* dropped from 310,000 in December 1994 to 78,000 in December 2001. The circulation of other national literary journals declined as well, and in December 2001 *Moskva* published 5,480 copies, *Molodaia gvardiia* 4,300 copies, and *Neva* (Neva) 3,800 copies. As many copies of literary journals are acquired by foreign libraries and individual subscribers, it becomes clear that only a small number of libraries in Russia have these journals on their shelves.

The exposure of the reading public to good literary texts is further complicated by the changing tastes of readers, and by the perverse publication and marketing practices of most major Russian publishing houses. Artistic and educational quality is no longer the determining factor of publication policy. Private publishing houses are in the business of making a profit rather than educating or entertaining readers. In 2001 12,484 books and pamphlets in the category of artistic litera-ture, with a total edition of 115,6 million copies, were published in Russia. Close to 60 per cent were thrillers, detective novels, and other pulp narratives. The question, 'What kind of books do you read most often?' was posed in a public poll conducted in 1998 among 2,401 respondents from different socio-demographic groups. Thirty-two per cent of the participants replied that they read predominantly detective novels, and only 6 per cent read contemporary Russian prose. Thirty-five per cent declared that they read nothing whatsoever.[22]

More than a third of all titles published in 2001 were printed in small editions of less than 500 copies each, close to 10 per cent in editions of between 501 and 1,000 copies, and 21.0 per cent in editions ranging from 1,001 to 5,000 copies. Only 0.7 per cent of all books published in 2001 appeared in editions of over a 100,000 copies. The average num-ber of copies published per title dropped from 11,628 in 1996 to 7,710 in 2001.[23] Since many authors cannot find a publisher willing to accept their manuscripts, self-publication has become an alternative. In 1988 the state publishing houses were given permission by the government to accept publication orders from private citizens, and in the decade between 1988 and 1998 more than 7,000 books were published at the authors' expense.[24] Self-publishing, however, is an expensive endeavour, and few Russian citizens can afford it, especially since the author usually has little possibility of recovering some of the expenses incurred by distributing and selling the privately produced books.

It is necessary to point out, however, that the situation is not as dire as it might appear. The appearance of a multitude of new small publishing houses and numerous new journals of limited circulation, especially in the provinces, demonstrate that literary activity is still vibrant. In addition to the well-known Moscow and St Petersburg periodicals, and established provincial literary journals such as *Ural* (Ural), *Volga* (Volga), *Don* (Don), and *Sibirskie ogni* (The Flames of Siberia), there are many new periodicals and almanacs, again especially in the provinces, such as, *Russkoe ekho* (Russian Echo; Samara), *Den' i noch'* (Day and Night; Krasnoiarsk), *Rodnaia Kuban'* (Native Kuban'; Krasnodar), *Okean* (Ocean; Vladivostok), and many others.

The Internet

The technological revolution and the expansion of the Internet in Russia is a slow process. Economic conditions and Russia's antiquated telephone system hamper its development. Moreover, there is a fear that telephone rates for Internet users will be increased, and rumours that the Russian security service will soon begin registering all Russian Internet sites, leading to unofficial censorship. As late as 2000, only 5 per cent of the Russian population had direct access to the Internet. And yet, literature in Russia has created a special niche for itself on the Web.

Russia's first literary websites appeared in 1996, and today there are probably more literary sites in Russia than anywhere else in the world. Close to five hundred new verses and poems, and two hundred stories and novellas, appear on the Internet in Russia daily.[25] Most Internet publications are, of course, unedited and of poor literary quality. Some authors have tried earlier, unsuccessfully, to have their works published in the printed press. Others wanted fast results, and refused to wait for the required editorial and critical decisions. Original texts appearing on the Internet can be viewed as a variation of the *samizdat*, with the only difference being that self-publishing was formerly conditioned by political circumstances, while today it is determined by artistic and economic considerations.

Literature on the Internet is a democratic endeavour, and access is free and not restricted to professionals. Anyone can publish whatever he or she wants, with no restraints. Hence, graphomania predominates and no more than 10 per cent of all texts published on the net has any artistic value at all. There are, however, rare instances when works appearing on the Internet find their way into the printed media. And lately, even works of some well-known Russian writers, such as Marina Palei and Nikolai Kononov, have appeared on the net.

Literature on the net is not limited to the publication of original prose and poetry. Since the late 1990s the Internet has served as a useful reference source, communication medium, library, and archive. Many literary websites provide viewers with information about cultural and literary events; publish reviews of new books and publications in the literary journals; and conduct exchanges of readers' opinions, as well as competitions for the best works originally published on the net. Many participants in the Internet literary process may be amateurs who lack the skill of professional reviewers and writers, but most of them are open minded, sincere, and have no need to camouflage their views.

Russian literature on the Internet was once the domain of graphomaniacs, but lately many leading professional Russian literary critics have established their own websites, and important literary journals and newspapers have produced Internet versions of their publications. Today, not only the well-known Moscow periodicals *Novyi mir, Znamia, Oktiabr', Druzhba narodov* (Friendship of People), and *Kontinent* (Continent) appear on the net, but Russian provincial journals such as *Volga* (Saratov) and *Ural* (Ekaterinburg) also have their own websites. Among the most useful Russian literature websites it is worth mentioning www.infoart.ru/magazine, www.litera.ru, www.rema.ru/observer, www.guelman.ru/slava, www.vavilon.ru, www.magazines.russ.ru, www.russ.ru/krug/period and a few others, operated by literary critics such as Sergei Kostyrko, Sergei Kuznetsov, Viacheslav Kuritsyn, Dmitrii Kuz'min, and Boris Kuzminskii. There are also sites in the English language, such as www.english.russ.ru. General Russian Internet search engines, such as www. yandex.ru, www.rambler.ru, and www.aport.ru, also provide information about current literary and cultural activity.

The Internet does not contribute much to the growth of the artistic quality of literature in Russia, but it certainly helps to keep alive interest in culture and the arts, and it enables otherwise passive readers to become active participants in the literary process. For those who are not residents of Russia, in particular those who dwell overseas, the Russian literary websites provide not only a wealth of information, but also a window onto a distant reality.

2
The Seniors' Prose

The writers of the old generation share a Soviet upbringing and education. Many are graduates of Soviet institutions of higher learning, and
some, like Viktor Astaf'ev, Iurii Bondarev, or Grigorii Baklanov, served
in the Soviet army during the Second World War. With the exception of
Aleksandr Solzhenitsyn and Georgii Vladimov, who were expelled
from the Soviet Writers' Union and exiled from the USSR, all others
discussed here worked within the Soviet system and their works
appeared in official Soviet publications. Some occasionally questioned
Soviet policy, but they never openly challenged the regime. They
learned to compromise and acquiesce, the only way to survive in
Soviet conditions.

All writers included in this chapter, who were still alive in the 1990s,
are over seventy (Andrei Sergeev [1933–98], who perished in a car accident at the age of sixty-five, is the only exception). Some of them, such
as Anatolii Pristavkin (b. 1931) or the now deceased Sergei Zalygin
(1913–2000) and Anatolii Anan'ev (1925–2001), produced little of any
literary significance in the late 1990s. The recent prose of Bondarev (b.
1924) is discussed in the chapter dealing with the literature of the conservative 'patriotic' camp.

Chingiz Aitmatov

Chingiz Aitmatov (b. 1928), the bilingual Kirghiz-born Russian Soviet
writer, was always ahead of his time. As one of the best Soviet writers,
who supported Communist Party policy, he was occasionally allowed
to overstep the officially established boundaries and publish innovative and experimental narratives. At the centre of Aitmatov's best-

known early novellas, including 'Proshchai, Gulsary!' (Farewell, Gul'sary'; 1966) and 'Belyi parokhod' (The White Steamship; 1970), are elements of folklore and Kirghiz mythology, as well as the juxtaposition of the grandeur of nature with the insignificance of humans. Moreover, there is an understated criticism of the existing system of government in the USSR and the Soviet way of life.

With the ascent of Mikhail Gorbachev to power, Aitmatov became actively involved in political life, serving first as an elected delegate to the USSR Congress of People's Deputies, subsequently as a member of President Gorbachev's Advisory Committee, and finally as Soviet ambassador to Luxembourg. After the collapse of the USSR Aitmatov served as Kirghiz ambassador to Belgium. In the second half of the 1980s, when censorship was relaxed, and there was no longer any need for subterfuge, Aitmatov published the novel *Plakha* (Execution Block; 1986), in which he uncovers the evil and corruption prevalent in Soviet society and contrasts the Christian ethic with the ethics of contemporary Soviet life. In the late 1980s and early 1990s Aitmatov attempted to rewrite some of his old narratives and explore new possibilities. Not until the mid-nineties, however, did he manage to produce a new, and what he regards as significant, work of art.

Aitmatov's novel *Tavro Kassandry/Iz eresei XX veka/* (The Brand of Cassandra [From the Heresies of the XXth Century]),[1] written after the disintegration of the USSR, appeared in print in December 1994 but reached the reading public and generated critical reaction in 1995, and later. In his earlier works Aitmatov, the accomplished craftsman, always set his narratives in his native Kirghizia and vicinity. His main characters were always local, simple people, and reality was integrated with elements of myth, folklore, and fantasy. Much of his new novel, instead, is set in the West and in outer space. The main characters are intellectuals, some of them foreigners, and certain aspects of the novel belong to the realm of science fiction.

The novel begins with an open letter from the Russian cosmic monk, Filofei, who is in a spacecraft circling the earth, to the Pope in Rome, and to mankind in general. Filofei's real name is Andrei Kryl'tsov. He is a Russian scientist, sent into orbit in the days of Gorbachev. In his letter to the Pope Filofei describes an important discovery which enables him to send special rays from outer space to identify each pregnant woman who bears a foetus in which evil outweighs goodness. A mark on the forehead of the future mother is to indicate that she is carrying a child which, after birth, will create evil, and which, in a sense, does not even want to be born. According to Filofei, evil in human nature is passed on genetically and endless evil will lead to self-destruction and the end of the world. People, however, refuse to regard themselves as the source of evil and continue to procreate.[2] In principle, Filofei opposes abortion, but not when a mother has a brand on her forehead and carries a child that is evil.

Robert Bork, an American futurologist, supports Filofei's findings, but the simple people in America are against both Bork and Filofei. They view Filofei's conception as a new ideology and maintain that by destroying innocent, allegedly evil, embryos he wants to force people to live in a new, utopian, perfect society.[3] Most Americans oppose Filofei's interference in their family matters, and his intrusion into their earthly affairs. Consequently, demonstrations and public riots take place in the United States, and Bork is attacked and killed. Filofei is disturbed. He realizes that his discovery is premature and that mankind is not yet ready to accept it. Instead of benefiting the people it creates discord and unhappiness. Filofei then decides not to return to earth, and he commits suicide by emerging from his space station into the open air.

In an epilogue to the novel Kryl'tsov relates, in the first person, his own life story. He was an orphan, abandoned by his mother, and there is a suggestion that his father was a German soldier stationed in the occupied regions of the Soviet Union during the Second World War. The young Kryl'tsov was an able and hard-working man and he managed to become a leading Soviet scientist in the field of biology and medicine. Eventually, he became involved in a major scientific project, the objective of which was to create artificial human embryos which would bear the features and traits which the Soviet regime required for its perfect citizenry. These artificially created individuals were to be called 'iksrods.' They would have no parents or roots, and no allegiance to anyone or anything but the Soviet state. Their aim would be to establish world communism and to conquer and lead other nations. The women to be inseminated with these artificially created embryos were prisoners in Soviet jails. One of them refused to submit, or to accept the leniency offered to those who bore 'iksrods.' She even managed to convince Kryl'tsov that his endeavour was wrong and immoral, if not criminal. In the end she was killed while attempting to escape from prison.

The subject of social depravity and the disparity between good and evil is not new in Aitmatov's works. Both the setting and the subject matter in his new novel, however, are completely different from those employed in his earlier works. Aitmatov remains faithful to his humanitarian traditions, but his pessimism and disenchantment with the present human condition are obvious. Even the title of the novel indicates negativism: although disregarded by most of her contemporaries, Cassandra is the prophetess of disaster. Previously, Aitmatov sought harmony and contentment in the uniformity of humans with their natural environment. In *Tavro Kassandry* he seeks satisfaction in the ethical application of scientific knowledge and in the harmony among different religions and nationalities. Aitmatov raises a number of important scientific problems, such as artificial insemination, surrogate motherhood, and the abuse and manipulation of genetic engineering for political and ideological purposes. But he turns these subjects from medical and biological issues into psycho-philosophical and ethical dilemmas, posing the eternal question of how to alter human nature with the purpose of creating a better world. No wonder Aitmatov refers to the Tolstoian idea of self-improvement. He realizes, however, that so much has changed in the century since Tolstoi developed his thoughts, that Tolstoi's explications may now seem too simplistic.

Aitmatov's new novel received a mixed critical reaction in Russia. While all agree that his language, style, and composition are of high artistic quality, some question the new directions taken. Boris Evseev, for example, rejects Aitmatov's pessimism and asserts that the new novel has been written for the Western reader, rather than for Russians. According to Evseev, the purpose of the novel is to prove that Aitmatov is able to transcend local national boundaries and produce a narrative of universal appeal. Evseev further claims that the new novel contradicts the ideas postulated in Aitmatov's earlier works. Aitmatov's art formerly contained elements of universal truth, while in his recent novel there are only simple inventions. Moreover, Evseev claims, since no one ever believed the prophesies of Cassandra, there is no reason to believe in the inventions of Filofei and Aitmatov.[4] Similarly, V. Serdiuchenko asserts that in order to infuse people with the vision of Aitmatov's hero one would have to place individual humans in complete isolation, and in arduous conditions of life. Otherwise, the objective of 'Aitmatov's visionary novel is futile.'[5]

Other critics are more generous. Vladimir Korkin argues with Evseev and accuses him of treating Aitmatov's new novel not as a work of art, but rather as religious dogma. Korkin commends Aitmatov for addressing global and universal issues, and he suggests that since each heresy is always a first step on the way to the truth, Aitmatov's explications of the current state of the human condition are acceptable.[6] Aitmatov himself was disappointed by the critical reception of his novel by the Russian press. In the Soviet days, a new novella by Aitmatov always commanded attention, but *Tavro Kassandry* was almost completely ignored. Aitmatov admits that he fears for the future of mankind, and he claims that in his new novel he attempted to rise above everyday life, above politics and nationality issues, and to seek answers to the current difficult situation in Russia, both in the writers' community and in the country in general.[7]

Regardless of the critical reaction to *Tavro Kassandry*, Aitmatov remains a great master of the word, and his prose is lucid and transparent. It is also clear, however, that the social and political changes of the 1980s in Russia have affected his personal life, and the environment in which he lives. Moreover, these new developments prompted a certain change in his world-view and his artistic craft. Discussion of issues of good and evil in Aitmatov's earlier novels was usually placed within the limited confines of the physical setting of a given narrative. Today, these problems are set within unmanageable parameters of a universal scale and are influenced by current scientific and technological developments. The so-called *mankurts* from his early novels, created by local evil conquerors, have been replaced by artificial *'iksrods'* created by the government in power with the purpose of conquering the world.

The ideas and issues that Aitmatov addresses in his new novel are important and relevant, but the attempt to turn medical and biological issues into a philosophical and ethical dilemma requires further investigation and elucidation. Moreover, the correlation between biology, psychology, and ethics remains obscure. Aitmatov tries to integrate elements of myth and natural imagery with his main subject. The dying whales in the ocean, observed by Robert Bork, represent the disappearing human conscience, and the fateful owl in Moscow represents the dying wisdom of humans. These images, however, are secondary to the plot, and not central as, for example, the horse in 'Proshchai, Gul'sary!' or the deer in 'Belyi parokhod,' are.

Aitmatov's artistic roots are still visible in his new novel, but a transformation in his art is also evident. It remains to be seen whether he will return to his past or continue to experiment with new subject matter and new artistic approaches. Aitmatov was always an innovator within the permitted Soviet bounds. Today, there are no limits his creative freedom, but too much freedom can become a burden with inherent dangers.

Viktor Astaf'ev

Viktor Astaf'ev (1924–2001) is one of the best-known Russian writers of the post-Stalin era. Born in Siberia and orphaned early in life, Astaf'ev faced much hardship in his childhood and youth. Drafted into the Soviet army he managed to survive the Second World War, but he returned home from the front heavily wounded, without an education, and without the necessary means to support himself and provide for his young family. After demobilization Astaf'ev worked at various odd jobs and began to write prose. His first story appeared in print in 1951; his first collection of prose, *Do budushchei vesny* (Until Next Spring), was published in 1953.

For over twenty years Astaf'ev wrote the loosely connected autobiographical narrative *Poslednii srok* (The Last Respects; 1978), a tribute to his grandmother and to the simple people of his native Siberia. In *Tsar'-ryba* (Queen Fish; 1976), also set in Siberia, Astaf'ev mounted a passionate defence of the natural environment and contrasted the utilitarian approach and predatory nature of humans with the harmony, beauty, and uncorrupted essence of nature. Astaf'ev's prose of the 1960s and 1970s is close in spirit to that of 'village prose' of the same period. Unlike other village writers, however, he challenged the idealized image of the Russian peasant and the notion that evil and corruption have been introduced into the Russian village from the outside, from the urban environment. In this respect Astaf'ev follows in the steps of Dostoevskii, who asserts that the seeds of evil are present in everyone.

With the advent of Gorbachev and of *glasnost'*, Astaf'ev sacrificed artistic quality for a social cause and published the novel *Pechal'nyi detektiv* (A Sad Detective Story; 1986), in which he decries the evil, injustice, falsehood, and corruption prevalent in Soviet Russia. Moreover, he became embroiled, with other former village writers, in conservative nationalistic and chauvinistic activity. In 1992 Astaf'ev published the first volume of a tragic narrative about the Second World War, *Prokliaty i ubity* (The Cursed and the Slain) and he continued, until his death, to produce narratives based primarily on his war and life experience. Many of his later stories are set in two distinct time spans and locations: at the front in the army, and, after demobilization or injury, back in Russia.

In 1995 Astaf'ev published the novella 'Tak khochetsia zhit' (What a Desire to Live).[8] It tells the life story of Koliasha Khakhalin, the product of a Soviet boarding school for orphaned children, who, despite his physical handicap, is conscripted to army service during the Second World War. In the first two chapters Astaf'ev describes Koliasha's family background, his activity at the front, and his work at a military post office where he meets and impregnates his future wife, Zheniara Belousova. He also depicts their trip back to Russia, to the village where Zheniara's mother lives. In the portrayal of the war episodes Astaf'ev stresses the effort and dedication of the simple Russian soldiers in the difficult, inhuman conditions of war. He also criticizes aspects of the general Soviet war effort, and reveals the ineptness of Soviet commanders.

Chapter 3 covers the period up to 1995 and the life of the young family in Belousova's mother's village. Life in the countryside, in particular in the post-Soviet era, is difficult. Corruption is rampant, just as it was under Soviet rule, and money and economic well-being have become more important to many than family, friends, and integrity. Astaf'ev does not, however, blame the system of government for the transgressions of individual citizens. He maintains instead that some people are good, while others are evil, and that each person is responsible for his or her own deeds. Koliasha himself is no angel, but as he grows older he always weighs carefully the consequences of his actions and seeks fulfilment in poetry and religion. There is no nostalgia in the story for the Soviet past, merely a longing for bygone youth, when there was still hope and time to arrange for a better future.

Koliasha appears to express many of Astaf'ev's own ideas and emotions. There is in the novella a vivid identification with the suffering of the people, and some episodes in the story are infused with dramatic tension. There are also, however, a number of artistic shortcomings in the narrative. Its structure is loose, it lacks focus, and most characters are sketched only superficially. Some events and periods of time receive detailed attention, while others are mentioned only in passing. Astaf'ev does not fail to criticize foreign influence in Russia today, but he declines to indicate whether Russia itself has the desire and potential to improve the lot of its people.

The novella 'Oberton' (Overtone; 1996)[9] is, in a sense, an offshoot of 'Tak khochetsia zhit.' Some of the characters are the same and the location is similar, but most of the action in the story takes place in the immediate aftermath of the war. While the war is over, its repercussions affect the lives of the young, demobilized soldiers. Love aroused during the war does not come to fruition, and hope nurtured in the trenches of war is seldom fulfilled. Thus, many young people in postwar Russia grope in the dark, and some, like Liuba, one of the heroines of 'Oberton,' commit suicide. The language of the story, which is narrated in the first person by one of the characters, is simple. There are no major conflicts in the novella and portrayal is fleeting. There is just a hint that life is unpredictable and that circumstances and chance most often determine human fate.

'Veselyi soldat' (The Happy Soldier; 1998),[10] the title of another novella by Astaf'ev is, in a sense, a misnomer. A wounded soldier returns from the front and has nothing to be happy about. He has no home, no money, and no hope for a better future. Moreover, wherever he turns for help he is humiliated, abused, and ignored. Astaf'ev, a war veteran himself, is sensitive to the fate of his comrades-in-arms. He decries the fact that those who contributed most to the Soviet defeat of Nazi Germany were forgotten by their motherland as soon as victory was achieved.

The last two of Astaf'ev's stories, published before his death, 'Trofeinaia pushka' (A Trophy Cannon; 2001) and 'Zhestokie romansy' (Cruel Romances; 2001),[11] are also about the Second World War. In 'Trofeinaia pushka' the narrator recounts a war episode in which the extreme eagerness of one Soviet warrior to rout the enemy leads to the futile death of many other Soviet soldiers. It illustrates the great paradox of many war situations, when excessive bravery is more dangerous than cowardice, and when good intentions without adequate experience lead to tragic consequences. In 'Zhestokie romansy' the hero, Junior Lieutenant Chugunov, is a happy-go-lucky, uneducated fellow who is accepted to the officers' school with fake documents. At the front line, without proper qualifications, he is unable to calculate properly the command to his gunners, and instead of aiming at the position of the enemy, he directs a Soviet artillery volley at his own position. Having lost both legs in this brush with death, he returns to his native Siberia and becomes leader of a gang of criminals and hoodlums.

Astaf'ev's later prose is thematically different from that of the 1960s and 1970, and these stories, which are influenced primarily by his personal war experience, are grim, heartbreaking, and often shocking. No longer is he concerned with the natural environment, or the relation-ship between city dwellers and the Russian countryside. Instead, he concentrates on tragic episodes of individual behaviour in the fero-cious conditions of war, as well as on the shabby treatment of simple soldiers by their superiors, and the dreadful conditions of post-war life of those who made the Soviet victory possible.

Astaf'ev is a compassionate observer who writes without embellish-ing the facts. His prose is realistic and his imagery is harsh, but touch-ing. He contrasts happiness and despair, humility and hate, and he denounces the prevailing atmosphere of the universal lie which, he asserts, dominates contemporary Russian life. Despite some moral and intellectual limitations, Astaf'ev is able to portray conflicts of consid-erable dramatic intensity, and to pour out his emotional bitterness, repudiating both the Soviet regime and the current order of things in Russia. With the passing of Astaf'ev Russia lost one of its eminent writers of the older generation, and Siberia its native bard.

Anatolii Azol'skii

In the days of Brezhnev's rule Anatolii Azol'skii (b. 1930), a St Peters-burg writer of the older generation, had difficulty publishing his manuscripts. His novel *Kletka* (Cage), published in the 1996 volume of *Novyi mir*[12] and subsequently awarded the 1997 Booker Russian Novel Prize, was originally submitted to *Novyi mir* in the 1960s, but after a long delay was refused publication by the censors. No wonder – the novel dealt with subjects taboo in official Soviet literature.

The title of the novel is symbolic and alludes to the Soviet state as a cage in which one can move around and hide, but from which there is no escape. It refers also to *kletka*, or biological cell, and to the study of genetics, in which some protagonists in the novel are involved. The action covers a stretch of time between the early 1920s and 1960, approximately. The hero, Ivan Barinov, is the son of well-educated par-ents who are afraid of being purged, and therefore abandon their home in Leningrad to resettle in Belorussia. During the Second World War Ivan becomes a Soviet partisan fighting the Nazi occupiers. In the pro-cess he is caught by the Gestapo, but he pretends to be dead and man-ages to escape. After the war he serves in the Soviet security forces but is betrayed by his colleagues and accused of being a spy and a Nazi collaborator. After having successfully escaped Soviet prison Ivan becomes active, together with Klim, a purged relative, in the study of genetics, a science not favoured at that time by the Soviet authorities. Ivan and his associates are constantly on the run, their lives always in danger. In fact, Klim and his wife are murdered by bandits. At the end of the novel Ivan is in Siberia. Tired of running and hiding all his life, he contemplates suicide, but is apparently saved by the news that he may soon become a father. Ivan manages to survive against all odds. He eludes the Gestapo, he runs away from the NKVD, and he manages to avoid ordinary bandits, but the price he has to pay for his life, and for relative freedom, is very high indeed. It includes mental anguish, extreme stress, and the sacrifice of people who are dear to him.

Azol'skii's description of how the Soviet security forces operate is very disturbing. In order to nurture its own existence the Soviet security apparatus created a myth of a major 'danger' to the Soviet state. Azol'skii reveals the shallowness and stupidity of members of the Soviet security organs, and the life of these individuals who, justly or unjustly, are pursued by the Soviet regime and forced time and again to change their personal identities and places of residence.

Andrei Nemzer refers to *Kletka* as to a 'miracle.' He is impressed by Azol'skii's 'well adjusted architectonics, his intricate motivational ligature, ... [and] his surgical insight into the dark sides of the human soul.'[13] Nemzer may, however, be too generous. While the author demonstrates familiarity with and understanding of the material covered, this novel is no great work of art. Characterization is inadequate, and we learn little about the internal make-up of the heroes. The plot of the novel is inventive, but sometimes confusing, and the language is dense and not always easy to follow.

Azol'skii's next novel, *Monakhi* (Monks; 2000),[14] is similar in style but differs in substance. Much of the plot is set abroad, in the United States, and the main characters, Buzgalin and Kustov, are two Soviet secret agents operating in North America on behalf of the Soviet security organs. At one point the two appear disguised as ancient Catholic monks. The spies are under tremendous pressure, both from their Soviet handlers and the foreign environment, and Kustov breaks down, loses his mind, and becomes a traitor. Consequently, Buzgalin's objective is to deliver his deranged colleague, in one piece, back to the USSR. At the end of the novel both spies are at home in retirement. Kustov is tried as a traitor, but he is treated with consideration because of his mental condition. The life of the former spies, however, is trivial and in no way commensurate with the important service they provided to the state.

The plot of *Monakhi* mirrors Soviet reality, and much of it reflects the workings of the Soviet security organs. And yet, there is a certain artificiality in its construction. The story, while interesting, is contrived, and it fails to move the reader. Azol'skii knows Soviet life well. Formerly a naval officer, he is absorbed today by the activities of the Soviet security apparatus. His stories, usually straightforward, third-person narratives, contain elements of surprise, suspense, and some melodrama, but his language is simple and compressed. Sentences in his novels are very long, and paragraphs often extend to several pages. The denseness of Azol'skii's language and the tangled structure of his plots often obscure the main thrust of his argument and make reading his works a difficult task.

Grigorii Baklanov

The well-known writer of Soviet war prose, Grigorii Baklanov (b. 1923), is still active. His new novella, 'Moi general' (My General),[15] however, despite its title, is not on a military or war topic, and it is not a major work of art. The general in question is the father of one of the main characters. He does not appear in the narrative, having perished in an air crash. The novella opens with an episode of current Moscow life. The narrator stumbles on the half-naked body of a dead man lying abandoned on a Moscow street. In a flashback we are told about the life of the first-person narrator, Oleg Nikolaevich. Initially a young reporter for a small journal in central Russia, he falls in love with Nadia, the wife of a co-worker, and becomes attached to her small son, Vitia. Many years later Oleg, the husband of Tania, and the father of a teenaged daughter, meets Nadia and Vitia again. Nadia is now married to a Russian diplomat, and her renewed relationship with Oleg is platonic. Vitia, a handsome young man, is invited to stay with Oleg's family in their cottage. It then becomes clear that Vitia is addicted to narcotics, and Oleg becomes concerned that his daughter might fall in love with the young man. The end of the story is tragic. Constantly under the influence of drugs, Vitia is terribly injured in a car accident, and it appears that the dead body that Oleg discovers on the Moscow street is that of Vitia.

The focus in the short novella is on the rapid recent changes in the life of Moscow inhabitants. On the one hand, there is total freedom of expression and movement, and no shortage of consumer goods, but corruption, deprivation, and drug addiction ruin the future of the younger generation. Baklanov's war prose is realistic, vigorous, and straightforward, but his recent novella delivers a harsh message about current life in Russia in soft, occasionally sentimental, language infused with elements of melodrama. The narrative is charged with dramatic tension, but the portrayal of human relationships is superficial, and the story lacks psychological insight. The main focus is on the general human experience, rather than on the personal perspectives of the main characters. As in many other contemporary Russian narratives, artistry in 'Moi general' has been sacrificed for topicality.

Fazil' Iskander

Fazil' Iskander (b. 1929) is one of the veterans of Soviet literature currently still active on the Russian literary scene. Best known for his epic narrative *Sandro iz Chegema* (Sandro of Chegem; 1983), a loose collection of stories and novellas set in Abkhazia, Iskander managed to survive the Soviet era intact because his art was, in a sense, outside the mainstream of Soviet literature. His stories are at once comic and ironic, realistic and fantastic, and full of adventurous, often absurd characters. Iskander satirizes and mocks the Soviet bureaucracy and opposes injustice, falsehood, and corruption everywhere. The prose of the mature Iskander of the post-Soviet era contains a number of elements and artistic devices characteristic of his earlier stories, but much of it is more serious and sombre. In some of his recent works there is less humour and fantasy, and an underlying sense of tragedy and pessimism with little hope for the future.

In 1997 Iskander published a collection of prose[16] which includes the novella 'Sofichka' (Sofichka). The novella is a third-person, realistic narrative in which the life story of the Abkhazian woman Sofichka is described. Sofichka falls in love with the young Rouf, who is half Abkhazian and half Turkish. Sofichka's relatives scorn Rouf, but Sofichka marries him despite the family's opposition. She is a good wife and loves her husband dearly, but Rouf is hated by her kin, and her brother Nuri kills him. Sofichka refuses all advances and does not remarry, remaining true to her husband into old age. Moreover, she repudiates her brother Nuri who, time and again, begs her for forgiveness. In the end, she forgives Nuri but cannot forgive herself. She becomes depressed, believing that she has betrayed her husband, and then becomes ill, and dies. Like most of Iskander's early narratives 'Sofichka' is set in the environs of Chegem. The customs and the lore of the people there have changed little, but the humour and banter of Iskander's early prose have disappeared. Instead, sadness, adversity, and unhappiness prevail. The character of Sofichka, who embodies devotion and goodness, goes down in defeat, and it is juxtaposed with other characters who are jealous, greedy, and rapacious.

In the late 1990s Iskander produced several short narratives which can be seen to exemplify the slowly changing spirit of his prose. The action is no longer set in Chegem, but rather in Moscow, and the main characters are Russians. Moreover, the effect of recent social and political changes on the life of Russian citizens is addressed. 'Dumaiushchii o Rossii i amerikanets' (One Thinking About Russia and the American; 1997)[17] is presented in the form of a casual dialogue between a Russian man and an American Slavist who visits Russia with his wife. The purpose of the Russian is to entertain and occupy the American so that the Russian's friend and business partner can sell the American woman a fake icon.

The discussion is highly intellectual and covers a wide range of subjects, including politics, economics, culture, literature, religion, and even love. The Russian is pleased that the American prefers Pushkin to Byron, and he insinuates to the visitor that the young Mikhail Sholokhov could hardly produce a novel of the calibre of *Tikhii Don* (The Quiet Don). Many ideas expressed by the nameless Russian are original and thought provoking, and the discussion exposes the naivety of the American and his wife. The crux of the matter, postulated by the Russian, is that most Russians are impractical thinkers, dreamers, and thieves, all at the same time, while no foreigner is able to fathom the Russian mind. Most of the dialogue is narrated in a humorous tone. It intertwines episodes from real life and intellectual deliberations with fantasy. Under the surface, however, there is obvious criticism of Soviet rule, as well as of the situation in Russian today.

In 1998 Iskander published the novella 'Poet' (Poet),[18] another example of the changing spirit of his prose. The novella tells the life story of the Russian poet Volkov. During Brezhnev's rule he cannot publish a single book. His poetry, while harmless, is still suspect. After the collapse of the Soviet Union, Volkov becomes famous. He publishes many books, and is awarded the State Prize for Literature. The novella satirizes the Soviet system of government, ridicules Soviet officials, and mocks human frailty. The narrative, however, lacks focus. Iskander's attempts to expose the reader to a multitude of social, economic, and political problems are superficial. Moreover, the abrupt change of narrators and the unexpected transition from one time sequence to another are confusing.

In 'Kozy i Shekspir' (The Goats and Shakespeare; 2001),[19] the action initially returns to Chegem. The young protagonist herds goats, reading Shakespeare at the same time, and ignoring his charges, who invade a neighbour's garden. Soon a tale about the simple life in Chegem evolves into a story about life in Moscow. The narrator is now a student in the capital, and he deliberates about life in conditions of tyranny and oppression. According to the author humour and self-irony make life and survival possible in these improbable conditions. Iskander suggests that 'in order to become a master of good humour one has to become at first extremely pessimistic, to peep into the darkness of the abyss, realize that there is nothing, and then step by step begin the trip back.'[20]

The abolition of censorship in Russia has clearly led to a change in Iskander's creative approach to his prose. Today everything, including the pervading sense of dejection and resignation, is on the surface. Iskander's prose is still humorous, but it often arouses laughter through tears. Age apparently also influences Iskander's state of mind. He deprecates the Soviet past in his recent works, but he is also frustrated by the current situation in Russian society. Hence, despite Iskander's denunciation of Soviet rule, there is a hidden nostalgia for the past, when it was still possible to dream about a better future.

Andrei Sergeev

The poet and translator Andrei Sergeev (1933–98) produced in 1995 a manuscript entitled *Al'bom dlia marok. Kollektsia liudei, veshchei, slov i otnoshenii (1936–1956)*[21] (Stamp Album: A Collection of People, Things, Words, and Relationships [1936–1956]). The narrative combines reminiscences, observations, notes, and entries in a diary which the author kept for a number of years. He begins with recollections about his childhood and his early perception of political events of major significance, such as the Molotov-Ribbentrop pact, and the 1939 war between the USSR and Finland. Despite the political and social pressures of daily life in the pre-war Soviet Union, the narrator grows up in a happy and satisfying family environment. But he asserts that Soviet education and propaganda have been an accumulation of lies, and he provides numerous examples of dull brainwashing, illustrating, at the same time, the disparity between the contents of children's books and real life.

The author's family history consists of formal documents, as well as stories overheard by the child during adult conversations. Both of the author's parents have been married before, and it appears to him that his parents' marriage is a mismatch. The author declares that he had no special relationship with his father, yet he writes about him with love, respect, and sensitivity. Initially, the author-narrator enrols for study in the Moscow Institute of Cinematography. He observes the situation at school and provides some impressionistic sketches of his schoolmates. Soon, however, he decides to leave the Institute without having completed his studies. The atmosphere is stifling, nothing can be questioned, and there is no freedom of creative expression. The author then continues his higher education in a Soviet Institute of Foreign Languages.

A separate section in the narrative is devoted to the intricacies of creative activity, and the complicated means and ways by which a young poet tries to find a place in the Soviet literary scene. The narrator recalls his meetings with a number of leading Soviet poets, including Boris Pasternak and Nikolai Zabolotskii. Surprisingly, numerous comments are made about national minorities, in particular Jews, who are neighbours of the author or live elsewhere in the Soviet Union. Most of these remarks are negative. The narrator's mother hails from an old Russian gentry family, and her inherent anti-Semitic behaviour and attitudes are only too obvious. Jews are implied to have been instrumental in causing the Bolshevik revolution, and, therefore, Russia's current troubles. The narrator's mother scorns Jews and looks down upon them as at lower creatures. Many others, including some young and aspiring Russian poets and writers, refuse to have anything to do with Jews, shunning even those converted to Christianity, such as Boris Pasternak.

The Andrei Sergeev's memoirs cover some thirty years of his life, and were written over a period of roughly the same length. Most of the narrative is based on fact, and there is apparently very little fiction in it. Since much, however, has been written from memory, many years after the events described, the contents of some of the stories may have been changed, perhaps even embellished. The entries in the book are not in chronological order, and most characters are portrayed in a superficial manner. Most individuals discussed in the narrative pretend to be dedicated Soviet citizens, while deep in their hearts they despise the Soviet system. The language of the narrative is smooth, and sometimes poetic, but portrayal is casual and impressionistic.

Although Sergeev's narrative is no great masterpiece, and neither a novel nor fiction, it was awarded the 1996 Booker Russian Novel Prize. This is a clear indication that, in the mid-1990s, the Russian novel was, at least temporarily, in artistic decline.

Aleksandr Solzhenitsyn

In 1994, twenty years after his exile from the Soviet Union, Aleksandr Solzhenitsyn (b. 1918) returned to his native Russia. Most of his important works, including *Rakovyi korpus* (Cancer Ward; 1968), *V kruge pervom* (The First Circle; 1968), and *Arkhipelag GULag* (The Gulag Archipelago; 1973–4), once forbidden in the Soviet Union, were published during Gorbachev's rule. Today, Solzhenitsyn, who is well over eighty, is one of the oldest writers still active in Russia. His creative output illustrates that he has always been interested in writing both artistic prose and narratives of an autobiographical, historical, social, and political nature. Works published after his return from exile indicate that the diversity of his interests has not changed. His recent publications include political pamphlets, historical studies, autobiographical sketches, some prose fiction, and even literary criticism. Among others, he published critical essays on Evgenii Zamiatin, Varlaam Shalamov, and Iosif Brodskii.

In Solzhenitsyn's early prose the discussion of moral problems is almost always socially oriented, but most protagonists in his narratives are round, psychological investigation is precise, and the characters are treated with a subtle irony. Solzhenitsyn's recent prose fiction is different. First, it is motivated primarily by his political inclinations, and it also appears that Solzhenitsyn is not yet acquainted adequately with the life of the young who are at the forefront of economic activity in the country. Thus, the story 'Na izlomakh. Dvuchastnyi rasskaz' (On the Splinters. A Story of Two Components; 1996)[22] is composed of two separate parts which are uneven and divergent. In the first part, narrated in the spirit of socialist realism, the main character is the seventy-year-old Emtsov, a former Soviet production leader, who, with hard work and dedication, becomes first a *komsomol* and Communist Party bureaucrat, and later a manager and leader of a major enterprise in the Soviet industrial military complex. Solzhenitsyn stresses, however, that Emtsov always strives to be active in the production line, rather than in administration, because he believes that productive activity is the mainstay of the national economy and that it generates real wealth.

In the new conditions of the market economy, despite his advanced age, the experienced Emtsov remains a useful citizen in command of a newly developing production enterprise.

In the second part of the story, which is much shorter than the first, the main character is the thirty-year-old Tolkovianov. Enticed by the possibility of getting rich fast, he abandons his higher education studies and becomes an entrepreneur and a partner in a bank. Unfortunately, the bank is on the verge of bankruptcy, and Tolkovianov barely manages to escape an attempt on his life. In the end, Tolkovianov is in a quandary, and he seeks out Emtsov for some practical advice. The message of the story is obvious. It suggests that only education, determination, and productive hard work, rather than speculative activity, can bear positive results. There is little optimism for the future, and Solzhenitsyn implies that the brisk rise to power and the acquisition of wealth, without hard work, lead to corruption and inevitable failure.

Artistically, 'Na izlomakh' is a far cry from Solzhenitsyn's early stories. The image of Emtsov is drawn with confidence. Yet, where in the past Solzhenitsyn showed little kindness to Soviet bureaucrats and members of the *nomenklatura*, he now idealizes the former Soviet manager and sets him up as an example for the young and hapless Tolkovianov to emulate. The character of Tolkovianov, moreover, is poorly developed and lacks depth. It is a clear sign that Solzhenitsyn still lives in the past, that he cannot recognize the recent changes in the country, and that he is little interested in the new aspirations of the young generation of Russians. The language in the story is refined, and the narrative flows smoothly, but the treatment of the main conflict is superficial, and there is no psychological investigation, nor is there any attempt to understand what motivates the actions of the young protagonist.

In 1998 Solzhenitsyn published in *Novyi mir* a continuation of his biographical saga, originally recounted in *Bodalsia telenok s dubom* (The Calf Butted Against the Oak; 1974).[23] He describes events from his personal life and his experiences after his expulsion from the USSR, as well as his meetings with various personalities, representatives of the Western world, and members of the Russian émigré community. He also devotes some space to discussion of the political situation in the world and his relations with individuals such as Vladimir Maksimov, Andrei Sakharov, Andrei Siniavskii, and Nikita Struve. It is interesting to note that Solzhenitsyn initially intended to settle, after his exile from the USSR, in Canada, somewhere in Ontario, not far from the St

Lawrence river. He even travelled by train across Canada to Alaska to look for a place for himself, but in the end he decided to settle in Vermont, in the United States.

In 1999 Solzhenitsyn published 'Zheliabugskie vyselki. Dvuchastnyi rasskaz' (The Zheliabug Settlements. A Story of Two Components).[24] The first part of the story describes a war episode in which an artillery battalion partakes in the battles at the Kursk Bulge in 1943. In the second part, set fifty-two years later, the narrator visits the city of Orel to celebrate its liberation. There is, however, little to be joyful about. Life there is difficult and people complain. In another story, 'Adlig Shvenkitten' (Adlig Shvenkitten; 1999),[25] the author reminisces about his wartime experiences and describes a variety of combat situations. The main emphasis, however, is on human life and personal relationships, and the fact that even in the arduous conditions of war there is little justice. Those who deserve most to be decorated perish in battle, or are overlooked by those in charge, while military bureaucrats who have never faced the enemy in battle, and who are employed at staff offices, are nominated for decoration. In another episode Solzhenitsyn relates the story of how a number of Soviet soldiers are poisoned by wood alcohol on an alleged victory drinking binge.

It is well known that Solzhenitsyn, the great creative artist, has always aspired to become a major historian. It is, however, also known that the artistic quality of his short novellas such as Odin den' Ivana Denisovicha (One Day in the Life of Ivan Denisovich; 1962), or 'Matrenin dvor' (Matrena's House; 1963) is vastly superior to the historical value and quality of narratives such as Krasnoe koleso (The Red Wheel; 1993). Most of Solzhenitsyn's attention in the last decade has nonetheless been devoted to Russian political, national, social, and historical issues. These are the subject of Kak nam ob''ustroit' Rossiiu (How to Arrange Things in Russia; 1990), Russkii vopros: k kontsu dvadtsatogo veka (The Russian Question: At the End of the Twentieth Century; 1994), and Rossiia v obvale (Russia in Collapse; 1998), as well as Solzhenitsyn's last major work, the two-volume historical narrative Dvesti let vmeste (1795–1995) (Two Hundred Years Together [1795–1995]), published in Moscow in 2001–2.

Solzhenitsyn's recent narrative is an attempt to produce a definitive history of Jewish life in Russia, with particular emphasis on the relationship of the Russian tsarist and Soviet governments with their Jewish subjects. Volume 1 covers the period from 1795 to 1917, volume 2 the February Revolution in 1917 to 1995. In the introduction to the book the author states that his most important duty is to be objective. Yet complete objectivity is impossible. Solzhenitsyn tries hard to be fair to the Russian Jews by making extensive use of Jewish sources, but he uses the material selectively. He admits that the tsarist government did not do enough to protect the Jews in the so-called Pale of Settlement. He absolves it, however, of any responsibility for the pogroms and Jewish suffering, because, as he claims, most pogroms were spontaneous, or provoked by the Jewish self-defence. In other words, he blames the victims for their troubles. Solzhenitsyn further asserts that Jews were not persecuted in tsarist Russia, they were merely limited in their rights. Moreover, he justifies this inequality and deprivation by claiming that the Russian peasants were worse off than the Jews. According to Solzhenitsyn, everything is relative. Since the tsarist government enslaved the Russian peasants, the Jews had nothing to complain about, and Solzhenitsyn defends the tsarist government not because it was perfect, but rather because it was better than communism.

In the second volume Solzhenitsyn states clearly that, despite the leadership of Trotskii, neither the February nor the October revolutions of 1917 were created by the Jews. Russian themselves, he claims, were responsible for the overthrow of the tsarist regime. Jews, however, were instrumental in helping to organize and in participating in the new Soviet administration. Solzhenitsyn asserts that the Bolshevik Jews were renegades, rather than Jews in spirit. Solzhenitsyn deals in his study with the general history of Soviet Jewry, as well as with issues of assimilation, immigration, and the question of who is a Jew, and he suggests that there is a hand of Providence in the recent return of Russian Jews to the Holy Land. According to Solzhenitsyn, the objective of his book is to help Russians and Jews alike to better comprehend each other. As he hints, only mutual understanding can help heal the wounds of their common, difficult past.

The return of Solzhenitsyn to Russia was eagerly anticipated by both the liberals and 'patriotic' nationalists. The first remember Solzhenitsyn as a fighter for freedom and a vigorous opponent of the Soviet communist regime; the nationalists, in turn, have welcomed Solzhenitsyn's Russianness, his anti-Westernism, and his opposition to Boris Yeltsin's reforms. Solzhenitsyn has not joined any of the contemporary political or literary camps. Instead, he locked himself up in his reclusive residence on the outskirts of Moscow where, largely ignored by the establishment and the media, he continues to criticize the current order of things in Russia, and to call for changes in the country which, paradoxically, may coincide in many ways with the reactionary ideals of the Soviet regime formerly berated by him.

Georgii Vladimov

Georgii Vladimov is another of the few exiled Soviet writers who have recently returned to live in Russia. Expelled from the Writers' Union in 1977, Vladimov has become chairman of the Moscow chapter of Amnesty International. In 1983, he was invited to spend a year at the University of Koln, in Germany, to give a number of lectures on Soviet literature. A month after his arrival in Germany, Vladimov was informed that his Soviet citizenship had been revoked. In 1990, Iurii Andropov's order to banish Vladimov was repealed by Gorbachev, and his Soviet citizenship was reinstated.

Born in 1931 in the city of Kharkov, now in the Ukraine, Vladimov graduated from the Law Faculty of the Leningrad State University in 1963. Vladimov's early prose was imaginative and psychologically subtle, and his style vigorous. In 1961 his first publication, 'Bol'shaia ruda' (The Great Ore), appeared in *Novyi mir* and in 1969 *Znamia* published his novel *Tri minuty molchania* (Three Minutes of Silence). His most important work of that period, however, is *Vernyi Ruslan* (Faithful Ruslan; 1963–75), in which the central character is the labour camp guard dog, Ruslan. The dog cannot adjust to the changes after the Khrushchev amnesty of the late 1950s, when camp labourers are set free and are no longer prisoners. *Vernyi Ruslan* circulated in the Soviet Union in *samizdat* and in 1964 found its way into the West. In 1975 the novel was published in *Grani*, and in 1989 it officially appeared in print in the USSR for the first time. In the West Vladimov edited the journal *Grani* for several years and continued to write and publish.

In 1994 Vladimov published in *Znamia* his new major novel, *General i ego armiia* (The General and His Army),[26] which was awarded the Booker Russian Novel Prize in 1995. The main subject of the novel is the Soviet predicament in the Second World War, but the narrative differs from most other works of Soviet war prose and it should be approached rather as a historical novel. The narrative combines fact and fiction. While the names of battle locations are fictitious, many protagonists have real prototypes, with whom anyone acquainted with the history of the Second World War is familiar. When fact and fiction are freely intertwined in this way, there is always a danger of confus-

ing artistic realism with actuality, and the possibility of different interpretations by various critics and historians.

According to Vladimov, General Chibisov, the commander of the
38th Soviet Army, located, at that time, at the beach-head for attack at
the Dnepr' river shore, was the prototype for the main character of the
novel, General Kobrisov.[27] Kobrisov is an individualist who opposes
General Georgii Zhukov's strategy of victory at any price. He refuses
to become engaged in military escapades in which the risk of human
sacrifice outweighs the military and territorial advantage to be gained
even in case of success. Paradoxically, the other important protagonist
in the novel is Major Svetlookov, a 'Smersh' or counter-intelligence service operative who constantly snoops on Kobrisov, who before the war
was jailed by Stalin. Svetlookov tries hard to recruit Kobrisov's orderly,
aide-de-camp, and chauffeur into his service.

General Andrei Vlasov is another controversial character introduced in the novel, albeit not in a major role. Initially, Vlasov distin-
guishes himself in the defence of Kiev and in the battle for Moscow,
but when he is taken prisoner by the Germans he becomes the commander of the so-called ROA, or Russian Liberation Army, composed
of Soviet war prisoners captured by the Germans. The objective of the
ROA is to join the *Wehrmacht* in its war against the Soviet army.
According to Vladimov, Vlasov is not an important character and he
became a traitor by sheer chance. Had he not been taken prisoner by
the Germans he would probably have become a decorated Soviet mar-
shal. Vlasov naively believed that he could become the leader of some
third force, opposing both Stalin and Hitler. In the end, he pays for this
delusion with his life.[28]

In the concluding pages of the novel Kobrisov is on his way back to
Moscow. Another senior officer is now in charge and leads the army
Kobrisov formerly commanded in the risky attack of which the latter
does not approve. When Kobrisov hears, however, on the radio that
the town in question has been taken, and that he is rewarded and promoted anyway, he rejoices regardless of his previous stand.

Despite the fact that half a century has passed since the end of the
Second World War, the appearance of this novel met with a heated and
polarized critical reaction. Most liberal critics, in particular those of the
younger generation, treat the novel as a work of art, while members of
the conservative nationalistic camp attack it for its alleged distortion of
historical facts. Thus, Mikhail Lobanov condemns Vladimov for ideal-
izing the image of the German General Guderian while painting the

General Zhukov in negative colours. Similarly, Lobanov accuses Vladimov of falsifying facts by insinuating that counter-intelligence officers in the Soviet army were ordered to spy on high military commanders. In support of his allegations Lobanov quotes an article by the writer V. Bogomolov, a Second World War participant who allegedly presents verifiable facts to counter Vladimov's evidence.[29] Other critics assail Vladimov for raising the issue of the Vlasovite traitors, and accuse him of creating a positive picture of German generals while failing to mention the Nazi atrocities.

N.L. Leiderman and M.N. Lipovetskii detect another, allegedly artistic, shortcoming in the novel. They claim that since Kobrisov is ready to serve the Soviet state but not the communist regime, Vladimov 'fails to provide a clear artistic answer of how one is to serve the state without supporting the regime.'[30] Moreover, they assert that the fact that Kobrisov is jubilant upon hearing about the local victory and his promotion, despite his initial opposition to this risky operation, proves that 'the decoration and high esteem transform his [Kobrisov's] words about saving Russia, for the price of Russia, into words only, and no more. Because not having subdued the general by force, the regime buys him with an expression of appreciation. This in turn destroys the whole edifice of the novel, and the "arch" which unites the different episodes in the novel collapses, turning it into a vulgar simulation of "the truth".'[31] One can argue, of course, with this proposition, but it appears to be clear that under Stalin's rule one could not serve the state without serving the regime. The state machine was an expression of the communist regime, and the slightest hint of any vacillation was fraught with terrible consequences. Andrei Nemzer is more charitable. He likes the contrasting parallels between the three tragic heroes, Kobrisov, Guderian, and Vlasov, and he approves of the diction, plot, psychological insights, and illogical hope in the novel. To Nemzer, *General i ego armiia* is a 'great novel.'[32]

As a work of art the novel has both merits and flaws. It falls short, however, of the artistic level reached by Vladimov in *Vernyi Ruslan*. The language is occasionally verbose, the narrative is rambling, and the author interrupts too often with his comments and interpretations. Moreover, most characters, including Kobrisov, are not adequately developed. The novel deals with acute, dramatic collisions of great magnitude and tension, yet this intensity is absent in the portrayal of direct human relations. Since *General i ego armiia* is a novel, rather than a historical text, the author has some latitude in using historical material. And yet, since the subject is so sensitive, it is the author's responsibility to make sure that he is truthful, and that important historical facts are not distorted. It is implied in the novel that most Soviet war prisoners who join Vlasov's army do so because they hate Stalin and want to avenge the atrocities and suffering to which their families were exposed in the Soviet Union before the war. In reality, however, many of those who joined the ROA did so to avoid hard labour, abuse, and starvation in the German camps for Soviet prisoners of war.

Despite the criticism and certain shortcomings, the appearance of Vladimov's most recent novel was an important literary and cultural event. The novel addresses many important issues which were previously taboo. Many of the problems discussed, however, require further elucidation and clarification in order to prevent the history of the Second World War from becoming a bone of contention between the different political parties and warring writers' communities in contemporary Russia.

3
The Mature Generation

Most writers of the mature generation discussed in this chapter are now in their late fifties and sixties. They all matured in the Brezhnev era of stagnation and were educated in the spirit of the Soviet totalitarian myth. Some complied hesitantly with the publication requirements of the Soviet regime; others refused to accept official ideology at its face value and were forced to go underground. Thus Leonid Borodin was denied publication and imprisoned in the Soviet GULag, while Viktor Erofeev was victimized by the Soviet authorities and expelled from the Writers' Union. Eduard Limonov, on the other hand, went into exile. He stayed for several years in the United States, and subsequently moved to Paris.

The writers of the mature generation are a diverse group with varied thematic, artistic, social, and political interests. Some of them limit their activity to literature, while others are actively involved in political, social, and religious affairs. In all instances, however, the creative output of the mature authors reflects, in a sense, their life experience, and their current non-literary inclinations.

Leonid Borodin

Leonid Borodin, born in 1938 in Irkutsk, occupies a special place in contemporary Russian literature. A social and political individualist, he became an opponent of the Soviet regime early in his life. He was not, however, a liberal or pro-Western dissident, and his main interests lay in the areas of religion, Slavophilism, and Russianness. In 1967 Borodin was arrested, convicted, and sentenced to six years in a labour camp for being a member of the illegal 'All-Russian Social-Christian

Union of the Liberation of Nations.' After his release from prison Borodin continued to oppose the regime and in 1982 he was again arrested, tried, and sentenced to ten years in prison. Early in the 1980s Borodin was offered a choice between prison and emigration, but he preferred jail in his native land to loneliness in exile. With the rise of Gorbachev to power, and the release of all political prisoners, Borodin was set free and resumed his literary activity. In 1992 he was appointed editor-in-chief of *Moskva* (Moscow), a journal with an obvious Russian Orthodox bent, and early in 2002 he was awarded the prestigious Solzhenitsyn Prize for his literary activity and dedication to his native land.

Borodin's first mature works of prose, the stories 'Povest' strannogo vremeni' (The Story of a Strange Time) and 'Vstrecha' (The Meeting), were written in prison. Since, under Soviet rule, Borodin was denied publication, most of his works of that time were published in the West. Today, Borodin continues his literary activity as a free man. As the editor of *Moskva* he has changed considerably the face and subject matter of the journal. At the same time, he is producing narratives of significant artistic and social merit.

In 1998 Borodin published the novel *Triki, ili khronika zlobnykh dnei* (The Three 'K's, or the Chronicle of the Wicked Days).[1] The three Ks are the first letters of the surnames of the three main characters of the novel. Krutov, Klimov, and Krapivin are close school friends in a provincial Russian town. Krapivin becomes an influential KGB officer in Moscow, and with his help the other two also move to the capital. Krutov works as a school teacher of literature; Klimov becomes editor of a scientific journal, writing poetry in his spare time. Both Krutov and Klimov are involved in underground dissident activity. They attend meetings of a select group of Moscow intellectuals at which issues of philosophy, ideology, Slavophilism, and cultural nationalism are discussed. Krutov eventually becomes involved in the publication of an illegal Slavophile journal. Consequently, he is arrested and sentenced to a lengthy prison term. Klimov, whose father-in-law is an important literary bureaucrat, manages to avoid arrest by becoming an informer and assisting the security to assemble their case against his friend. Krapivin, a lieutenant-colonel in the KGB, has many important contacts, but does nothing to help Krutov. Moreover, when Krutov is in jail, Krapivin visits his wife, who subsequently bears Krapivin a son. In the days of *perestroika* Krutov returns home from jail and is faced with this new family reality. At first he suspects that Klimov is the culprit, only to realize later that Krapivin, who introduced Krutov to his wife, is the real offender. Krutov is, of course, furious, and seeks vengeance against his former friends.

The novel opens with a scene in which the drunken Klimov is ready to kill himself in anger and desperation. In another scene Krutov, who hates Klimov, arrives, allegedly to avenge himself on his enemy. Most of the novel, which concludes in 1993, when anti-government opposition forces barricaded in the building of the Russian parliament are attacked by the Russian military, consists of a flashback that tells the story of the three friends. After many years they meet accidentally on that ominous day at the Russian White House, and Krutov eventually forgives his old friends.

The novel combines exposition of the illegal activity of those who have sought answers to Russia's problems in religion, Slavophilism, and the return to Russian national roots with an intricate personal and family drama. It also contains elements of a detective novel, with special reference to the work of the Soviet internal security forces, and allusions to the workings of the Soviet literary bureaucracy and the censorship apparatus. It is equally evident that Borodin draws on his personal experience and bestows on his main hero, Krutov, some of his own character traits. Like Borodin, Krutov is a truth seeker. He is not vindictive, and he is ready to forgive those who hurt him. He wants to become a true believer, and he seeks God and a special path for Russia's future. Borodin is a compassionate observer of the human predicament. He seeks solutions to human problems in Christian understanding rather than in political action. He is indulgent to the failings of his characters, trying to understand what motivates their actions.

Triki is a straightforward third-person narrative. The language is refined, the plot is inventive, with some dramatic intensity, and characterization of the three protagonists is adequate. There are, however, certain compositional problems. Structural sequentiality is sometimes confusing, and some of the intellectual discussions presented are superficial and leave the reader wondering about the real beliefs of those who risk their freedom by becoming involved in underground dissident activity.

In Borodin's next novella, 'Povest' o liubvi, podvigakh i prestupleniakh starshiny Nefedova' (A Tale About the Love, Exploits, and Crimes of Sergeant-Major Nefedov; 1999),[2] the action takes place during, and immediately after, the Second World War, in a small town on the shore of the Lake Baikal. The hero, Nefedov, an attractive, middle-aged man, is in charge of a military detachment stationed there to protect the nearby railway station. All women, mostly widows, or with husbands at the front, are in love with him. After Nefedov is demobilized, he settles down and falls in love with a woman named Liza. Unfortunately, Nefedov then becomes entangled in a love affair with a teacher in the local school, and Liza's son, who adores his stepfather, becomes desperate. He runs away from home and sits on a remote dangerous cliff. Nefedov returns to Liza, saves the boy, and blows up the cliff. For using explosives without permission, however, Nefedov is jailed and he is only reunited with Liza and her son after Stalin's death.

This realistic story is told by a first-person narrator who has allegedly been a student at the local school in those ominous days of the Second World War. The novella illustrates the harshness of Stalinist rule. But neither here, nor in *Triki*, does Borodin write directly about camp and prison life in the Soviet Union. Instead, he usually deals with issues of justice, and shows how good people are brutally punished for alleged minor transgressions. The focus in Borodin's prose is always on individual human experience. He does not absolve his heroes of responsibility for their deeds, but he provides them with the ability to seek understanding, to admit their guilt, and ask for, or grant, forgiveness.

Boris Ekimov

By the early 1980s the so-called Soviet Russian village prose had exhausted itself as a literary trend. Some Russian writers, however, continue to set their novellas and stories in the Russian countryside, and devote their main attention to the current situation in the Russian village. Boris Ekimov (b. 1938), a resident of the Volgograd region, is one such writer. Ekimov is exceptionally free of political or ideological biases, and both the liberals and representatives of the conservative 'patriotic' camp praise his work. He is a traditional realist, untouched by recent postmodern departures from established literary norms, who focuses his attention on the social and moral problems of contemporary Russian village life. Ekimov is an impassioned observer of the current changes in the Russian countryside, and he does not pretend to have any solutions to the problems he exposes. He also allows his characters to speak for themselves.

Ekimov's story 'Fetisych' (Fetisych; 1996)[3] is set in the early post-Soviet days at a farmstead in central Russia. The hero of the story is the nine-year-old Iakov, nicknamed Fetisych to indicate that his maturity is unusual for his young age. Life in the countryside is in disarray. Iakov's mother works hard, while his stepfather spends his time in lazing and drinking. Iakov himself is industrious and diligent. He helps around the house, and attends the local school where there are only five young pupils. When their elderly female teacher dies unexpectedly, Iakov, the senior pupil, feels the burden of responsibility, and keeps the school running. He approaches the principal of a school some ten kilometres away and asks her to send a replacement for the former teacher. Instead, the principal is so impressed by Iakov that she offers him a place in the local school, and a bed in her house. At first, Iakov is exhilarated by this generous proposal, but when he returns home he becomes depressed. He realizes that he cannot desert the other children in the local school. Without him the school in the farmstead will be closed and its premises plundered by the members of the disintegrating collective farm.

Ekimov does not judge the actions of his characters, nor does he analyse the reasons for their deeds. He simply describes an episode of life in the Russian village and contrasts the behaviour of Iakov who, despite his young age, has a mature conscience and a firm sense of responsibility, with that of his stepfather and others, who are corrupt, irresponsible, and prefer to steal rather than to work. There is no overt message in the story, but there is an oblique suggestion that the future of Russia lies with the young, those little affected by the influence of Soviet depravity, and still untouched by the new Russian corruption.

In the story 'Vozvrashchenie' (The Return; 1998)[4] the main character is an old woman in the Cossack land. She is hard-working, lonely, religious, and constantly praying. One day someone steals her icon with the image of the Holy Mother. The old woman is devastated. A girl who stays with her is inspired to draw a picture of the Holy Mother to replace the icon, and the health of the sick old woman improves. The old woman is drawn in the tradition of Solzhenitsyn's Matrena and Rasputin's Daria. She is thoroughly selfless, forever helping others and expecting little in return; she always forgives those who wrong her and prays for them. The language in the story is laconic and it flows smoothly. Appropriate simple peasant talk and metaphors create an atmosphere of humility.

In 'V stepi' (In the Steppe; 1998)[5] the first-person narrator driving in the steppe sees a man trying to rebuild his farmhouse, apparently destroyed while he was in hospital. The man wants to restore the past, but his effort is futile, especially since he appears to be ill. His wife brings him food and cries, not because the house is destroyed, but because her husband is obviously mentally deranged. The scenario described is symbolic. The recent changes in Russia have generated some positive developments, but they have also devastated a way of life and destroyed the security to which ordinary people were accustomed. There is no direct denunciation of the current system of government in this story, just a simple picture of Russian country life which is more informative than any intellectual deliberations about social and economic conditions.

One of Ekimov's most important recent publications is the novella 'Pinochet' (Pinochet; 1999),[6] in which he describes the disintegration of the collective farm system within the framework of a family drama. The protagonist is the chairman of a *kolkhoz* (a collective farm), Korytin, a professional who returns from the city to the village to take on this thankless job. Korytin's father, the former chairman of the *kolkhoz*, had extracted at his death bed a promise from his son that after his father's death the young Korytin would return to manage the farm. The son tries hard to fulfil his obligation. He introduces strict labour discipline, fights thievery and corruption, and takes away stolen property. The times, however, have changed. Peasants fear nothing, and they are members of the *kolkhoz* not to work, but to steal. They hate Korytin. He, and his rigid controls, are in their way. Hence, they nickname him Pinochet.

Korytin has a twin sister, a physician living somewhere in Siberia. When she comes to visit her brother and his family, the peasants complain to her. They denounce Korytin's fierce ways, but she cannot understand why everyone hates him. Moreover, she wonders why he has taken this troublesome job in the first place. Korytin does not tell her that their father extracted a commitment from him, and he tries hard to minimize the effects of the social conflict on their family relations.

The third-person narrative reads well and its language is conventional Russian. The plot of the story is simple, covering no more than a week in the life of the Korytin family. In a flashback we are told about the family past. Under the surface there is an inherent intensity to the story. The tension is evident in the life of the peasants, and in the family life of the Korytins, as well as in the relationship between the social and private lives of the characters. The description of peasant life in Russia today is truthful and precise, without embellishment or exaggeration. Ekimov does not moralize, nor does he preach. He does not even hint at any possible solutions to the dilemmas presented.

Ekimov continues to be active. In the last few years he has published a number of new sketches about the Russian village under the general titles of 'Ocherki nashikh dnei' (Sketches of Our Days) and 'Zhiteiskie istorii' (Everyday Stories). In these stories he writes about the current state of agricultural production is south-central Russia. Life in the countryside, he asserts, is difficult, but most people are still good. Ekimov respects the emotions of his characters, and he treats them with understanding.

Ekimov pays little attention to the changes in contemporary Russian literature. He claims that innovation is good, but it is more important to write well than to innovate at any cost. In literature, he asserts, everything must be simple, and clear to every reader.[7] According to Ekimov, sincerity is one of the most important features of both literature and life, and his attitude to religion is indicative of his personal honesty: 'he cannot simply choose and become a believer. Another childhood, another upbringing. One has to be honest with oneself. He is jealous of those who are true believers, because it is easier for them to live, and to die.'[8]

Viktor Erofeev

Viktor Erofeev (b. 1947), an author and literary scholar, and the son of a highly placed Soviet diplomat, was admitted to the Writers' Union in 1978. As an editor of, and contributor to, the infamous literary almanac *Metropol'* (Metropol'; 1979), which defied the Soviet literary bureaucracy and challenged the officially established criteria for Soviet literature, he was soon expelled, but in the days of *perestroika*, when censorship in the USSR was abolished, Erofeev reappeared on the literary scene. His article 'Pominki po sovetskoi literature' (A Funeral Feast for Soviet Literature; 1990), which provided a provocative, albeit somewhat biased, critique of the Soviet literary past, shocked the Russian literati, both liberal and conservative. Erofeev also published a number of prose fiction works, including the well-known short narrative, 'Popugaichik' (Parakeet; 1989), and the multidimensional novel *Russkaia krasavitsa* (Russian Beauty; 1990).

Erofeev is a sophisticated and skilled artist who refuses to adhere to conventional Russian artistic norms. His prose of the 1980s and early 1990s, in which reality and fantasy intermingle freely, is grotesque, absurd, full of explicit physiological and sexual detail and displays of sadistic cruelty. Spatial and temporal confines in his works are always vague, and his language is full of slang, obscenities, and naturalistic portrayal. The language and style of Erofeev's most recent works has changed little since the early 1990s, but the substance is different. In most new narratives the author-narrator, who speaks in the first person, is at the centre. Moreover, despite the fact that most of Erofeev's recent novels combine fact and fiction, they are topical and firmly rooted in contemporary life.

Piat' rek zhizni (roman reka) (Five Rivers of Life [A Novel River]; 1998)[9] is a blend of reality, fantasy, personal travel experiences, and deliberations on the human condition. The five rivers explored by the narrator, the Volga, Rhine, Ganges, Mississippi, and Niger, are located in four different continents, in Europe, Asia, North America, and Africa respectively. Each chapter in the book is set in a different part of the world. In some, the narrator travels down the river by boat. In others, he travels by land as well. The Russian first-person narrator is accompanied by a German friend, but other characters occasionally appear.

Characterization in this novel is inadequate and except for the narrator himself, most other protagonists are soon forgotten. The language employed is simple, but full of obscenities and foreign expressions, and many ordinary Russian words are often changed with the apparent purpose of adding a foreign flavour to the text. Similarly, depravity and sex scenes are utilized to attract the unsophisticated reader. Some intellectual observations and deliberations about the essence of faith and ritual, in particular in the remote regions of Asia and Africa, are interesting and witty, but they are usually superficial, and analysis of the events described lacks depth. In some instances the narrator assumes the pose of a prophet and calls for the creation of a new, unifying universal metaphysical religion for all mankind. No idea in this book, however, is fully developed. The author glides from one notion to another with the same ease as he flows down the river stream, leading the reader to conclude that human life flows as smoothly as the river itself. In the beginning, both life and the river are clear and pure, but with time, they become polluted and foul. Since water, just as air, is indispensable for our existence, the river symbolizes the desired unity of all humans.

In 1999 Erofeev published a collection of prose entitled *Muzhchiny* (Men).[10] According to the author, he was initially invited to write a regular column for the Russian *Playboy* magazine. He agreed, and sub-sequently decided to produce a book, including in it the articles published in the journal that have a common theme. Erofeev admits, however, that for the first time 'he has perceived a social responsibility for what he writes, because the material in the book is explosive. It deals with issues which run counter to the Russian tradition of male-female relations.'[11]

Muzhchiny is a collection of thirty-seven sketches, essays, and stories which include the author-narrator's views, impressions, and observations, most of which are related to his personal life. The first story sets the tone. It is about the 'morning miracle,' the masculine daily morning erection. The last story concerns the virtues of men and manhood. In between there are stories on a variety of unrelated subjects, as well as sketches of a number of Soviet writers. Special attention is devoted to Mikhail Bulgakov, Mikhail Lermontov, Semen Babaevskii, Vasilii Aksenov, and Evgenii Evtushenko, among others. Erofeev has little positive to say about Evtushenko, but he is much more charitable to Aksenov. The longest, and perhaps the most interesting, essay is auto-biographical. In it Erofeev recounts his family background, his father's position as a highly placed official in the Soviet diplomatic service, and his work as an interpreter for Iosif Stalin and an assistant to Viacheslav Molotov. The young Erofeev tries hard to comprehend the complex personality of Stalin and to understand the way his parents perceive him.

In other stories Erofeev deals with the relationship of men with women. In one instance he asserts that women in Russia are mistreated and shown little respect. On another occasion, however, he claims that women rule men, and that men are often ignored in Russia. In general terms the author is critical of Russia and its way of life, but he tends to judge other individuals more harshly than himself. The narrative is a combination of fact, invention, exaggeration, parody, satire, with a good dose of sex, all presented without chronological sequence or the-matic consistency. Some of the author's observations, however, are subtle, and despite his personal biases he provides some interesting insights into Soviet and Russian literature and life.

Erofeev's most recent narrative, *Entsiklopediia russkoi dushi. Roman entsiklopediia* (The Encyclopaedia of the Russian Soul: A Novel with an Encyclopaedia; 1999)[12] is not a conventional novel. It is rather an attempt to explore and analyse the Russian psyche and mentality, the Russian way of life, and the effect of past experiences on the current state of the Russian mind. At the centre of the narrative is the author-narrator, but the most important fictional character is an individual named Seryi, who appears to be the collective image of a common Russian, a member of the so-called *narod*. Seryi appears in many scenes. He dies, comes back to life, and dies again. The name Seryi, which literally means grey, alludes to the grey, dull, and often depressing life of the average Russian. The author clearly has a love-hate relationship with his native land. He is critical of many Russian habits and customs, yet he could not live anywhere else.

According to Erofeev the Russians are a talented people, but by nature they are both smart and stupid, suspicious and trustful, jealous and altruistic, lazy and eager to do something useful, moral and immoral, all at the same time. Moreover, Russia is the meeting point of the East and the West, it is inherently opposed to the influence of any outside culture. The narrator asserts that Russia exists in a state of delusion. It is assumed that the country is in the process of transition from one social system to another, from socialism to capitalism. He claims, however, that this is total nonesense, because there has never been real socialism in Russia, only state despotism, and there is no capitalism in Russia today, just a transformed state autocracy.[13] There may be an external appearance of democracy and free elections, but in essence the government system and the rule of power have changed little.

In his various narratives Erofeev makes a number of sensitive and insightful observations about the essence of the Russian national character. He is unable, however, to identify precisely how the Russian soul differs from that of other peoples'. Since the Russian term *dukhovnost'*, or spirituality, which is closely related to the notion of *nravstvennost'*, or moral and ethical principles, is difficult to define, the author has no qualms in stipulating that the Russian character is unpredictable, and Russia a country of paradoxes.

Erofeev's recent prose, in which social issues are highlighted, appears to have been greatly influenced by the current conditions of the Russian book market. This prose is still sophisticated, thought provoking, and, at times, shocking, but artistic perfection is not the author's main concern. Art has become for Erofeev primarily a means to produce a marketable product. That is not to say that Erofeev's recent narratives are devoid of meaning. In fact, in many ways, they are more serious than his earlier fiction. Erofeev's explications, and the contents of his books, are, however, not to everyone's liking. Thus

Boris Sokolov suggests that Erofeev has managed to reveal a new truth for Russian literature, namely, that if humans are stripped of their moral casing, only sexual instincts motivate their actions.[14] There is no question that there is an abundance of sex scenes and naturalistic portrayal in Erofeev's prose, but it is an oversimplification to contrast, in absolute terms, sexuality with morality, as Sokolov does. Human nature and social intercourse are much more complex than Sokolov implies, and Erofeev uses sex and sexuality in order to elicit a variety of different emblematic deductions of a personal, as well as of a social nature.

Evgenii Evtushenko

The famous Soviet poet Evgenii Evtushenko (b. 1933) is today better known, particularly in the West, for his recent novels, rather than his poems. The poet who writes prose usually draws his or her inspiration from the same roots that nurture the poetry, but this prose is invariably influenced by certain poetic traits. Such prose is ordinarily charged with emotional nuances, and has a distinct lyrical poetic atmosphere. Evtushenko's prose, like his poetry, is topical, highly individualistic, and contains a pertinent social message.

Most of Evtushenko's early prose, of the 1970s and 1980s, consists of journalism, but some narratives combine reality and fiction. His first novel, *Iagodnye mesta* (Wild Berries; 1981), is set in Siberia in the Brezhnev era, and it centres on the activity of a geological expedition. Evtushenko's second novel, *Ne umirai prezhde smerti* (Don't Die Before Your Death; 1993), is a deliberation on Soviet life during Gorbachev's rule.

Evtushenko's most recent narrative, *Volchii pasport* (Blacklisted Passport), published in Moscow in 1998, is a mélange of autobiography, memoirs, and literary history. It also includes ruminations on the general human condition and life in the Soviet Union and in Russia of the 1990s. These reflections are presented from a personal, and occasionally biased, vantage point, and the author admits that no autobiographical musings should be taken too seriously. As he asserts, 'we forget what we do not want to remember ... Hence, all memoirs, including my own, should be believed ... with reservations.'[15]

The narrative begins with the investigation of Evtushenko's family roots and his expulsion from school with a so-called *volchii pasport*, a ticket with no return. Born in 1933 in Stantsiia Zima, or Zima Junction, in Siberia, Evtushenko comes from a family of mixed German, Russian, Polish, Ukrainian, and Belorussian heritage. His grandparents were forced into exile from their Ukrainian village by the Russian tsarist government. Evtushenko's father, a geologist by profession and an amateur poet by inclination, is the prototype for one of the protagonists in *Iagodnye mesta*. The family saga also includes the story of the author's four marriages. Evtushenko does not blame any of his former wives for their marriage breakdowns, and he claims that he still loves all of them.

In the days of Brezhnev's rule Evtushenko was one of the best-known Soviet poets, and his works have been translated into seventy-two foreign languages. His position and prestige enabled him to travel all over the world and gave him the opportunity to meet a number of important Soviet and foreign dignitaries, as well as leading poets, writers, and artists. The list of foreign personalities encountered includes such luminaries as the writers John Steinbeck and Gabriel Garcia Marquez, and public figures such as Robert Kennedy and Jacqueline Kennedy. Evtushenko also writes about his meetings with important Soviet personalities, including Nobel Prize winners Aleksandr Solzhenitsyn, Boris Pasternak, and Mikhail Sholokhov, as well as Andrei Sakharov.

The history of the creation and publication of Evtushenko's poems and his continuous struggle with official censors and representatives of the Soviet ideological bureaucracy is also discussed in the book. Evtushenko describes in detail the background of one of his boldest poems, 'Babi Iar,' which inspired Shostakovich to create his 'Thirteenth Symphony,' and he recounts the particulars of his cooperation with the composer.

The most contentious issue in Evtushenko's autobiographical narrative is his relationship with the Soviet regime and the Soviet security forces. He describes how, in 1957, the KGB tried to enlist his services as an informer, but states unequivocally that he refused the offer. Many of Evtushenko's contemporaries, however, in Russia as well as in the West, wondered why the Soviet authorities were more tolerant of Evtushenko than of most other Soviet writers and poets, including the Nobel Prize winners Solzhenitsyn and Pasternak. Iosif Brodskii asserts that Evtushenko 'throws stones only in the directions that are officially sanctioned,' and David Remnick describes him as 'slippery and periodically brave.'[16] It may be some time before literary scholars and historians are fully satisfied with the accuracy of Evtushenko's account of his relationship with the Soviet authorities.

In the final pages of the narrative the author muses about the complexities of old age and about the human predicament in general. The last chapter is, in a sense, an appendix to the novel. It has not been written by the author himself, and consists of a number of critical quotations from articles and statements made by friends and enemies alike, published over the years.

This book is a lyrical publicistic novel in which the author and his social environment occupy centre stage. The material is not presented in chronological order, and the author rambles in space and time. There is a constant emphasis on the relationship between the Soviet regime and the intelligentsia, and the author stresses continuously his critical assessment of the Soviet system. Evtushenko is also critical of the current situation in Russia, and he has little positive to say about the Russian leadership of the 1990s. He admits, however, that to a certain degree he himself succumbed to Soviet brainwashing, and that it was some time before he could rid himself of that pernicious influence.

The narrative is informative and engaging, but uneven. Some chapters present original material with some new insights; others are hastily written and include discussion of events and personalities previously covered in *Ne umirai prezhde smerti*. Evtushenko suggests that Soviet censors helped many writers to master their literary skills, but this book would have benefited from the assistance of an experienced editor. It may be of interest, and of some use, to students of Russian and Soviet literature and society of the second half of the twentieth century. It is not, however, a substitute for serious Russian literary and social history.

Anatolii Kim

Anatolii Kim (b. 1939) is one of the writers who formerly belonged to the so-called *sorokaletnie*, or forty-years-old. Kim spent much of his youth in the Russian Far East, serving as a soldier in an internal security military detachment which escorted convoys of prisoners and guarded labour camps, and gaining valuable life experience at the same time. His first incursion into the world of the creative arts involved an attempt to write poetry. This was followed by an interest in painting, and study in a school of applied arts. In 1971 Kim graduated from the Moscow Literary Institute, and by 1973 his first published work had appeared in Leningrad. Kim's art blends his Korean and Asian heritage with his Russian experience and Soviet upbringing.

He believes that all mankind is composed of one nationality, *chelovek*, or human being. He claims that his language is the general language of the human heart, which everyone understands.[17]

Kim's fictional world is not exactly in the mainstream of Soviet and contemporary Russian literature. Both the structure of his plots and his language are unconventional. His prose is grotesque, lyrical, and inculcated with Romantic irony, and his novellas are full of exotic images, angels and demons, devils and saints. Kim's narratives, which are usually a mixture of reality, fantasy, and myth, pose important philosophical, religious, and ethical issues, making the reading of his prose always worthwhile, if not always easy to follow.

The title of Kim's novel, *Onliriia* (Onliriia), published in the 1995 volume of *Novyi mir*,[18] refers to a perfect world after resurrection, and apparently to the location where the dead reside. The novel begins with a story about Christ, who gives his flute to a suffering hungry shepherd boy who is waiting for his meal. Over centuries, the flute is passed on from hand to hand, and the tune that the young Christ plays could save the world. The initial myth about the flute evolves into a fantastic story about demons and angels who live among ordinary people, and about certain humans who have the ability to fly without wings.

Early in the novel we are told that the so-called hour *IKS*, or X, is the time when the end of the world is supposed to come. Sometime later the hour X arrives and everyone dies. Most people immediately resurrect, but the demons do not. Their appetite for earthly women is so great that they cannot abstain, and they are condemned to perish. The narrator, however, still hopes that evil can be overcome, and that the Creator will eventually forgive the demons who want to resurrect. It is also suggested that loneliness is a trait inherited by humans, angels, and demons from their Creator. He is one and all, others are essentially alone. He creates his own enemies to challenge Him, knowing well in advance that they will be defeated. The *Kniaz'*, or Prince, who leads the demons, receives his power from the Creator, even the power to kill His beloved son, but in the end he too is defeated. The novel concludes with a proclamation that faith, and the notion of immortality, can influence the behaviour and action of humans in a positive sense.

Onliriia is a mixture of fantasy, myth, and philosophical contemplation in which it is possible to detect parallels and allusions to life in the Soviet Union and in Russia today. From the fact that humans resurrect, while demons are doomed to perdition, we can infer that humanity is immortal and goodness triumphs over evil. The final message in the novel, the possibility of resurrection, which is the moving force of earthly life, is delivered only in the author's Afterword. Kim thus tacitly acknowledges that it is beyond his ability to integrate this important message within the main body of the novel.

Kim's prose flows smoothly, but the plot of the novel is intricate, and there are abrupt changes in the sequence of time, locations, characters, narrators, and themes. Third-person narration alternates with narration in the first person by both humans and demons, and the tangled structure of the novel makes it, at times, difficult to follow the course of events.

Kim's complex prose always generates critical interest. Some critics, however, have become impatient with his complicated plots. Thus, Andrei Nemzer criticizes the artistic quality of the novel and claims that there is no point in trying to summarize the contents of *Onliriia* because it has no definite plot. Moreover, he suggests that except for 'grotesque monstrosities' and some clichés, there is not much else in the novel.[19] Mariia Remizova, on the other hand, attacks Kim's philosophical approach to his subject. She claims that his philosophizing smacks of amateurism and accuses him of the 'distortion of Christian ideas, which are intermingled [in the novel] with contemporary reality, and fantasy.'[20] All critics, however, even those who are more indulgent of Kim's serious philosophic prose, refuse to accept his negativism, and the sadness and hopelessness which permeate this novel.

In 1998 Kim published a new novella, 'Stena. Povest' nevidimok' (The Wall: A Story of Invisible Beings)[21] which is vastly different from his other recent works. While there are many stylistic parallels with his earlier prose, the setting is realistic and the main characters are real people. The action in the story takes place in our own times and the narrative provides an account of a love affair, and a failed marriage. Anna is thirty years old and has a child from a previous marriage. Valentin is forty-six; he lives with, and has looked after, his elderly mother for many years. At first, it appears that Valentin is devoted, sincere, and in love with Anna, while Anna is unfaithful to him. It subsequently becomes clear that Anna is both unfulfilled and rather exhausted by Valentin's constant demands for sex. Valentin seems to be consumed with sexual passion, but apparently not much real love, for Anna. Initially, Anna likes Valentin's advances, but she also resents them. A family conflict is simmering and the partners try to straighten out their differences, but lack of communication and too much dissension preclude any reconciliation. Hence, despite their passionate attachment to each other they decide to divorce and build a wall in the house in order to separate their living quarters. Eventually Valentin leaves the provincial town for Moscow and accepts teaching jobs in foreign countries.

After their separation it becomes clear that both Valentin and Anna are afraid of rejection, and that both initially miss each other. Valentin's passion proves so strong that he finds he cannot live without Anna. Wherever he goes he is followed by her phantom, and no other woman can replace her. He starts to see Anna, to converse with her, even make love to her in his imagination. But when Valentin returns to Russia and goes to look for the real Anna, he is told that she is dead, that she was murdered. He cannot believe it. How can she be dead, when he is talking to and seeing her daily, in his dreams and hallucinations?

'Stena' provides a psychological investigation of a failed relationship between two apparently incompatible individuals. At times, however, it is difficult to distinguish what actually happens from Valentin's morbid imaginings. In the end, it is obvious that Valentin is so overcome by his passion that he cannot accept reality, and his vision becomes blurred. Stylistically, Kim is true to himself. The novella is not a straightforward narrative and it is told variously by Valentin, Anna, and a third-person narrator, as well as by a collective narrator, 'we,' who speaks in the name of both man and woman. In some instances the different narrators alternate even within a single paragraph.

In 2001 Kim published a new novel, *Ostrov Iony* (The Island of Jonah),[22] which has some parallels with *Onliriia*. In it the author relates the biblical story of Jonah, who disobeys the Creator's order and refuses to preach to the evil-doers. Jonah is punished by being swallowed by a whale, repents, and is saved by the Lord. In *Ostrov Iony* the prophet who allegedly continues his polemic with the Creator is granted immortality and banished to a remote island somewhere in the far East.

Most characters in this novel are phantoms, rather than real people. The 'I' narrator is a mystical invisible image, the so-called Guardian of the Word. He inspires and orders the allegedly realistic character A. Kim to write a novel about the expedition to seek out the prophet Jonah on his abandoned island. The writer A. Kim is one of the participants in this expedition. The conclusion of the narrative is anticlimactic, because the emphasis throughout the novel is on verbal exchanges between unrealistic characters, rather than action. The religious message is obvious. Humans are immortal, because they resurrect and continue their existence in the so-called Onliriia, but the writer A. Kim produces works of art only because he is inspired and empowered by his invisible Master to do so.

Onliriia and *Ostrov Iony* resemble religious and philosophical treatises rather than works of art. At the centre of these novels is intellectual discourse between poorly developed characters who are to be remembered by what they say, rather than by what they do. Kim's recent prose has been influenced by his obsession with issues of religion and faith, and the quality of his art has been sacrificed for intellectual theological effect.

Stylistically, Kim's recent prose has much in common with his earlier work, but thematically it abounds in new overtones, and in some of his narratives the influence of Tolstoi's philosophy is perceptible. Kim is an individualist who preaches cosmopolitanism. He asserts that people have different colours, faces, and religions, but similar feeling and emotions. He believes that nature and God determine human destiny. Kim declares that each individual is alienated from the masses, and that, therefore, he writes only about himself and about the psychological and emotional processes within himself. He asserts that his fictional heroes are followers of the aesthetic school of impressionism, and that he wants to explore the uniqueness of each individual. Moreover, he wants to portray the unique rather than the typical. He states that he is 'a writer of human uniqueness, and that he is drawn in his aesthetics not by the blunt symbol of the eternal, but rather by the trembling nuance of the fleeting.'[23]

Anatolii Kurchatkin

Anatolii Kurchatkin (b. 1944) is another member of the former *sorokaletnie*. A native of the city of Sverdlovsk, currently Ekaterinburg, he is a graduate of the Moscow Literary Institute, and now lives in Moscow. His first published work appeared in print in 1967, and he currently writes fiction and journalism on a variety of topics. His early prose is realistic and straightforward, but in the days of *perestroika* he diversified his style and produced the novella 'Zapiski ekstremista' (Notes of an Extremist; 1990), a narrative with an anti-Utopian vision which blends with an allegorical fantastic tale. In 2000 Kurchatkin published another fantastic narrative with an allegorical subtext, entitled 'Schast'e Veniamina L.' (The Luck of Benjamin L.).[24]

The main character of the story, Veniamin L., is a feeble-minded person. He is caught by humanlike rats and taken into the city's underground to meet their leader. The rats assign to Veniamin the job of negotiating and making peace with the people in the city. Once the peace is achieved, the blood-sucking human-rats come out from hiding. They rob and murder the people in town and take over the rule of the city. Veniamin L. is respected and protected by the rats as an honoured citizen, but he notices that he is slowly acquiring rats' features and turns himself into a humanlike rat. The mutation of people into rats becomes a natural process in the city. The rats justify their murderous and destructive actions by claiming that they represent a new stage in the evolution of nature.

Kurchatkin asserts that the urge to write the novella came to him not from literary recollections, but from the Russian soil, and from the difficult life in Russian today.[25] The story is obviously a satire on the recent economic and political changes in the country. After the collapse of the Soviet state, the former Soviet black marketeers emerged from their economic, criminal, and political underground and took over the country's economy, driving the majority of ordinary citizens into poverty. It appears that today, just as in Kurchatkin's story, adaptation and acquiescence are the only means of physical and emotional survival.

Kurchatkin's 'Sfinks' (Sphinx; 2000)[26] is very different. The story centres on Nina, a woman of consummate sexual passion and feminine power, who has the ability to entice any desirable man. She cannot be satisfied in a monogamous relationship, and at different times in her life she is a partner in different love triangles. Her sexual attractiveness is of such magnitude that her husband pretends ignorance and disregards her love escapades. At one point, Nina is involved in a car accident. Her husband is killed, and her own face and body are mutilated and deformed, but her sexual appeal does not diminish, and her former, presently married, lover is trapped again. Kurchatkin provides a realistic picture of female sexual passion which is used to seduce, manipulate, and subjugate men of different stations in life. He fails, however, to address the psychological aspects of female sexuality, and the essence of a relationship which is based not on love but on sexual attraction. Moreover, the title of the story, which is by no means complimentary to the heroine, requires further elucidation.

In 2002 Kurchatkin published a new novel set in contemporary Russia. Margarita, the heroine of *Amazonka* (The Amazon),[27] is an educated, intelligent, good-looking, single young woman. She tries hard to make ends meet, remaining honest at the same time. Unfortunately, time and again, she falls prey to various shady characters who use and abuse her. Life in Russia is difficult, and there are few opportunities for young female members of the former intelligentsia who are unwilling or unable to submit to those in power. Kurchatkin attempts in this novel to expose the corruption of the Russian state and business environment, but except for Margarita his characters are treated sketchily. Moreover, in order to keep the readers' attention, he concentrates on unimportant detail, rather than analysis, and employs a number of shoddy melodramatic devices.

Kurchatkin is an interesting writer who tries to innovate and diversify his thematic range, but in some narratives he repeats himself, while in others the characters are poorly developed, and the treatment of the conflicts and issues addressed is superficial.

Eduard Limonov

Eduard Limonov (b. 1943) is one of the Soviet writers who was exiled or emigrated from the Soviet Union and returned to Russia after the collapse of the Soviet empire. He is also among those returnees active not only in literature, but also in political activity. Limonov's plots have always been inventive, and his prose autobiographical, aggressive, full of scenes of perversion and sexual activity, and characterized by expressive language of high intensity. Little has changed from the early days. In his novel *Palach* (The Executioner; 1998)[28] which is set in New York in the late 1970s and early 1980s, Limonov wants to expose and denounce the corrupt and perverted way of life of the upper middle class in America. By providing a graphic picture of the sexual and sado-masochistic exploits of American women, the author also wants to attract the attention of the lower class of Russian readers who, in the Soviet days, were deprived of the possibility of reading such literature.

The novel obviously contains a number of autobiographical elements and much of it is apparently based on the author's own experience in New York in the late seventies. Many characters have real prototypes, and some of them, like Andy Warhol, even appear under their real names. Oscar Khudzinskii, a former student of philosophy and an aspiring Polish émigré, is one of the heroes, and his rise and fall is one of the main subjects of the plot. But the conclusion of the novel, in which Khudzinskii is murdered by an anonymous killer, and thus removed from the scene, is poorly motivated. Limonov fails to investigate the social or psychological reasons for his characters' actions, although he does not miss a single opportunity to describe the sexual proclivities of his heroines.

The fantastic novel *316, punkt 'V'* (316, Point 'V'),[29] published in the same year, is set in the year 2015, eight years after an alleged devastating nuclear encounter between Russia and the United States. Both countries have become police states, controlling the whole world, and close allies. Nuclear contamination has destroyed most food reserves and control of population growth is state policy. In the United States everyone over sixty-five, except for a few distinguished citizens, is to be killed; in Russia, everyone over sixty-eight is to face death. The bizarre, fantastic plot evolves around the internal struggle for power in America. Jenkins, the head of the department of demography, which controls population growth, organizes the murder of the President with the purpose of usurping power. Luk'ianov, a half-Russian writer of detective novels, looks exactly like Jenkins, and becomes his double. Ultimately, Luk'ianov manages to outsmart Jenkins and he becomes the ruler of America. Luk'ianov, who is sixty-five and was originally to have been killed himself, is even more zealous in enforcing the population control policies than his predecessor Jenkins had been. His sole objective is to strengthen his power and gain complete control over the country. The novel illustrates that the thirst for power and the struggle for physical survival is inherent in human nature. Today, in the age of nuclear proliferation, it is highly topical. As in Limonov's other narratives, the emphasis is on the detective elements of the story, rather than on characterization and psychological investigation.

Smert' sovremennykh geroev (The Death of Contemporary Heroes),[30] also published in 1998, is set in Europe. The three main characters, two men and a woman, meet in Paris. One man is an American journalist and editor of an English-language magazine in France. The other is a South American, from Columbia, apparently a gigolo who lives in Paris, and the woman is a drug runner and the daughter of a British lord. The three, who meet accidentally, decide to travel together to Venice. There, the Columbian and the woman are murdered in their hotel room. The American becomes frightened for his life and returns to his family in America.

Limonov is a prolific writer with a vivid imagination, and he is certainly a talented individual, but a great artist he is not. The action in the three narratives discussed above, all of which are set in foreign countries, is usually artificially concocted and poorly delineated. There is little logical sequence in plot development, and the ideas expressed are little connected with the actions of the heroes. Graphic portrayal of intimate sex scenes, and the profanation of the human body, is manifest in all three novels. Limonov's prose is dominated by his emotional drive and aplomb, which often prevent him from approaching his characters and plots in a detached and sincere manner. Similarly, the tone of his journalistic sketches is bitter and bellicose. This is particularly evident in his book of memoirs, given the odd title *Kniga mertvykh* (The Book of the Dead; 2000).[31] It is a book charged with tension and narrated in an angry voice. In it Limonov deliberates on the fate and actions of his contemporaries, most of whom are dead and have no chance to defend themselves.

The tone of much of what Limonov has recently written is influenced by his political views. After his return to Russia Limonov became directly engaged in political activity, and subsequently the organizer and leader of the Russian Nationalist-Bolshevik Party. Recently he has been accused of purchasing arms for this organization, arrested, and put in jail. The Russian PEN has published a statement in which it disassociates itself from, and denounces, Limonov's political views, but it calls for objectivity and openness in the investigation of his case.[32] Somewhat later Limonov published an open letter from prison, in which he recounts his literary accomplishments and asserts that he is the victim of political persecution and corporate vengeance.[33] Whatever the reasons for Limonov's political activity and his arrest, it is clear that he wastes his talent, and that artistic creativity is currently not his primary concern.

Vladimir Makanin

Vladimir Makanin (b. 1937) is one of the best-known, and most prolific, writers of the former so-called *sorokaletnie*. Born in the city of Orsk, in the Ural region, he arrived in Moscow in 1954, at the age of seventeen, to study mathematics. After graduating from the Moscow State University he soon abandoned his profession and embarked on a career in literature. Makanin's first narrative, *Priamaia liniia* (The Straight Line), set in a small scientific laboratory, was published in 1965, but before the 1980s his prose received little critical attention. Makanin avoided subjects of political significance, and shunned involvement in the internal conflicts in the Soviet writers' community. He was neither openly pro-Soviet, nor anti-Soviet, but he valued highly his personal freedom and integrity. He acted, in a sense, as an alienated individualist, keeping always to himself whether on the job as a scientist or as a teacher in the Moscow Literary Institute, preferring, at the same time, to experiment in his creative work with new themes, styles, and genres.

In the 1980s and early 1990s Makanin produced several anti-utopian, allegorical novels and devised plots of impressive philosophic significance. Action in these novellas is secondary to metaphysical deliberation, and human experiences serve only to illustrate the author-narrator's philosophical ruminations. In December 1993 Makanin was awarded the Booker Russian Novel Prize for his 'Stol, pokrytyi suknom i s grafinom poseredine' (Cloth-Covered Table with Carafe in the Middle; 1993). Since this was not a novel, but a forty-four-page *povest'* (novella), there were numerous allegations that the jury had violated the basic rules of the competition. Indeed, it was obvious that the Booker Prize was awarded to Makanin for the quality of his creative output as a whole, rather than for the novella in question. Five years later, in 1998, Makanin was awarded the prestigious German Pushkin Prize of Alfred Topfer, in the amount of 40,000 DM. In this case the prize was for Makanin's general creative contribution to Russian literature, rather than for a single text.

In the April 1995 issue of *Novyi mir* Makanin published a new story entitled 'Kavkazskii plennyi' (A Captive in the Caucasus).[34] Although Makanin once avoided burning political issues of the day, the subject of 'Kavkazskii plennyi' is topical. For the first time he sets the action in the Caucasus, where there is constant warfare between Russian soldiers and the so-called Chechen freedom fighters, who are allegedly battling for Chechnia's political independence. The title of the story recalls that by Leo Tolstoi, but the substance is different. In Tolstoi's story there is a semblance of humanity, and some basic rules of ethical conduct are still observed; in Makanin's narrative this is not true.

The story is composed of several externally unrelated episodes which are, however, thematically closely connected. Several trucks with Russian soldiers are stopped by a gang of unidentified Caucasian fighters who refuse the Russians passage through the canyon unless they are paid something in return. Two soldiers, Rubakhin and Vovka, return to their detachment, approach one of their commanders, Lieutenant-Colonel Gurov, and ask him for food or money to pay ransom to the fighters. Gurov, however, refuses to help. He has nothing to give, and is short of food even for his own soldiers. Rubakhin is distraught and decides to catch a Chechen prisoner, hoping to exchange him for the right of passage through the canyon. He apprehends a beautiful Caucasian boy who perishes, however, during a skirmish with another gang of Chechen fighters. In fact, Rubakhin kills the boy himself in order not to endanger his own life. Paradoxically, Rubakhin has already served his time in the Caucasus and was due to return home. He had decided to remain because he was attracted by the beauty of the region.

Unlike Makanin's other recent stories, in which most characters are abstract, inert, and often detached, here the characters are realistic and full-blooded individuals. Rubakhin is fascinated by the enticing beauty of the captive boy as well as the beauty of the mountains. In the end, he is so enamoured by the boy that their relationship acquires homosexual overtones. Oleg Pavlov questions, however, the captive's homosexual inclinations, because gays are abhorred by the mountaineers, and would never be accepted into a detachment of armed warriors.[35] The story ends inconclusively, but its message is clear. External beauty can attract, entice, and enchant, but it will not save the world, because physical beauty is seldom tantamount to the beauty of action. It can sooth the human spirit, and bring out the good in people, but it can also devastate and destroy.

On another level the story provides a sketchy picture of the war in Chechnia and the situation in Russia. Russian generals in Moscow are little concerned with the fate of Russian soldiers in Chechnia, and Russian commanders there are forced to sell weapons to the enemy in order to buy food for their soldiers. Precisely at the moment when Rubakhin arrives, Gurov negotiates a deal with the Chechen, Alibek, who is ready to provide Gurov with food in exchange for Russian weapons and ammunition. Russians arm the Chechens in order not to die from starvation, but the Chechens use those weapons to kill and maim Russian soldiers. Russian survival is in question, because Russian commanders unwittingly arm the enemy.

The most important of Makanin's post-Soviet-era writing is his new novel, *Andergraund, ili Geroi nashego vremeni* (Underground, or the Hero of Our Times), published in the 1998 volume of *Znamia*.[36] The first-person narrator, Petrovich, who is known only by his patronymic, is the hero of the novel. He has been married in the past, and has a daughter, but we know nothing about them; they do not appear in the novel. The story Petrovich tells us covers some thirty years of his life, but not chronologically. There is a constant alternation of time, space, and characters. In 1991, the last year of Gorbachev's rule, Petrovich is in his mid-fifties. He interweaves stories about his present experiences with flashbacks about his past, as well as with internal monologue and ruminations which inform us about his state of mind. He was for many years a writer whose manuscripts were constantly rejected by publishers because he was a *'drugoi,'* or an outsider, someone who did not belong to the fold, whose narratives did not conform with the requirements for official Soviet literature. Hence, Petrovich becomes a recluse, driven into the literary underground and forced to write for the drawer.

Unable to earn a living by publishing his prose, Petrovich becomes a watchman and takes care of temporarily vacated apartments in the so-called *obshchaga,* or communal dwelling. He has a brother, Benedikt Petrovich, or Venia, who is three years younger. Venia was once a talented painter, a genius, but as a student he was denounced and unjustly betrayed by a KGB informer, and consequently confined to a psychiatric ward. Anyone in the Soviet Union who was allegedly critical of the Soviet paradise was regarded as mentally unstable and in need of psychiatric treatment. Venia entered the hospital in good health, but the abuse and the so-called treatment in the institution turned him into a feeble, mentally unsound individual.

The novel is set in Moscow and the action alternates among three distinct locations. The first is the communal block of flats, where Petrovich moves from apartment to apartment, taking care of the possessions of original residents who are vacationing or away on business. The second is the psychiatric hospital where Venia resides, and where Petrovich himself is a patient for some time. The third is the cheap lodging house into which Petrovich is forced to move when the flats in the apartment block are privatized and his services are no longer required.

The novel is divided into five parts and twenty-six sections, each of which could be read as a separate story. In these sub-chapters Petrovich introduces the reader to an array of characters, including tenants of the block of flats, as well as some of his former colleagues, writers and painters. Some of the residents are local people, others are transients. Some are destitute, others are rich 'new Russians.' Some are single, others have families, and Petrovich, the friendly recluse, does not fail to take advantage of every possible opportunity to enter into a sexual relationship with his female acquaintances, even those who are married. The secondary characters in the novel are described only fleetingly; their role is limited to their brief interaction with Petrovich, and some disappear almost immediately. We encounter them in their relations with Petrovich, at different stages of his life: in the Brezhnev era, and later in post-Gorbachev Russia. Some have become successful business people, others have ended in the gutter.

Despite Petrovich's seeming amiability, it is clear that he is no angel, and that he has a violent streak. In fact, he is a murderer, and kills two people. In the first instance, Petrovich stabs a Chechen through his heart from behind. The Chechen had asked Petrovich for money, they drank together, then they fought. The second assassination is also cold-blooded. Petrovich kills a former art critic and KGB informer, Chubisov, who has altered his ways and is the father of two young sons. In both instances the victims appear to be innocent. Petrovich kills them in a cowardly manner, allegedly to protect his dignity and resist abuse. Moreover, the murder of Chubisov is for Petrovich apparently a symbolic act of vengeance over the system that has driven him into the underground and destroyed the life of his brother.

After the murders, Petrovich appears to have a guilty conscience and feels a need to confess his crime. Yet, at the same time, he does not genuinely feel guilty; he just wants to rid himself of the internal mental discomfort caused by his actions. At one point, he is suspected of murder and placed in a special psychiatric ward where alleged criminals are induced to admit to their wrongdoings. Despite his mental vacillations, however, the ego, the 'I' of Petrovich, turns out to be stronger than his conscience. He does not break down, nor does he confess.

Most important in the novel is Makanin's attempt to enter Petrovich's psyche and investigate his state of mind. Since the entire novel is narrated in the first person by the protagonist, we are only able to learn how Petrovich perceives his own actions, how he judges himself. Some of his deeds and thoughts, however, tell us about his logic, his values, and his assessment of himself as a human being. Initially, Petrovich goes underground to protect his art from corruption. The underground also provides him with the internal freedom to remain himself, to protect his 'I.' One is absolutely free when one has nothing, including living quarters. The importance of living quarters, or space, is an important subject in Soviet literature, specifically addressed in the prose of Iurii Trifonov. Without an address, without a personal living space, a human being is nobody. Homelessness absolves people, however, from any responsibility, and frees them from social obligation. It thus appears that Petrovich's retreat into the underground is not only an act of defiance, but also an escape and an admission of weakness and defeat. Unable to find a place for himself in the real world, he becomes superfluous. As G.S. Smith suggests, 'For Petrovich, there seems to be nothing worth fighting for beyond a solipsistic sense of personal identity.'[37]

In the end, it becomes clear that absolute personal freedom, alienation, and escape from reality cannot provide the individual with fulfilment and happiness. Hence, the novel concludes with the tender scenes of Petrovich's kinship with his sick brother. Friends, acquaintances, and casual sexual partners come and go, but relations between brothers endure. There are many parallels between the fictional Petrovich and the writer Makanin. Both are approximately the same age, and both leave the Ural region to study in Moscow. In contrast to Petrovich, however, Makanin learns to compromise and does not go underground.

Makanin's recent narrative is not a traditional novel, and its structure is rather unconventional. His prose, however, is realistic and the description of most characters and events is logical and to the point. The language employed is harsh, detached, and infused with irony, but there is little slang. The language is simple but exact, and the author obviously prefers precision to beauty. The accumulation of sketches of individuals, scenes, and encounters, as well as the gatherings of painters and writers, mostly social outcasts, both before and after *perestroika*, create an atmosphere of gloom and doom, and a feeling that an entire generation of talented people has been lost. Unfortunately, those who suffered most under the old regime have benefited least from the recent political and social changes. Moreover, there is little hope for them in the future. They are old, disillusioned, and unfit to continue their struggle.

As usual, Makanin finds the subject matter more important than the mode of description; consequently the predicament of Petrovich, and of the other characters to whom we are exposed, raises important ethical questions, such as what is right, and what is wrong, or what is honourable and what is unjust. The answer to these questions, however, is not immediately obvious and difficult to discover in the maze of human fates. Most characters are self-centred, and concerned solely with their own well-being. Even Petrovich is self-righteous as well as self-reliant.

Makanin's new novel has received much critical attention in Russia. Most reviews are positive, and the novel has been acknowledged as one of the major literary events of the year. Some, however, criticize Makanin severely, and point out that the novel is not true to life. Viktor Toporov writes in *Znamia* that 'Vladimir Makanin is a particularly gloomy writer, and that it is difficult to find anything more gloomy than 'Andergraund ...' The critics showed much kindness to him. There are and will be awards. The writer is talented, but his work is unreadable ... [and] an ethically false masquerade.'[38] While one can reproach Makanin for various artistic shortcomings, the novel appears to be gloomy because life in the Soviet Union, especially for those who dared not to conform with the demands of the system, was difficult and depressing.

Makanin's next story, 'Bukva "A"' (Letter 'A'), published in the April 2000 issue of *Novyi mir*,[39] is even more depressing, because it is set in a Soviet labour camp where the situation is horrid and the fate of the prisoners shocking. Prisons and labour camps in the USSR were not intended to rehabilitate and re-educate the inmates. Incarceration was simply a means of ridding society of the undesirable. Prisoners were exploited, abused, and humiliated; some were driven to madness and deprived of any hope for a better future. Makanin provides the reader in this story with a glimpse into the life of a labour camp in the Brezhnev era, and with a picture of the terrible waste of human potential. Except in the case of a homosexual who is terrorized by guards and prisoners alike, we learn little about the past of the prisoners. Makanin's main focus is on the general atmosphere in the camp and on its dehumanizing effect on both guards and prisoners.

The title of the story, 'Bukva "A",' refers to a letter engraved by the prisoners, in their own free time, on a rock just outside the camp. This appears to be a meaningless endeavour, yet the fact that the engraving is the result of their free labour, which the prisoners can view from a distance in their spare time, provides them with a temporary escape from their enslavement. The generalized image of the prisoners, and the allusion to the fact that those who guard them are made from the same clay, point to the criminality of those in charge of the Soviet system of justice, and the criminal nature of the Soviet state.

In 2001 Makanin published another topical experimental story with a fantastic plot. In 'Odnodnevnaia voina' (One-Day War),[40] Islamic students in the city of Kazan, the capital of the Tartar autonomous republic in Russia, rebel and Russian tanks move to suppress the rebellion. A resolution of the United Nations demands immediate Russian withdrawal and Russian economic centres are attacked. The Russians retaliate and launch a nuclear weapon on Chicago, wiping out half the city. The presidents of Russia and the United States are impeached, arrested, and expect trial.

Makanin's prose is simple and straightforward, and his style is versatile, but his narratives often have a complex and intricate structure. His plots are inventive and infused with dramatic tension. His images are vivid, and his heroes are portrayed in a dispassionate manner. In his recent works most characters are placed in extraordinary and difficult situations, and the author tries to investigate the effects of external pressure and internal stress on the behaviour of his heroes. He does not moralize, however, and rarely deviates from the main topic. As before, Makanin continues to be apolitical, yet most social problems posed in his narratives can be solved only with the help of political means. Moreover, in his last few narratives Makanin has exhibited a new interest in political and social issues of universal significance which may affect the survival of mankind.

4

The New Writers of the Perestroika *Era*

The authors who appeared on the Russian literary scene in the days of Gorbachev's *perestroika*, and in the immediate post-Soviet period, represent today the most active and vigorous group of Russian writers. Most of the writers discussed here are relatively young, currently in their thirties, forties, with a few in their fifties. Most of them reside in Moscow, although Mikhail Kuraev and Aleksandr Melikhov live in St Petersburg, Aleksei Slapovskii lives in Saratov, Oleg Ermakov lives in the Smolensk region, and Mikhail Shishkin in Zurich, Switzerland. Some authors, such as Aleksandr Ivanchenko and Valeriia Narbikova, who made a mark in the days of *perestroika* and in the immediate post-Soviet period, have lately published little of literary significance. Others, like Leonid Gabyshev, have disappeared completely from the literary scene.

The writers included in this group represent different artistic trends, they are stylistically diverse, and their works are thematically distinct. Thus, for example, Aleksei Varlamov and Sergei Kaledin produce works in the tradition of Russian conventional realistic prose. Valentin Pelevin, Vladimir Sorokin, and Iurii Buida, on the other hand, exhibit a predilection for postmodern artistic devices. In many instances, as in the case of Mikhail Butov and Shishkin, authors combine realistic narration with modernist techniques, creating novels in which style, narrative techniques, and creative modes overlap.

Iurii Buida

Iurii Buida (b. 1954) was born in the region of Kaliningrad, formerly Konigsberg, East Prussia, and is of mixed Russian, Polish, Ukrainian, and Belorussian parentage. He graduated from the Kaliningrad University, and until 1991 he lived and worked as a journalist in that city. At the same time, he made attempts to produce literary prose. In 1991, when the Soviet Union disintegrated, Buida moved to Moscow and published some of his previously written works. It was not long before he became known in Moscow as a prolific and original writer. In 1993 Buida published the novella 'Don-Domino' (The Zero Train), a tragic allegorical tale about people at a remote railway station deep in the Russian hinterland, and a strong indictment of the Soviet regime. In 1994 'Don-Domino' was short-listed for the Booker Russian Novel Prize.

In the mid- and late 1990s Buida published several novels and a number of short stories diverse in style and on a variety of different subjects. Some stories are set in Buida's native places and deal with the complex issues connected with the Soviet conquest of German territory. In others Buida concentrates on the fate of downtrodden individuals abused by fellow humans and neglected by fate. In still other works he attempts to come to terms with the Russian historical past, in particular the cruelty and violence of Russian rulers and princes. The style and artistic means in Buida's prose vary from story to story. Traditional critical realist texts may unexpectedly evolve into metaphoric narratives, and conventional realism often alternates with myth, fantasy, the grotesque, and the absurd.

Buida's best-known novel is *Ermo* (Ermo; 1996),[1] a sophisticated narrative play of words, events, and ideas placed within a realistic setting and written in elegant Russian. The hero, George Ermo, a Nobel Prize winner in literature whose real name is Georgii Ermo-Nikolaev, is the son of a highly placed official in the Russian tsarist government. Born in 1914, Ermo turns up after the October Revolution in the United States. After the Second World War, he usually lives in Europe. The life story of Ermo and his relationship with his two wives, Sofia and Liza, is interspersed with the history of his literary career. Passages from Ermo's novels are inserted into Buida's narrative, but these differ little in style and language, and one may wonder whether Buida and Ermo are not one and the same person. The prototype for Ermo may be Vladimir Nabokov, but the latter is not a Nobel Prize Laureate. Ermo's ties with Russia are weak, and his national and intellectual inclinations are rather of a cosmopolitan nature. While Ermo is often compared in the novel to Ivan Bunin and Vladimir Nabokov, his preferred author is Dante. Among Soviet writers Ermo likes Andrei Platonov, and approves of Mikhail Sholokhov's novel, *Tikhii Don*, but he dislikes Mikhail Bulgakov and Boris Pasternak.

Ermo spends much of his life contemplating the relationship between art and reality, invention and actuality, but he does not arrive at any ground-breaking conclusions. The story of Ermo's personal and family life is more interesting than the account of his literary activity, but even this is descriptive rather than analytical. Most important in the novel is its form, composition, style, and language, which may captivate the intelligent reader. That does not mean, however, that Buida's novel satisfies the expectations of all critics. Andrei Nemzer approves of the structure and style of the novel. He also likes the combination of erudition and fantasy in the narrative.[2] Evgeniia Shcheglova, on the other hand, asserts that the novel lacks dynamism, and that the author is emotionally detached from his characters. *Ermo*, she claims, 'is not a novel, but a richly instrumented phantasmagoria, painted in beautiful colours, but absolutely dead.'[3] The above notwithstanding, one cannot deny that Buida is a master of the word, and that the subject of the Russian cosmopolitan intellectual émigré is today topical and relevant.

In 1997 Buida published the novel *Boris i Gleb* (Boris and Gleb),[4] in which he attempts to re-assess five centuries of Russian history. The novel tells the story of a family in which the names of the brothers Boris and Gleb recur in every second generation. The narrative is a historical phantasmagoria, set within a religious and mystical context, in which cruelty and violence never end.

In 1998 Buida published a collection of prose entitled *Prusskaia nevesta* (The Prussian Bride),[5] which is regarded by some as a novel in novellas. The spatial and structural centre of most stories in this collection is a small town in the Kaliningrad region, but the style of each story is different and varies from fantasy and the grotesque to naturalistic realism. Most characters are simple local people. Some are eccentric, aiming at the impossible; others are engaged in a futile search for love in the wrong places. The narrator does not judge his characters; he accepts them the way they are, but in order to stress the effect of their behaviour he often resorts to the use of the literary device of shock. The stories are compact, with little redundant detail, providing, in an expressive manner, the most significant elements of human character and fate.

Buida's most recent prose is similar in form and substance to his earlier stories. Thus, 'Summa odinochestva' (The Sum of Loneliness; 1998)[6] is a series of sketches. Some are fictional, others rooted in reality. Some sketches deal with Russian lore and the so-called famous Russian *vran'e*, or habitual lie, common among the simple folk. Others explore highly intellectual and historical issues such as, for example, the genesis of Christianity. The peculiar phenomenon of human alienation and loneliness, even in the crowd, is emphasized in most stories.

In 2000 Buida published another series of short stories under the general title 'U koshki deviat' smertei. Povest' v rasskazakh' (The Cat Has Nine Deaths: A Narrative in Stories).[7] The action in most of these stories takes place in the post-war Kaliningrad region, and one story is set in Germany proper. 'U koshki deviat' smertei' is a tragic tale of a single lonely girl who searches for happiness in the wrong places, and in the end is seduced and abused by a gang of criminals. In 'Shkola russkogo rasskaza' (The School of the Russian Story) the author attempts to investigate the psychology of misunderstanding, lack of communication, and the generation gap in what appears to be a family of intelligent people. In other stories Buida dwells on the fate of the unhappy, the abused, and those who cannot find their way in the quagmire of human relations.

The prose of Buida is innovative, expressive, and often challenging. Buida is detached and non-committal, and the lack of much descriptive detail in his works often leaves the reader with hints not always easy to decipher. His language is refined, and his plots are well constructed, but his approach to the relationship between fact and fiction, reality and invention, is, just as in the case of Ermo, still in the process of evolution. Many of his stories have a moral underpinning, but equally important to Buida is the aesthetic aspect of his literary creation.

Mikhail Butov

In 1999 the Booker Russian Novel Prize was for the first time awarded to a young and aspiring author. Mikhail Butov (b. 1964) was selected for this honour for his novel *Svoboda* (Freedom; 1999).[8] Butov is a graduate of the Moscow Electromechanical Communication Institute, and a member of the *Novyi mir* editorial board. His first stories, published in the periodical press, appeared in 1992. *Svoboda* is Butov's first novel. It opens with the chronological introduction of the anonymous narrator's past, of his ancestors, and family history. Soon, however, the novel becomes a disorderly narrative without a clear beginning, middle, or end. The narrator claims that he 'started this narrative as a chain of humourous stories without suspecting that as it grows it will turn into a farewell to his youth.' Elsewhere he asserts that 'freedom begins where things stop hinting at anything, but themselves.' Hence, in order to achieve self-knowledge the hero feels an insatiable, unconscious urge of self-exploration, and a need to be left by himself, in a kind of self-exile. The disjointed narrative is the author-narrator's expression of extreme freedom, of his liberty to live, and to conduct his affairs, in the manner he wishes. Hence, the course of his life is determined by chance, by circumstances, and by intuition, as well as by the actions of friends, relatives, and strangers.

The narrative is not a conventional novel. It is rather a compilation of a number of self-contained stories, held together by the characters of the narrator and his friend Andriukha. Sporadically, other characters – neighbours, friends, and relatives – are introduced, but they soon disappear from sight without having made any significant impact on the development of the plot. The narrator attempts to discuss, albeit superficially, some topical issues of current life in Russian society, such as business activity, crime and the mafia, and immigration, as well as the political situation in the country. He also contemplates the human predicament, and the relationship of humans with nature.

The language and style of the novel are realistic, with an admixture of some slang, neologisms, and foreign words. The structure and composition, however, are postmodernist. Butov is an excellent observer. He is extremely good at describing in minute detail different elements of the natural world, as well as various aspects of daily human existence. His philosophical deliberations and the discussion of complex intellectual issues, however, are often convoluted and lack clarity. Butov's novel reflects, in many ways, the current attempt by many young Russian intellectuals to redefine themselves. Faced with a new reality in which values are no longer predetermined by those in power, some seek contentment in faith and religion, while others, like Butov's narrator, search for answers to the question of how to live within themselves.

Butov's newest story, 'V kar'ere' (In the Quarry; 2002)[9] is a short narrative with a definite setting and characters. A nameless father and his six-year-old son go deep into the countryside in search of rare stones and calcified bones of rare, ancient animals. Father is a professional engineer, but he has turned to the business of collecting rarities and selling them to Western buyers. Many Russians involved in this business have made a lot of money, but most of them wasted it all. Now, there are no longer any valuable stones remaining, nor any buyers to acquire them. The father appears to be an excellent parent with a deep understanding of his young son's mind. The boy, in turn, exhibits a maturity beyond his years, and is a keen observer who searches for answers to his father's complicated past.

As in the novel *Svoboda*, personal freedom appears to be the force that moves the actions of the protagonist. In retrospect, the father realizes that he could have arranged his life in a better and more useful manner, but he accepts the fact that it is impossible to rule fate in a preconceived fashion. In the background of the story there are hints at the current economic and social situation in the country, when Russians sell off their natural resources and rare valuable commodities to foreigners without concern for the future of their motherland.

The warm and sensitive relationship between father and son finds expression in dialogue, and their constant exchange of words reflects dedication, consideration, and mutual respect. Butov pays little attention to the external appearance of his characters, but he projects well their inner state, the conditions of their internal environment, and the historical past of our old and multifarious universe.

Oleg Ermakov

Oleg Ermakov (b. 1961) is another writer of the *perestroika* generation. He made his literary debut in the late 1980s with the publication of a number of stories and sketches about the Soviet debacle in Afghanistan. His best-known work is the novel *Znak zveria* (Sign of the Beast; 1992). It is a realistic third-person narrative set in Afghanistan, and interspersed with lyrical digressions, flashbacks, and internal monologue. Despite some compositional and stylistic shortcomings and the absence of thorough psychological analysis, Ermakov manages to provide an objective picture of the harrowing war experience in Afghanistan and the loneliness of the Soviet warrior in this hostile, alien world.

Diversification and the transition from one thematic realm to another is always a problem for young realistic authors, in particular those who draw their material and inspiration from real life experience. The case of Ermakov is no different. After demobilization, and the end of Soviet involvement in Afghanistan, he returned to his native Smolensk region in central Russia, and his role of a chronicler of the Afghan war was thus completed. Hence, Ermakov the writer finds himself in search of a new theme, and his new novel, *Svirel' vselennoi* (The Reed-Pipe of the Universe; 1997–9), published in three parts entitled 'Transsibirskaia pastoral' (Trans-Siberian Pastoral),[10] 'Edinorog' (Unicorn),[11] and 'Reka' (River),[12] respectively, is set in the 1970s, long before the Soviet invasion of Afghanistan. The main character, Daniel Men'shikov, is in the beginning of the novel seventeen years old. Like Ermakov, he is a resident of central Russia, but he hates his native place. He abandons home, moves to Siberia, and settles in the region of Lake Baikal. Men'shikov works for a while in a forest reserve and is attracted to the natural environment, but not for long. Soon he becomes bored with his monotonous existence and yearns for something new.

Before long Men'shikov is drafted into service in the army, but he decides to desert. For a while, he is on the run without any clear objective in life. At one point, he contemplates a return to his army unit, but he is hesitant and indecisive, and it is some time before he rejoins his army detachment. Surprisingly, Men'shikov is not punished for his desertion. He is viewed by his commanders as emotionally unstable and discharged from the army. The ending of the novel is inconclusive. Men'shikov is all alone in the *taiga*, drifting aimlessly in time and space. He reveres the natural environment and enjoys his absolute freedom without any responsibilities.

Ermakov's hero is a romantic dreamer, alienated from the real world and attempting to escape from the pressures of actual existence. It is clear that Men'shikov cannot find any satisfying outlet for his energies or a place for himself in the Russian Soviet environment. Hence, his concentration span and patience are of limited duration, and he is in the constant process of escaping reality. It is also obvious that, since Men'shikov is not a man of action, he is constantly wavering and unsure of the course of conduct his life is to take.

The passivity and indecisiveness of the hero also affect the artistic quality of the novel; without dynamic action the narrative becomes monotonous and repetitive. Moreover, the reader begins to wonder about the extent to which the hero reflects the state of mind of his creator. It is possible only to surmise from Ermakov's recent novel that he identifies, up to a point, with his protagonist, and that he is still in the process of his post-Afghan transition, and in search of a positive outlet for his new creative impulses.

Aleksandr Kabakov

Aleksandr Kabakov (b. 1943) is one of the new Soviet authors to appear on the literary scene in the days of *glasnost'* and *perestroika*. A mathematician by profession, he began to write fiction in the early 1980s, but only after the publication of *Nevozvrashchenets* (No Return; 1989) did he become better known in Moscow literary circles. In his early novels Kabakov tries to capitalize on the new opportunities of the Gorbachev era, and attempts to bridge the Soviet past with the unpredictable future of Russia. He creates anti-utopias, as well as narratives in which reality and fantasy, melodramatic love stories, and elements of the detective novel are all mixed together.

Kabakov's novel *Poslednii geroi* (The Last Hero; 1995)[13] is not much different. The novel is composed of three parts. Parts one and three are set in contemporary Russia; part two is set in the distant future, in a new Russia where public opinion is controlled by a special administrative office of social thought, and which is ruled by dictators. The main character and narrator, Mikhail Shornikov, is a Russian-Jewish writer, poet, and actor. Married three times before, he currently carries on simultaneous love affairs with a number of different women. At one point, all his former lovers get together with the purpose of discussing and sharing their love experiences. In the end Shornikov becomes involved with criminal elements, loses his living quarters, and becomes a homeless vagabond.

Life in the future Russia, as it is portrayed in part two of the novel, is strictly controlled by the government, and the truth is hidden from the people. Personal love and sexual intercourse are forbidden and children are produced to order, the product of artificial insemination. The narrator and his lover decide to uncover the truth and educate the people. They stealthily penetrate the local television station and make love on the stage in view of the masses. When the people learn the truth about sexual intercourse they demonstrate in the streets, but their expression of dissent is not welcome, and it is silenced with the help of tanks and arms.

Much of the space in the novel is taken up by introspection, internal monologue, and the discussion of intimate human relations, yet we know very little about the characters, of how they look, or what determines their actions. In the early prose of Kabakov the author, narrator, and hero are frequently fused together, often obscuring the main thrust of the story. In *Poslednii geroi* the author also becomes a participant in the action. At first, the narrator writes a letter to the author complaining that the picture of reality presented is not truthful. Sometime later the author replies, and tells the narrator that if he does not like what it is written he will produce even something more outrageous.

In the late 1990s Kabakov continued to produce experimental narratives in which he explores problems of artistic creation, and of the author's relation with his or her readers. In *Pozdnii gost'. Istoriia neudachi* (The Late Guest: A History of Failure; 1998–2000)[14] the author-narrator is the alter ego of his protagonist who tries, without much success, to create literary plots which can be utilized in practical life. Deliberations about life, and the place of the individual in our complex world, are intertwined with the notion of loneliness and the emptiness of human existence. The material is presented in the form of short stories about love, infidelity, perversion, drunkenness, and an attempt to fill the vacuum which pervades human existence with some meaning. Unable to fulfil his objective the hero, a dreamer, and a rebel, tries to escape from reality into nowhere. Circumstances force him, however, to return home, because one cannot break loose from oneself. One can escape a physical environment, but one's soul and mind irrevocably follow.

The narrative has no definite plot and much of it is presented in the form of internal monologue. Similarly most characters, including that of the hero, are elusive, and ill defined. It is obvious that a great deal of the material in the novel is autobiographical, and it may reflect the author's own state of mind. Kabakov is now sixty years old and he apparently finds himself at a crossroads in his life and work, searching for new themes, creative means, and a new way of life.

Another story by Kabakov, published recently, may substantiate this proposition. In the Introduction to 'Den' iz zhizni gluptsa' (A Day in the Life of a Fool; 1996–8)[15] the author asserts in the first person that many years ago he wrote the beginning of a novel which he has unfortunately never had the opportunity to finish. Now, he has decided to publish the incomplete work. The narrative is composed of two parts. The first part, a fiction of the author's imagination, is about a Russian architect, born in France, who decides after the collapse of the Soviet Union to retire and move to Moscow. The second part is about the author himself, and his attempts to change his lifestyle, to stop drinking, end his affairs with prostitutes, eschew debauchery, and move from emptiness into real existence. Unfortunately, just as in the case of his hero, the efforts of the author are futile. In *Pozdnii gost'* Kabakov imparts his personal problems and shortcomings to his hero, and does not participate in the action directly. In 'Den' iz zhizni gluptsa' he discards the pose and reveals, in the first person, his personal dilemmas for all to see.

Kabakov's prose may be original, ingenious, and topical, and the author may be good at creating anti-utopias, and satirizing life in Russia and the Soviet Union, but his narratives are repetitive, they lack depth, and his characters are poorly developed. One of the main subjects of *Poslednii geroi* is the problem of the intelligentsia in post-Soviet Russia, and the downfall of a Russian-Jewish intellectual who cannot find a proper place for himself in the new conditions. The style and the method of presentation in the novel, however, do not do justice to the subject. There is certainly more to the issue than sex, infidelity, and sheer fantasy.

Sergei Kaledin

Sergei Kaledin (b. 1949) is another Soviet prose writer who made his literary debut in the days of *perestroika*. His first publication, the novella 'Smirennoe kladbishche' (The Humble Cemetery; 1987) is a naturalistic sketch set at a city-cemetery; the characters are social outcasts and alcoholics who occupy the strange world where life and death, funerals and wakes, cohabit. Kaledin's narratives, including his novellas 'Stroibat' (Construction Battalion; 1989) and 'Pop i rabotnik' (The Priest and the Worker; 1991), are carefully constructed, and his plots are usually original and innovative.

His recent novella, 'Takhana merkazit' (Central Station; 1996),[16] is set in the state of Israel and deals with such topical issues as immigration, mixed marriages, and terrorism. The plot of the story is simple. Naum Nim, a divorced Russian Jewish scientist who presently resides in Israel, leaves in his will to his former Russian wife, Irina, and their daughter Natasha, his summer house located on the shore of a lake in Israel. Irina, in turn, approaches a relative, Petr Ivanovich Vasin, a professional carpenter, and asks him to go to Israel to assess the state of the villa, and if required to make the necessary arrangements for repair. Vasin, who is initially not friendly to the Jews, realizes in Israel that religion divides, rather than unites, people, and that the essence of existence is hidden in the nature of humans. While people can be good or bad, there is only one God.

Petr Ivanovich travels to inspect the villa with the son of a former Soviet citizen he encounters in Israel. On their way back to Jerusalem the bus in which they travel is blown up by a female suicide bomber and both Petr Ivanovich and the youngster who accompanies him are killed. The conclusion of the novella is unexpected and speaks to the unpredictability of human fate. Petr Vasin perishes at the very time when a transformation in his world-view takes place. Naum Nim, now an Israeli scientist, is still in love with his former, much younger, Russian wife. Similarly, many former Soviet Jews residing in Israel are still emotionally attached to their motherland. Although discriminated against in Russia, they continue to cling to its history, its culture, and to the memories of their past.

The narrative is realistic and flows smoothly. Most of the plot is obviously the product of Kaledin's imagination. There are also, however, some autobiographical elements. Kaledin lives in Moscow, but his son Dmitrii, who is also a writer, lives in Israel. Dmitrii's mother, apparently Kaledin's former wife, likewise lives in Israel. Naum Nim, to whom the novella is dedicated, is a close friend of Kaledin.

Kaledin's topical novella reflects the political changes in Soviet Russia in the last quarter of the twentieth century. The Soviet Union had been surrounded by the so-called Iron Curtain and no emigration was possible. At end of the century, in particular after the ascent of Gorbachev to power, the situation changed drastically, and citizens of the former Soviet Union are scattered today in a variety of countries all over the world. This migration has affected not only the demographic situation in a number of countries, but also the style, content, setting, and language of Russian literature, which is gradually becoming more universal and thematically all-embracing.

Mikhail Kuraev

Mikhail Kuraev (b. 1939) is another writer who made his mark in the late 1980s and early 1990s. In the late 1990s he produced little of any literary significance. His recent narrative, 'Razreshite proiavit' zrelost' (Please, Permit to Display Maturity; 2000),[17] is written in playful, ironic language. It is a story narrated in the first person by an alleged anonymous student who recounts his experience of studying the compulsory subject of Marxism-Leninism at the Leningrad State Institute of Drama. Special attention is devoted to the personality of the professor of Marxism, Ivan Vasil'evich Loktev. The narrator compares the teacher to a preacher who regards the subject of instruction as holy, and believes that its truthfulness is unquestionable. Moreover, whoever has the temerity to doubt the correctness of the party line at any given time is in danger of being expelled from the Institute.

The narrative captures the realities of Soviet higher education and indoctrination. The story is truthful to life, and it is narrated in simple Russian, in a jocular tone, and with much dialogue. The main conflict between the professor of Marxism and his wavering student is charged with dramatic intensity. In the end, however, the author-narrator points out that in retrospect the study of Marxism-Leninism, a subject of so little practical use, has certainly been a total waste of time.

Aleksandr Melikhov

Aleksandr Melikhov (b. 1947) is another prolific Russian writer whose name became well known in the days of *perestroika* and the post-Soviet era. He is a graduate of the mathematical-mechanical faculty of the Leningrad State University, and presently resides in St Petersburg. Much of his early childhood, however, was spent in Kazakhstan. Melikhov is the author of a number of novels, including *Izgnanie iz Edema: ispoved' evreia* (The Exile from Eden: The Confession of a Jew; 1994), *Roman s prostatitom* (A Novel with a Prostate; 1997), *Nam tselyi mir chuzhbina* (We Are Strangers in the Whole World; 2000),[18] and *Liubov' k otecheskim grobam* (The Love of Paternal Graves; 2001).[19] All of them are autobiographical, written in a confessional style, and contain the same characters, mainly members of the author-narrator's family.

Two major themes recur in all of Melikhov's novels, internal family relations, which are described and discussed candidly, and the problem of mixed Russian-Jewish marriages, in particular how they affect family connections and the future of progeny. The narrator's father is Jewish, his mother and wife are Russian. His children, who are only 25 per cent Jewish, are nonetheless affected negatively by their mixed ethnic background. According to the narrator the Russians form a unity, and the half-Jew wants to become part of that unity, but he is seldom accepted. Anti-Semitism is prevalent, and the Russian finds fault with the Jew even if the latter is perfect. The narrator is torn between the two conflicting sides of his personality. He often hates Jews, because they regard him as a Russian and hate him. The Russians, on the other hand, hate him because to them he is a Jew. Despite his close relation with his immediate family, the narrator is overcome by loneliness, and by the feeling that he is stranger in the whole world.

In *Liubov' k otecheskim grobam* one can also perceive the author's concern with the morality and ethics of life in post-Soviet Russia. He designates the present corrupt state of affairs M-Culture, or Masturbation Culture, meaning that positive values are debased, and there is noth-

ing real. 'Love in masturbation culture does not have any real equiva-
lent ... and masturbators seek God not to serve Him, but for self-
satisfaction.'[20]

Melikhov's prose is lucid, but since ideas, rather than events, are
usually at the centre of his narratives, his plots lack firm construction.
The material is presented as a slice of life without chronological
sequence, and narration shifts unexpectedly among different locations,
and from one group of characters to another. The characters of his
father and wife appear, however, in all of the novels, and the reader
perceives them only as the author sees and judges them. Their role is to
illustrate and elucidate the narrator's point of view, rather than to act
independently.

The author-narrator, who is also the main character in the novels, is a
romantic idealist who seeks happiness and harmony in a fractured
world. Melikhov is a serious writer who tries, through his protagonists, to unravel complex intellectual and social issues, such as the
relationship between the individual and the collective, the body and
the spirit, reality and imagination. Unfortunately, there are no easy
answers to the questions posed, nor are there readily available solutions to the rifts between different ethnic and national communities in
Russian society today.

Viktor Pelevin

The forty-year-old Viktor Pelevin (b. 1962) is today one of the best-
known contemporary Russian prose writers, both in Russia and in the
West. A former student of the Moscow Institute of Power Engineering
and the Moscow Literary Institute, he began writing fiction in his mid-
twenties, and his first collection of prose, *Sinii fonar'* (Blue Lamp), published in 1991, was in 1993 awarded the Russian 'Little Booker' Prize
for the best work of short fiction.

Pelevin's creative personality is peculiar. Brought up in a traditional
Soviet *nomenklatura* family, he quickly adapted to the changes in post-
Soviet Russia, rebelling, in a sense, against his own past. Today,
Pelevin is a semi-recluse in his native country, sporting a shaved head
and dark glasses. He disavows any social responsibility or moral role,
and says that he is disgusted with his own country. He shuns publicity,
does not participate in the activities of the Russian literary circles,
refuses to give interviews to Russian journalists, and spends months
meditating with Buddhist monks in Korea. He also publishes post-

modern fiction, speaking with a voice authentically his own. Despite his considerable popularity, Pelevin is one of the most controversial writers in contemporary Russia. Although he is one of the few authors able to survive on the income generated from the sale of their books, he has as many detractors as he does followers.

In the second half of the 1990s Pelevin published two narratives similar in style, but different in substance. The introduction to one of them, *Chapaev i Pustota* (Chapaev and Void; 1996)[21] states that the book was written in the mid-1920s in a monastery somewhere in Mongolia, and that the real author is anonymous. Moreover, the reliability of Dmitrii Furmanov's book *Chapaev* (Chapaev; 1923) is questioned. Thus, instead of clarifying the subject, the introduction deliberately confuses it.

The action in *Chapaev i Pustota* is set in two unrelated and alternating realms. In one, the hero and narrator, Petr Pustota, a minor Petersburg poet, is in danger of being arrested for the unconventional views expressed in his poetry. He escapes to Moscow, where he is caught up in a series of major upheavals, including murder and assuming a false identity, but he eventually enlists in the service of the legendary revolutionary commander Chapaev, as a political commissar. Petr Pustota travels, with Chapaev and his beautiful machine-gunner Anna, to the Ural to join in the civil war and engage in battle with the Russian White Army.

In the other realm Petr Pustota, who allegedly suffers from a split personality, is a patient in a mental institution. There he is first exposed to military psychiatric investigation, in the course of which he is drugged and hallucinates. Later he participates in sessions of group therapy, the objective of which is to rid Pustota of his 'second' shadowy personality. In the end Timur Timurovich, the psychiatrist, tells Pustota that he is cured, but Petr becomes aware that it is impossible to distinguish between what is real and what is an illusion, because reality itself is an illusion. Unable to resolve this dichotomy, Pustota escapes into the emptiness of Inner Mongolia.

The surname of the novel's hero, Pustota or void, is the main symbol of the narrative. Chapaev tells Pustota that 'every form is emptiness,'[22] and that there is nothing but oneself, which is also empty. The insecurity and uncertainty of Pustota also affect the reader, who is in constant doubt as to what is real in the novel and what exists only in Pustota's mind. Chapaev, Kotovskii, and Anna may be viewed as real historical figures at one point, while at other times they seem to be pigments of Pustota's morbid imagination. The narrative and its protagonists alternate between reality and dream, actuality and hallucination, and the reader is not sure whether the events in the novel, which take place in post-revolutionary and contemporary Russia, or the experiences of the protagonists, which are concerned with Russian and West European culture, philosophy, and the arts, have any realistic significance.

Pelevin draws on Soviet history, Buddhist philosophy, and contemporary Russian life in this novel. The four patients in the mental asylum represent four strata of Russian society. One is a member of the intelligentsia, another represents the simple masses, the third is a vagabond, and the fourth is a 'new Russian.' Their mental illness represents their individual emptiness, but it also symbolizes the emptiness of life in contemporary Russia in general. The notion of the futility of life, and the emptiness of the material concerns of human existence, find expression in Pelevin's personal immersion in Zen Buddhist philosophy, which apparently results from his belief that all reality is illusory.

Like that of *Chapaev i Pustota*, the introductory note to *Generation 'P'* (1999)[23] contains a disclaimer. The novel is dedicated to the middle class, but it is also suggested that 'the opinions of the author may not be the same as his view point.'[24] Moreover, in a quotation from Leonard Cohen we can perceive Pelevin's own voice exclaiming, 'I love the country, but I can't stand the scene. And I am neither left or right ...'[25] The introduction is again intended to confuse the reader and to convince him or her, from the very beginning, that the author is objective and non-committal. It suggests also, perhaps, that the whole story is a conceptual notion or a virtual invention.

The above notwithstanding, *Generation 'P'* has a realistic setting in contemporary post-Soviet Russia, and an array of characters which represent a certain segment of Russian society. Unlike many of Pelevin's works, this novel is topical and its subject contemporaneous. The biographical background of the protagonist, Vavilen Tatarskii, has much in common with the past of the author himself. Like Pelevin, Tatarskii studies engineering and later enrols in the Literary Institute to study poetry, and just as Pelevin is involved in the study of Zen Buddhism, Tatarskii is engrossed in the study of eternity. With the collapse of the Soviet empire both the author and his hero are faced with a new reality. The talented Pelevin becomes a successful prose writer, while Tatarskii, the poor poet, has a hard time adjusting to life in this new world. At first he works as a sales clerk in a kiosk owned by a ruthless Chechen. Somewhat later he is introduced by an old friend to the advertisement business, where he is employed as copywriter and creator of advertisements.

Generation 'P' exposes the corrupt nature of the Russian market economy, which has adopted and perverted many aspects of Western business. Advertisement, the main objective of which is to befuddle the consumer, is the new ideology of the Russian business class. In the West both those who order and those who produce advertisements intend to confuse the buyer. In Russia, the creator of advertisements also tries to deceive the businessman who orders the script. Tatarskii's involvement in different facets of the advertisement business reveals the technology of creating public opinion in Russia, and exposes the reader to the criminal elements and practices connected with this business. As the action in the novel evolves, in order to move the plot, the author introduces a number of gangsters, con men, drug addicts, and advertisement 'professionals' with whom Tatarskii occasionally associates. Tatarskii is a creature of the current age, and a product of the new Russian conditions, but he seeks narcotic stimulation in order to escape from this reality into a world of phantasmagoric invention and Buddhist exploration.

Pelevin's recent novel received a mixed critical reaction, in Russia as well as in the West. *Chapaev i Pustota* was disregarded by the judges in the 1996 competition for the Booker Russian Novel Prize in Literature, and *Generation 'P'* was ignored by the 1999 jury. And yet Irina Rodnianskaia asserts in *Novyi mir* that Pelevin is a serious and important literary figure, and that his last novel is a major literary event. Moreover, she regards Pelevin as a wise and serious individual.[26] Most other critics, however, including Andrei Nemzer and Pavel Basinskii, although they pay due to Pelevin the storyteller, criticize harshly the artistic quality of his prose. Nemzer, for example, states that Pelevin is an 'infantile writer producing books for an infantile society';[27] Maksim Pavlov writes in *Znamia* that *Generation 'P'* is contemporary and interesting, but it is also superficial and lacks truthfulness. He asserts that by replacing real life with the virtual space of television Pelevin manipulates the consciousness of the reader.[28]

The Lithuanian critic Roza Glintershchik is most outspoken in her criticism of Pelevin. She asserts that plot construction and storytelling form the basis of Pelevin's talent, but that the main objective of his art is to debase and malign the human character, and to debunk and ridicule all ideals, dogmas, and myths. She further argues that Pelevin rejects reality and transforms it, in his works, into nightmares and dreams of a tired consciousness. She asserts that Pelevin's images are coarse and abrupt, his prose is sloppy, and that it is written in the language of newspapers and cheap detective novels. Moreover, she claims, Pelevin is emotionally detached and pays no attention to detail, or to circumstances of time and place (chronotop).[29]

While most critics attack the extremes of Pelevin's postmodern art, N.L. Leiderman and M.N. Lipovetskii assert that by moving away from the basic tenets of postmodernism Pelevin is compromising his post-modern past. They suggest that his 'last novel illustrates the internal limitations of Pelevin's poetics. From the depth of post-modernism Pelevin turned in a paradoxical manner to the Russian classical tradition with its passionate urge of moralizing which is directed towards the creation of a religious-philosophical ideal, even utopia.'[30] In the West, where Pelevin has many fans, the criticism is more guarded, and yet Anthony Quinn, a critic for the London newspaper *The Independent*, writes that 'Victor Pelevin may have the goods on the state of contemporary Russia, and maybe even the state of contemporary advertising, but the flights of fancy that constitute the latter half of this book induce not so much moral vertigo as long-haul ennui.'[31] Pelevin generally ignores his critics, but in one instance he did not hesitate to humiliate Pavel Basinskii, the literary observer from *Literaturnaia gazeta*, by having him fall, in his last novel, into a heap of dung in a makeshift lavatory.

Today, Pelevin's art remains controversial in Russia, and many claim that it requires further study. His novels combine elevated subjects with the grotesque and the absurd, and his prose is crammed with ironic allusions to the Russian historic and cultural heritage, classical literature, and Buddhist philosophy. Yet he perverts the ideas explored. He reduces their meaning by rendering them subject to disputes by the mentally ill, buffoons, or individuals under the influence of hallucinogens. The notions expressed by his characters, in a serious tone, may be simplistic, but this may be precisely the reason why they attract the attention of his young, disaffected readers. Pelevin constructs his novels in the current idiom of the young generation. His language is cool and detached. He experiments and innovates, playing with words, style, structure, and composition.

There is no doubt that Pelevin is a talented writer with a vivid imagination, and that he has the ability to convince the unsuspecting reader that fiction and reality can be one and the same thing. Pelevin attempts to investigate the essence of reality and the crisis of identity, but in the end he concludes that there is nothing but emptiness. Indeed, solving philosophical problems and psychological analysis is not the prerogative of postmodern art. Hence, Pelevin is able to pose serious questions in his novels, but he does not have the necessary tools to answer them. Instead, drawing on his own reclusive experience, generated by his disenchantment with social existence, he implies that for those who are alienated from the mainstream of life, the solution is an escape into oneself. Real freedom, according to Pelevin, can be attained only in complete ignorance and emptiness. This is a negative solution, which leaves the ordinary individual in the dark, because there is no escape from the realities and pressures of daily life, and not everyone can take refuge in a monastery in Korea.

Pelevin is a product of his time. His works express his disgust, as well as fascination, with the new modes of life and consumer culture in post-Soviet Russia. But he makes ample use of the newly developed market economy to promote his books, some of which may have little artistic, literary, or social value.

Viacheslav P'etsukh

Viacheslav P'etsukh (b. 1946) is a professional teacher who began writing prose in the 1970s, but he became known to the reading public only in the days of *perestroika*. P'etsukh's plots combine reality and fantasy, fact and fiction. His main topics are Russian history, human nature, and the relationship between life and the arts. His prose is eclectic, and in many instances outside the mainstream of contemporary Russian literature. Among P'etsukh's characters we encounter political and historical figures, peasant drunkards and city homeless, as well as saints and angels, witches and phantoms. P'etsukh utilizes a variety of stylistic and artistic devices, including hyperbole, the grotesque, and parody.

In 1997 P'etsukh published a collection of prose entitled *Gosudarstvennoe ditia* (The Child of the State)[32] which includes stories about city and country life, as well as a tale of the same designation as the title of the book. The plots of the stories are simple, and they are usually narrated in the form of *skaz*, or non-literary narration. The protagonist of most of P'etsukh's works is a collective hero who represents the Russian people. P'etsukh searches for the inexplicable irrational essence of Russian national existence, and its guiding reference point, which is almost impossible to detect. Unfortunately, most serious issues addressed in P'etsukh's stories find no logical solution. The dramatic collisions are often absurd, weighty issues are trivialized, and the author treats important subjects in a humourous, playful manner.

P'etsukh's most recent story, 'Kryzhovnik' (Gooseberries; 2002),[33] is in many aspects similar to his earlier prose. The hero, Sasha Petushkov, is a *Komsomol* (Young Communist League) official in Moscow who is sent with a delegation to the city of Magadan, in the Far East, to inspect the work of the local administration. Upon arrival Petushkov gets drunk, joins first a gang of former convicts, and then a group of followers of a pagan religious cult, and returns to Moscow many years later. In the post-Soviet days Petushkov becomes a successful businessman, then a leader of a socialist-monarchist political party. After having failed in all his grandiose endeavours, he returns to his house in the countryside and grows various kinds of gooseberries. This new preoccupation affords him much satisfaction. Only then does Petushkov remember the pronouncement of an unfrocked monk in Siberia, who admonished that only foolish people are unhappy, because life itself is the endless source of happiness. Petushkov realizes how little one needs to attain real happiness.

As in most of his stories P'etsukh infuses his plot with a touch of common sense, peoples' wisdom, and simple human life philosophy. The language in the story is sprightly, imbued with humour, and steeped in fantasy. Unfortunately, P'etsukh has recently begun to repeat himself, and he often broaches the same ideas in stories with different subject matter.

Evgenii Popov

Evgenii Popov's (b. 1946) debut on the Russian Soviet literary scene is connected with the appearance of the clandestine almanac *Metropol'* (Metropol'), published in 1979. It forced the writer into the literary underground and caused his expulsion from the Writers' Union. In the days of *perestroika*, and after the dissolution of the Soviet Union, Popov published most of his underground narratives. His recent book, *Podlinnaia istoriia 'zelenykh muzykantov'* (The Real Story of the 'Green Musicians'; 1999)[34] has two parts. The first is the story of the 'green musicians,' allegedly written in 1974 but never published in Brezhnev's Russia. It is a narrative about the young Ivan Ivanovich who, under the influence of a newspaper editor, Popugasov, decides to become a writer. Unsuccessful in this endeavour he soon abandons the idea and becomes a bureaucrat. Popugasov introduced Ivan

Ivanovich to drugs and in one of his dream-hallucinations he sees the green musicians.

The second, much longer, part of the book consists of Popov's commentaries on the story about the green musicians, as well as on Soviet and current Russian life. Special emphasis is devoted to the author's involvement with literature and the arts. The commentaries provide a satirical and derisive picture of life in the former Soviet Union. Unsuccessful in his early determination to become a professional writer, the author-narrator himself is in all probability the prototype for Ivan Ivanovich. Indeed, Popov was refused admission to the Moscow Literary Institute twice, and to the Institute of Cinematography once, graduating in the end from the Institute for Geological Studies.

Popov's commentaries address a number of serious issues, such as morality, spirituality, and love and faith, but he treats these problems lightly, in an unobtrusive manner, and with humour. Popov's prose is expressive, and it flows smoothly, but the material is presented without temporal chronology or spatial sequentiality. The transition from one subject to another is abrupt and unexpected. It becomes clear that Popov is a dedicated democrat who advocates freedom, understanding, and tolerance for all.

Mikhail Shishkin

The award of the Booker Russian Novel Prize has become one of the most important events in the life of Moscow's liberal literary intelligentsia, and the choice of the winner is usually controversial. Little changed in 2000, when the novel *Vziatie Izmaila* (The Conquest of Izmail; 1999),[35] by Mikhail Shishkin (b. 1964), was awarded the prize. Shishkin appeared on the Russian literary scene in the early 1990s. His narrative *Vsekh ozhidaet odna noch'* (A Single Night Awaits Us All; 1993), published in *Znamia*, is modelled on the mid-nineteenth-century Russian novel. Its language and style are excellent, but it has little substance.

Shishkin's recent novel, *Vziatie Izmaila*, begins as a lecture in which stories and images from the times of antiquity are presented. This confusing introduction is followed by the stories of two families. One is about a certain Aleksandr Vasil'evich, a lawyer; the other is apparently autobiographical and relates the life story of the narrator himself. Under the surface there are some obvious parallels between the two plot lines. In the first Aleksandr Vasil'evich marries Katia, who bears him a handicapped child. Katia is dejected and suicidal. Unable to cope with the tragedy in her life, she is placed in a mental institution. Initially she intends to stay there only for a while, but in fact she never returns home. The narrator has also been married, to a woman named Sveta. They part, however, after their son is killed in a car accident. Subsequently, the narrator moves from Russia to Zurich with a female Slavist student from Switzerland whom he encountered in Moscow. Zurich is today Shishkin's place of residence.

Between the two realistically presented plot lines there is an array of disconnected passages, relating stories of various characters, as well as episodes from Russian and general history. At times these stories are heart wrenching and clear, at other times they are confusing, and difficult to follow. These unrelated sketches, images, and historical events are indiscriminately intertwined, creating a chaotic picture of reality. The language of the novel is refined and exquisite, but characterization is inadequate. Structure is unconventional and may be intended to imply that life, just as the composition of the plot, is chaotic, confusing, and unpredictable. The title of the novel may have some historical connotations, but it refers directly to a show in the circus where mice, attracted by chunks of cheese, climb over a fortress and allegedly take the fortification.

The award of the Booker Prize to *Vziatie Izmaila* generated much critical attention. Most critics, including the author himself, have guardedly expressed surprise. Some have even admitted that after having read the first fifty pages of the convoluted text they gave up, and stopped reading it altogether. One critic even claims that 'Shishkin could not give any answer to the question ... what his novel was about. Indeed, it is about everything and nothing ... it can be read beginning from any page – perhaps even better from the back forwards.' [36] And yet, the respected critic Karen Stepanian asserts that 'the power of artistic expressiveness, the depth and subtlety of psychological analysis' in the novel are such that there 'is nothing in post-Soviet literature of the last decade to compare with it.' [37] The language in the novel is indeed expressive and polished, but since characterization is superficial we learn little about the hidden character traits of the heroes, and have difficulty in perceiving the course of their actions correctly. Characterization in a novel is always associated with psychological investigation, because it is impossible to analyse the psychology of a character we hardly know. Shishkin tells us about the psychological implications of the tragic life experiences of the female characters,

Katia and Sveta, but he fails to demonstrate them. Thus, instead of being able to judge the relative actions of the characters by himself, the reader is forced to believe, or not, any inferences made by the omniscient narrator. This is not to say that Shishkin is not a talented writer. His plots are innovative, and he is an excellent stylist. He is not afraid to experiment with both language and substance, but his prose is almost plotless, often confusing, lacks logical affinity, and is not easy to read.

Aleksei Slapovskii

Aleksei Slapovskii (b. 1957), a resident of the city of Saratov and a graduate of the philological faculty of the Saratov University, is one of the many Russian provincial prose writers who became known in the early days of the post-Soviet era. Slapovskii is a prolific and versatile author who produces narratives in a variety of styles, and in genres which are often difficult to define. His *Den' deneg* (The Day of Money; 1999)[38] has a puzzling subtitle, *Plutovskoi roman*, which literally means a Rogue Novel. The rogue or picaresque novel has its roots in sixteenth-century Spain and its hero is usually a *picaro*, a merry rascal who lives by his wits. Realistic in manner, episodic in structure, and narrated in the first person, the picaresque novel is generally a vehicle for satire. Slapovskii's novel, however, has hardly any of the above prerequisites and barely conforms to the requirements of a conventional novel. And yet, it is an interesting story which provides the reader with a number of pertinent insights into contemporary Russian provincial life, with particular reference to the details of Russian habitual drinking parties and the associated amity and fraternization.

The plot of the novel is simple. Three old school pals and neighbours, now in different walks of life, find a wallet containing a lot of money, and begin to argue about how to divide and spend the cash. Since the only thing the three have in common is their fondness for alcohol, much of the narrative is taken up by the description of drinking bouts. The three lucky friends decide to give away the remaining money to the needy, to the poor, or to the famous. Most, however, of those who are offered the generous gift are suspicious and refuse to accept it. Some reject the money out of self-respect and vanity, most decline to take it because Russians believe that unearned money seldom brings good fortune and happiness. In the end, the original owner of the wallet appears, but since all the money has been spent on drink, he joins the others in merriment and drinking. Soon the party is over, and the novel is brought to a logical conclusion.

This grim story, with its ironic intonations, begins and ends with scenes of drinking, leading the uninitiated reader to believe that alcohol is the moving force of Russian provincial life. Alcoholism is indeed a major problem in Russian society, and Slapovskii's narrative emphasizes some important social and psychological traits connected with this phenomenon. Artistically, however, the novel is far from perfect, and it seems to have been hastily produced. The narrative lacks focus. Characterization is superficial, and we learn little even about the three protagonists. Authorial intrusions often distract the reader from the action and the inclusion of parody of various contemporary Russian writers and critics has more to do with the author's ego than with the subject matter of the novel. The above notwithstanding, Slapovskii has talent. His narratives are interesting and easy to follow. His plots are inventive, and he is not afraid to experiment with style and substance. It would be helpful, however, if he were to concentrate on analysis rather than description, and if he worked more closely within the confines of a particular genre.

Vladimir Sorokin

Vladimir Sorokin (b. 1955), a graphic artist by profession, began to write prose in the early 1980s. His first novel, *Ochered'* (The Queue) was published in Paris in 1985, but none of his works were published in Russia before 1991. In 1992 a small volume containing seventeen stories, and simply titled *Vladimir Sorokin* (Vladimir Sorokin), appeared in Moscow. It was soon followed by the publication of a number of Sorokin's works previously published in the West.

Sorokin is an unusual figure on the Russian literary scene. His prose is peculiar and eccentric, shocking and grotesque, and full of sexual deviance and physical abuse. At times, his stories are exciting and thought provoking, at other times they are obscure and irrational. Most of his novels contain passages written in elegant nineteenth-century Russian realistic prose, as well as paragraphs of incomprehensible gibberish. Sudden transitions from one narrative mode to another are always connected with thematic and contextual change which is usually unexpected and shocking.

In Russia Sorokin is regarded as a postmodernist as well as a conceptualist. Unlike postmodernism, which is an expression of relativism, conceptualism in literature is play with language signs which have no meaning. According to Sorokin, in conceptualist art 'the relation to the object is more important than the essence of the object itself. Conceptualism means a remote relationship to a work of art, and to culture in general.'[39] Sorokin's novels, published in Russia in the mid- and late 1990s, follow the well-established pattern of his earlier stories. In *Tridtsataia liubov' Mariny* (The Thirtieth Love of Marina), published in Moscow in 1995, but written in 1984 and published earlier in Germany and France, Sorokin remains true to himself. The two parts of the novel are different in style and in substance. The first part describes Marina's life since early childhood. She is raped as small child by her father, and she also witnesses her mother's debauchery (the mother unabashedly brings lovers into the house). Sometime later she is raped by a counsellor in charge of the Young Pioneers unit to which she belongs. Older girls teach her to masturbate and soon she is introduced to lesbianism. Over time she has twenty-nine different female lovers, as well as some affairs with men. The mature Marina becomes a music teacher at a House of Culture of a major plant, experiments with drugs, hates the Soviet system, and associates with political dissidents.

In the second part of the novel the father of a pupil, a certain Rumiantsev, who is the leader of the party organization at the plant, comes to pick up his daughter after the music lessons. When Rumiantsev sees that Marina is tired, shaky, and feels ill, he offers to take her home. He stays there over night, makes love to Marina, and for the first time in her life she experiences an orgasm with a man. Under the influence of this encounter Marina is instantly transformed into a diligent worker and a dedicated citizen of the Soviet state. The portrayal in the novel continues in the spirit of socialist realism. It deals with production accomplishments, Soviet politics, and the glorious leadership of Iurii Andropov. The title of the novel, *The Thirtieth Love of Marina*, obviously refers to Marina's love of the Communist Party and the Soviet state. The fact, however, that Marina's new inspiration comes from an illicit sexual affair with a highly placed party official, who is unfaithful to his wife, is never mentioned, because this would allude to the hypocrisy of Soviet leaders who preach one thing but practice something entirely different. It is clear that those who cheat on their spouses can hardly be trusted in other matters. Sorokin thus illustrates two different sides of Soviet life. The first is full of dissolute behaviour, abuse, and perversion, the second appears to be orderly, ethical, and patriotic. In reality, both sides are negative and corrupt, with the only difference being that in the first case depravity is readily apparent, while in the other it is hidden under the surface.

Sorokin's subsequent novel, *Goluboe salo* (Blue Lard; 1999),[40] combines science fiction, fantasy, and some distorted realistic detail. The narrative is set in two distinct time frames, the last years of Stalin's rule and the distant future, in the second half of the twenty-first century. Facts about historical figures and dates of real events are misconstrued and changed. The title of the novel refers to a special substance grown by genetically cloned humanlike creatures, who are kept in seclusion and named after famous Russian writers. The blue lard, which has been discovered by military scientists, is a substance of extraordinary power that does not freeze or melt under the influence of any temperature, and which can serve as an isolator in most complex circumstances.

In another fragment of the novel the Second World War ends with the victory of Germany and the USSR, who then divide Europe among themselves. England is destroyed by an atom bomb, and the six million Jews are killed by the Americans. Stalin and his family go, together with Khrushchev, to visit Hitler who rapes Stalin's little daughter, while Stalin himself has a homosexual affair with Khrushchev. In the next century China takes over parts of Russia and a new language, which is a mixture of many different languages, including Russian, Chinese, German, and English, is created. As usual in Sorokin's prose, the novel is full of bizarre scenes, callous, monstrous actions, numerous portrayals of perverted sex, and incongruous exploits. Its meaning, however, is open to interpretation. Early in 2002 the Russian conservative nationalistic organization, *Idushchie vmeste* (Moving Together), turned to the courts, accusing Sorokin and his publisher, 'Ad Marginem,' of engaging in the distribution of pornographic material. The director of the press defended Sorokin's freedom of expression and asserted that Sorokin is a practising Orthodox Christian who lives up to the demands of his faith. Sorokin himself declared that he is not interested in pornography and that artistic literature cannot be subjected to judicial interference.[41]

Sorokin's most recent novel, *Pir* (Feast; 2001),[42] is a bizarre collection of short narratives thematically connected by the subject of food consumption. The first, 'Nastia' (Nastia), sets the tone. In the beginning it appears to have a well-structured plot line, and it is narrated in refined nineteenth-century Russian prose. The heroine, Nastia, who is reminiscent of Turgenev's young female characters, celebrates her sixteenth birthday. Members of the Russian local nobility gather to mark this important event. Suddenly the language and course of action change drastically. According to some bizarre custom girls who reach the age of sixteen are grilled on the fire, and all those gathered for the celebration, including Nastia's parents, partake in the meal at which Nastia's grilled body is the main course. The language at the table is no longer polished or polite, but rather crude, abusive, and profane, and the good manners of those present give way to scenes of adultery, wanton murder, and physical abuse. Another section, 'Zerkalo' (Mirror), consists of the enumeration of various menus and comments that make little sense; it ends with the repetition, over the next several pages, of the note 'rot-anus' (mouth-anus), apparently referring to the possibility that the substance at both ends of the food consumption passage chain might be the same.

Vladimir Sorokin's prose is a peculiar phenomenon in contemporary Russian literature. Sorokin certainly has talent and he is a master of multiple styles, moving freely from nineteenth-century Russian classical language to the language of *Pravda* (Truth) and sots-art (socialist art). Nevertheless, he chooses, in many instances, to be incomprehensible and obscure. Viacheslav Kuritsyn suggests that Sorokin wants to 'destroy the metaphor' in his prose, removing real meaning from the writing, because he aims at transforming his text into complete violence.[43] According to Kuritsyn it is possible to read Sorokin's writing in a manner 'which is not connected with socialization, nor with semantic habits. It is possible to read Sorokin failing absolutely to understand the meaning of the words.'[44]

Supporters of Sorokin's prose try to remove him from the margins of contemporary Russian literature and place him in the mainstream. But not many can accept his assault on the reader's aesthetic sensibilities. Few can cope with the array of murders, scenes of cannibalism, sadism, sexual abuse, and verbal violence found in Sorokin's prose. And yet, Dmitrii Bykov declares that he believes that Sorokin is more of a moralist than a writer; despite the fact that Sorokin's prose is unvaried and full of clichés, he likes it because it is dynamic, hilarious, and comforting.[45] Iurii Buida also tries to find meaning in Sorokin's prose. He asserts that in Sorokin's narratives 'there are no real people, nor real actions, no real God ... He writes about a world after Auschwitz, where God died, and after Kolyma, where Man died. He writes about a world after reason, after humanism, and after pain – finally about a world which does not reject old values, but attempts to reassess them in the light of the new experience.'[46] Others wonder about Sorokin's appeal to certain readers, and his general place in the contemporary Russian literary scene. To that effect Pavel Basinskii states bluntly that 'literary criticism has not yet examined adequately the Sorokin phenomenon,' and he questions whether what Sorokin writes 'can be regarded as literature in general, and Russian literature in particular.'[47]

The question then remains whether Sorokin's graphically constructed plots, often incomprehensible outside Soviet life, which subvert, ridicule, and parody all that is dear to the human heart, as well as his functional language full of cynicism, sarcasm, and absurdities can contribute anything positive to the enlightenment, enjoyment, and education of contemporary Russian readers. Sorokin is a writer with a vivid imagination and great artistic potential, but his characters are indistinct and hardly memorable. Shock and surprise have always been the means by which Sorokin holds his readers' attention. But he or she now knows what to expect. Moreover, the long passages in which certain actions or slogans are repeated over and over again are boring and hardly meaningful. Sorokin is still a relatively young man and it will be interesting to see whether his artistic talent can evolve and change its direction.

Aleksandr Terekhov

Aleksandr Terekhov (b. 1966) was one of the youngest new writers to appear in print in the days of Gorbachev's *perestroika*. His first story, 'Durachok' (The Little Fool), was published in 1988. It deals with the so-called *dedovshchina*, or abuse of young conscripts by older members of the Soviet army. Most of Terekhov's early narratives are based on his personal experience as a soldier in the Soviet armed forces, or as a student at the faculty of journalism at the Moscow State University. He exposes in his novellas the harsh reality of army life, which is full of humiliation and deprivation, and the difficult life of Soviet students.

Terekhov's first novel, *Krysoboi* (Exterminators),[48] was published in 1995. In contrast to his earlier realistic stories, the novel is a phantasmagoric narrative set in the Russian provincial town of Svetloiar. The local officials expect the arrival of several important dignitaries from the capital, but the city is in a mess, inundated by rats. Rats are even falling from the ceiling in the hotel where the visitors are to stay. The local exterminators are usually able to manage the situation, but they are helpless in fighting the rats in the hotel. Hence, two specialists are summoned from Moscow. The younger one, who narrates much of the story, is more active and his role in the novel changes many times. Terekhov describes the nature and social structure of the rats' family, and analyses the different methods of extermination. It appears at the end of the novel that it is impossible to exterminate the rats, because rats are a metaphor for people, and one cannot exterminate the people.

Terekhov is obviously comparing the local unscrupulous bureaucrats in the town of Svetloiar to a family of rats. Both do more harm than good, and it is impossible to get rid of any of them. Terekhov, who is now in his mid-thirties, is a young writer of talent with a gift for satire. In his last novel he has attempted to diversify his creative output by experimenting with both the style and substance of his work, trying at the same time to retain the humourous and satirical bent of his prose.

Aleksei Varlamov

Aleksei Varlamov (b. 1963), a graduate of the Moscow State University, is one of the prolific new writers of the younger generation who adhere to the traditions of conventional Russian realism. He is also one of those who value their independence highly and refuse to become involved in the struggle between the different political and ideological camps in the writers' community. Varlamov asserts that his 'aim it to be a free writer, as much as possible independent from anyone and anything. He does not want to participate in the literary conflicts, because it is much more important to him to be involved in direct literary activity.'[49] Varlamov, who falls somewhere between the right and the left, between the conservatives and the liberals, is today accepted, as well as criticized, by both liberal critics and representatives of the conservative nationalistic camp.

Varlamov's first collection of prose, *Zdravstvui, Kniaz'!* (Good Day, Prince!; 1993), consists of a novella and several short stories. The action in the novella 'Zdravstvui Kniaz' begins in 1968 and covers a period of more than twenty years. The story is interesting, the narrative flows smoothly, and the language is simple. In a sense the novella can be read as a satire of the Soviet system of education, but the unpredictability of fate moves the plot, and chance becomes the driving force. Varlamov avoids, however, psychological investigation and some of the discussions in the story lack depth.

In 1995 Varlamov published his first novel, *Lokh* (Moron).[50] The action is set mainly in the 1980s and early 1990s, and it centres on the fates of the main characters Aleksandr Tezkin and Levka Goldovskii. Tezkin is a Russian dreamer, attracted to the ideas of *pochvenichestvo*, or the native-soil movement. Levka, who hails from a mixed marriage, inherits from his Jewish father a practical business mind, and from his Russian mother a deep attachment to Russian spiritual values. Tezkin, the sentimental idealist, is continuously searching for the right path in life, but his quest is never fulfilled because his yearnings are undefined. He is constantly depressed, and apparently lacks the internal character traits which make the attainment of personal happiness possible. Fate drives him from place to place in search of love and fulfilment. At one point he hopes that love for Katia, the woman who sacrifices her virginity to save him from military service in Siberia when he is dangerously ill, will redeem him. But this turns out to be another illusion. In fact, while he dreams about getting together with Katia, Tezkin has many love affairs with other women. In the end Tezkin dies young without having achieved anything significant in his life.

Both Tezkin and Goldovskii live abroad for a certain time, Tezkin in Germany and Goldovskii in the United States, but both return to Russia. It appears that a Russian belongs in his native land, and that the Russian soil and spirit which nurture the lives of the protagonists are more important to them than material satisfaction.

Between the passages in which the personal saga of the heroes is described there is an episodic portrayal of the political situation in Russia from the Brezhnev era to the days of Yeltsin's rule. The Soviet past is gone. There is freedom to think and act, but the life of the young is unsettled, with little positive in sight. The novel raises a number of important questions, including the issue of mixed marriages, which in the atheistic Soviet society were common, but which today have become a significant national and religious problem. The plot of the novel is inventive and the story is interesting. Unfortunately, little is acted out in the novel, and few convincing solutions are offered to the problems posed.

After the appearance of *Lokh* Varlamov published two novellas: 'Rozhdenie' (Birth; 1995)[51] and 'Gora' (Hill; 1996).[52] 'Rozhdenie' is set in Moscow at the time of the 1993 confrontation between the supporters of President Boris Yeltsin and the Russian Supreme Soviet. At the centre of the novella are the emotions of parents expecting their first child in these ominous days. 'Gora' is set at the Lake of Baikal and its main subject is the protection of nature, and the confrontation between poachers and their opponents.

Varlamov's next novel, *Zatonuvshii kovcheg* (The Sunken Ark; 1997),[53] is a book about the evils of sectarianism. At the centre of the novel is the history of two different sects. One which settles in total isolation in the *taiga*, is a splinter group of the mainstream Old Believers. It was formed in the eighteenth century, at the time of the construction of St Petersburg during the rule of Peter the Great. The other sect, of the so-called *skoptsi* or eunuchs, was founded by Boris Lippo, who was caught raping a young girl and punished by being castrated on the spot. All men in this sect are castrated and women have their breasts cut off. The leader of the sect of the Old Believers is sincere but blinded by dark faith, while Lippo is a charlatan. He pretends to be the saviour, but he is greedy for power and money, and he preaches total submission. According to Varlamov, all sects are harmful and dangerous. They distract people from real life, and enslave them by making them believe in easy salvation.

In an interview which follows the conclusion of the narrative, Varlamov explains his reasons for writing it. He asserts that the number of new sects in Russia multiplies daily. The leaders of most present an external image of piety and religiosity while in reality they are greedy, hungry for power, and unmoved by religion. He claims that sectarianism is dangerous in Russia. The collapse of the Soviet State has left a spiritual and ethical vacuum, and the young generation in particular is vulnerable to all kinds of harmful influences. There are even suggestions in the novel that sectarianism can lead to fascism and a national disaster.

Zatonuvshii kovcheg is a complicated novel, but the absorbing plot is well constructed. The rich material is well researched and the most important characters are vividly drawn. Some of the author's conclusions, however, especially those about the role of the new religious sects, are hasty and not always convincing. Moreover, the author's moralization and ideological digressions detract from the artistic quality of the narrative.

Varlamov's recent novel, *Kupavna* (Kupavna; 2000),[54] is in all probability an autobiographical narrative; its title refers to the name of a *dacha* settlement near Moscow where the main character, Koliunia, spends much time in his childhood and adolescence. The young Koliunia grows up under the tutelage and influence of his grandmother, who is wise, dedicated, and an unbeliever, yet a highly spiritual person. Most other characters, including Koliunia's father, who is a censor in Glavlit, are dedicated communists.

The main objective of the novel is to follow the development of the boy and portray the transformation of the mature Koliunia from an individual indoctrinated by the atheistic Soviet system of education into a believing Christian. Baptized as a mature man, Koliunia turns from an internationalist into a Russophile, and from an individual who initially wants to learn about the world into one who seeks spiritual and emotional fulfilment within himself and in Russia. Varlamov attempts to reach out to those Russian intellectuals who, after the disintegration of the Soviet Union, continue to live in a spiritual and intellectual vacuum. He is forced, however, to admit that the abrupt conversion of many former communists to Orthodox Christianity is not sincere and often hypocritical, because he believes that true faith can be instilled only in early childhood. Hence, the mature Koliunia begins the religious indoctrination of his son early in his life.

The novel is a straightforward third-person narrative. It begins in the early 1960s and concludes in the post-*perestroika* years, but chronology is inconsistent and sometimes confusing. The description of the emotional experiences of the boy and his perception of the external environment, nature, and people is interesting. Varlamov tries, however, to solve the ideological and psychological problems posed in the novel in a theoretical manner. Instead of showing us how Koliunia's transformation occurs, he tells us about it. He appeals thus to the reader's logical faculties, rather than to his or her emotions.

There seem to be many parallels between the author of *Kupavna* and its protagonist. Both grow up in the atheistic Soviet world, both become ardent believers. Religious and ideological motifs are found in most of Varlamov's works, as is, albeit under the surface, a Russian nationalistic message. Varlamov's prose is simple, yet not simplistic, but his portrayal is colourless. His multilateral plots are interesting and well researched, but often jumbled. His prose is deeply rooted in the traditions of Russian conventional realism and he aims at harmony in his work, as if in opposition to the chaos in the current Russian postmodern narratives.

5
Women Writers

In the days of Soviet rule women formed a small minority of the writers' community. No more than 15 per cent of the total membership of the Writers' Union was composed of women. Moreover, there was not a single woman among the best-known Soviet writers. This situation began to change in the days of *perestroika*, when a number of promising female authors, such as Nina Gorlanova, Irina Polianskaia, Nina Sadur, Liudmila Ulitskaia, Svetlana Vasilenko, and many others began to appear on the scene. In the late 1990s the list of active women writers was further expanded by the inclusion of prolific authors, such as Ol'ga Slavnikova and Marina Vishnevetskaia, as well as by a number of new aspiring female writers such as Marina Anashkevich, Valentina Tul'gina, Nina Turupova, and a few others.

Since most Russian women writers are not interested in advancing the cause of militant feminism as it is understood in the West, 'women's prose' is characterized by an intuitive approach to human problems. In practical terms that means that in the works of women writers the narrators and protagonists are usually women. The prose of most contemporary women authors can be recognized by its sensitivity, emotional tone, and personal touch. Moreover, issues of love and marriage, family and infidelity, children and parenthood are always at the centre of narratives by women authors. That does not mean, of course, that the prose of female writers is thematically limited. Aleksandra Marinina, Polina Dashkova, and Dar'ia Dontsova are among the best-known authors of contemporary Russian detective novels. Since the gender distinction, however, is not apparent in the mystery writers' group, their works are discussed in the chapter on detective fiction.

Nina Gorlanova

The prose of Nina Gorlanova (b. 1947) is in the mainstream of the auto-biographical and confessional literature popular today in Russia. Her novellas, however, differ from those by Melikhov, Gandlevskii, or Evtushenko. First of all, Gorlanova is a resident of the provincial town of Perm' in northern Russia, which provides the physical background of most of her narratives. In addition, most of her prose has been produced jointly with her husband, Viacheslav Bukur, who is also a writer. Gorlanova began to publish in the 1980s, but not until the appearance in *Novyi mir* of *Roman vospitaniia* (A Novel About Education; 1995)[1] did she become reasonably well known on the national literary scene.

Roman vospitaniia, and most other publications, whether produced by the husband-and-wife team or authored by Gorlanova herself, are similar in style and subject matter. At the centre of all her works are family affairs. In *Roman vospitaniia* the characters include four children and one adopted daughter, as well as friends, associates, and co-workers. Nothing significant happens in their lives, but the collage of momentary observations and a mosaic of factual occurrences create a truthful and sincere picture of family and intellectual life in provincial Russia. *Roman vospitaniia* turns on the fate of the adopted daughter, Nastia – Natasha. She is adopted at the age of seven, and taken away from her dissolute alcoholic mother. The dedication of the adoptive parents is boundless, but all their efforts are largely futile. Whether because of genetic inclinations, or the damage of early childhood experience, the young woman is thankless, and in the end abuses and abandons her benefactors.

Nel'zia, mozhno, nel'zia. Roman-monolog (Impossible, Possible, Impossible: A Novel Monologue; 2002),[2] authored by Gorlanova alone, is a confessional narrative in which the writer combines the story of her personal and family life with an account of her efforts to become a competent and recognized professional prose writer. 'Storozhevye zapiski' (A Janitor's Notes; 2002),[3] authored jointly by the husband-and-wife team, is narrated in the first person by a male protagonist who accepts a job of a janitor in the Perm' city synagogue. The narrator is a Christian, but he is proficient in the Hebrew language and Jewish studies and also acts as a teacher in the Jewish community. The novella is a compilation of casual observations about the life of the Jewish religious congregation and the narrator's relationship with his wife, Niniko, who teaches journalism at the Perm' city university.

The prose of Gorlanova and Bukur is interesting, and sincere, saturated with notes, reminiscences, accounts of family life, observations on social and professional life in Perm', on human relations and various events and situations, and on their continuous effort to become established prose writers. The picture that emanates reflects the struggle for a better future in the difficult conditions of post-Soviet life, in which idealistic striving alternates with periods of personal failure and depression.

The author and narrator in these narratives is usually the protagonist. The physical setting of all works is the city of Perm', but there is no spatial definition and little geographical reality. Similarly, there is no temporal sequence in most of the prose, but time is dealt with very specifically and in detail. The prose of Gorlanova is sketchy, soft, feminine, emotional, and full of details of everyday life. The language is simple, infused with some local dialect, and there is much dialogue. One wonders whether the wellspring of Gorlanova's life experience will ever exhaust itself, and if she will be able to diversify her thematic range. A recent story, 'Afrorossianka' (Afro-Russian; 2002),[4] relates the experience of a mulatto girl abandoned by both her parents and brought up by her grandmother in Perm'.

Irina Polianskaia

Irina Polianskaia (b. 1952), a native of the town Kasli, in the Cheliabinsk region, is a graduate of the drama school in the city of Rostov, and of the Moscow Literary Institute. She began to write verse and journalism in the 1970s. Today she is a versatile prose writer who has tried her hand at a variety of literary genres. She is the author of books for children, plays for the theatre, biographical narratives, and she even compiled an ethnographic encyclopaedia. Most important, however, are her prose fiction narratives, which are told in the first person by a female narrator and based on realistic, often autobiographical material.

The novella 'Predlagaemye obstoiatel'stva' (Proposed Circumstances; 1988) provides an account of a tragic family drama, in all probability that of the author's own family. *Prokhozhdenie teni* (The Passing of a Shadow; 1997),[5] which was short-listed for the 1998 Booker Russian Novel Prize, is, in a sense, a continuation of the same family story. It combines the youthful narrator's family saga with an account of her experience of living and studying in a music school somewhere in southern Russia. At school the narrator is placed by chance in a study group with four blind musicians. Initially, Polianskaia intended to publish two separate novels, keeping the subjects of her family life and that of the blind students apart. In the end, however, she merged the two thematically diverse topics into a single novel. The extended narrative is interesting, but the story often becomes confusing.

Married before the war, the father of the nameless narrator is an eminent nuclear scientist taken prisoner by the Germans in the Second World War. He works for a while as a scientist in Berlin, and has an affair with a German woman who bears him a child. After the war he returns to the Soviet Union, where he is imprisoned by the Soviet authorities. Somewhat later he is transferred to a so-called *sharashka*, an institution where incarcerated Soviet scientists and scholars conduct secret research on the development of new, including nuclear, weapons. The author-narrator relates the complicated story of growing up as a child of a former Soviet political convict who is never trusted by the authorities, and is forced all his life to move from place to place in search of work. (Polianskaia herself was born in the days of Stalin's rule in the GULag, in the Cheliabinsk region, in the Urals.) The family life of the narrator's parents is tangled. Both are unfaithful, both lose their lovers in tragic circumstances. Paradoxically, however, the blood of the dead victims cements the renewed love of the narrator's parents.

The music school that the narrator attends is apparently located in the city of Orzhdonikidze. The four blind students are all members of Soviet national minorities. The most impressive and attractive of them is the Georgian Kosta. Both the narrator and her roommate Nelia are in love with Kosta. Nelia enters their room when the narrator appears to be intimate with Kosta. She is shocked and jealous, and she denounces the narrator to the school administration. The narrator is then summoned to the office of the school director, but she runs away in panic. She abandons her studies and leaves town several months before graduation.

The structure of the narrative is loose, and there is no chronological or thematic consistency. It begins with the arrival of the narrator at the music school, and ends with her escape. In between chapters about the family alternate with chapters about the blind music students, and chapters about the family's past with chapters about their present life. Occasionally, there is transition from one subject to another in the same chapter, even on the same page. The author is a good observer. She claims that when she was assigned to a study group with blind students she became interested in their experience and kept a diary, making notes about their behaviour, habits, and mentality. In her novel

Polianskaia explores the inner world of the blind, and asserts that their relationship 'with the outside world is based on absolute trust. It is a zone of pure moralism.'[6]

Polianskaia is an accomplished artist who is interested in a variety of life experiences and their influence on human fate. She is, however, more interested in the effect of external events on the human soul than in the practical side of life. Her investigation of the world of music and that of the blind, as well as the irrational power of love, is accomplished, her perspective is subtle and insightful, and she has a good grasp of the complexity of human relations. Her language is poetic, often figurative, and infused with musicality of expression. *Prokhozhdenie teni*, however, has its share of artistic shortcomings. The loosely constructed plot, and the abrupt transition from one subject to another, often make it difficult to follow the main thrust of the story. The conclusion of the novel is inadequately motivated, and the relationship between Kosta and the narrator is not elaborated clearly. Moreover, long digressions and verbose passages of abstract deliberations on unrelated subjects, while intended to clarify, often obscure the plot.

In 1999 Polianskaia published in *Novyi mir* a new novel, *Chitaiushchaia voda* (The Reading Water).[7] The narrator, Tania, is a graduate student in a school of the arts. She relates in the first person the story of her relationship with Viktor Petrovich, a famous film director, producer, and teacher. She approaches Petrovich under the pretext of an alleged intention to write a book about him, and they become friends. The narrative is a story of a personal relationship which can also be read as a poorly organized history of Russian and Soviet theatre and cinematography in the first half of the twentieth century. Those, however, not familiar with the personalities or the films discussed in the novel may fail to grasp the essential meaning of the narrative. Long historical passages alternate with biographical and autobiographical detail, descriptions of encounters, and exchanges of opinions between Tania and Viktor Petrovich. The narrative ends with Petrovich's lonely last years and death.

Polianskaia's recent prose makes it clear that her talent is descriptive rather than imaginative, and that it is nurtured by personal experience centred primarily on issues connected with her family's past and the arts. She also draws inspiration from her affinity with music. Her narratives are often fragmentary and impressionistic, but she is sensitive to the fate of her characters, trying to understand the psychological and intellectual motivation which determines their actions.

Liudmila Petrushevskaia

Liudmila Petrushevskaia (b. 1938) belongs to the mature generation of Russian women writers. A graduate of the faculty of journalism of the Moscow State University, she began to write prose in the early 1960s, but not until the late 1980s could she publish any of her works in official Soviet journals. Her first collection of stories and novellas, *Bessmertnaia liubov'* (Immortal Love), was officially published in the USSR in the days of *perestroika*, in 1988. Petrushevskaia had a hard time publishing during Soviet rule, because her narratives emphasize the negative aspects of Soviet life. They stress the social despair and moral decay prevalent in Soviet society, and most of Petrushevskaia's characters are single women abused by fellow humans and ignored by fate. In the 1990s, after the collapse of the Soviet empire, the tone of Petrushevskaia's prose mellowed somewhat, and the intensity of her social criticism softened, albeit slightly.

The mother-child relation has always been an important theme in Petrushevskaia's narratives. The mother is usually downtrodden, but in her misery she loves and protects her child, expecting in return compensation when the need may arise. In the story 'Mladshii brat' (The Younger Brother; 1996),[8] the young Vladik is lazy, he likes to sleep late, and he has trouble at school, but his mother, Diana, adores him anyway. There is little happiness in Diana's life. Her husband abandons her for another woman, and she has little contact with either her daughter or her alcoholic husband. Vladik, who becomes a graduate student, is Diana's only joy. Eventually, the old Diana becomes ill, apparently with a stroke, and Vladik suddenly wakes up. He looks after his sick mother with dedication and refuses even to let her be taken to the hospital, hoping that he will be able to provide better care at home. The conclusion of the story has a moral message different from those of Petrushevskaia's early novellas: people without responsibilities may turn into useless sluggards, and mothers who are too protective of their children may do them more harm than good. Moreover, difficult life conditions may stimulate ingenuity, and reveal the hidden human potential for action and achievement.

In another story, 'Laila i Mara' (Laila and Mara; 1996),[9] there is an obvious reference to the dangerous life in the Northern Caucasus, and to the war in Chechnia. Previously, Petrushevskaia rarely touched upon issues of political significance. In 'Belye doma' (White Houses; 1996)[10] Petrushevskaia returned to her past and produced a story in the spirit of

Soviet *byt* literature. Infidelity, moral and social decay, and the price the children pay for their parents' dissolution are at the centre. Most of the characters in this story are intelligent, educated people, but they are all negative, and many are themselves responsible for their shattered lives. The story is a straightforward third-person narrative involving little psychological analysis. The facts speak for themselves. Petrushevskaia depicts the harsh reality and the manipulative ways of her characters, but she does not spare any of them.

Lately, Petrushevskaia has published a number of new short stories on a variety of topics. Most are set in real life and are a reaction to the current economic and social changes in Russian society. Thus, the beginning of 'Zapadnia' (A Trap; 2000)[11] deals with the problems of mixed marriages and emigration. As the story progresses, however, it evolves into a portrayal of lawlessness, criminality, and the abuse of defenceless ordinary Russian citizens. In many stories Petrushevskaia provides a picture of moral depravity, infidelity, and family instability. In 'Naidi menia, son' (Find Me, Sleep; 2000)[12] one of the main characters is a respectable scholar, a married man in poor health, and a womanizer who dies during one of his sexual escapades. 'Detskii prazdnik' (Children's Holiday; 2000)[13] describes life in a colony of artists. The parents appear to be concerned about the well-being of their children. Nevertheless, their teenage daughters become pregnant and bear children without being able to establish the paternity of their infants. In 'Dva boga' (Two Gods; 2000)[14] a child born out of wedlock is the result of a casual sexual encounter between two decent humans. Despite their difference in age – she is thirty-five and he is only twenty – they move in together and take care of their son.

'Dom s fontanom' (The House with a Fountain; 2000)[15] brings the reader back to current Russian reality, and the hazardous life in the new age of universal terrorism. An explosion takes place on a bus in Moscow. A fifteen-year-old girl appears to be dead and is taken to the local morgue. In the fantastic conclusion the father's determination, and the professional reanimator's skill, bring the allegedly dead girl miraculously back to life.

In general terms Petrushevskaia is true to herself. Her prose is always frank and disheartening, and in most instances true to life. Her collisions are rough and often absurd and her naturalistic language is intertwined with slang, colloquialisms, and vulgar expressions. Yet she is still the purveyor of a dire message, and the creator of a reality in which there is material poverty, family desolation, and a world in which love is rare and loneliness is the cause of the deprivation of the spirit. In the days of Soviet rule there was no possibility of publishing anything with such a negative, depressing message, and even today, when the life of ordinary Russians is still complex and arduous, most readers prefer to read something that is invigorating and provides a positive message infused with hope.

Galina Shcherbakova

Galina Shcherbakova (b. 1932), a graduate of the Rostov State University, is one of the oldest contemporary Russian female writers. Initially a schoolteacher and journalist, she began to write fiction in the 1970s. The style and substance of her prose has changed little since her first publications, but with the collapse of the Soviet state, and the abolition of censorship, there is no longer any need to adhere to Soviet principles in the construction of her plots or in the selection of characters. In the late 1990s Shcherbakova continued to be true to herself. As before, her main characters and narrators are usually women, and the subject of her novellas is typically love and infidelity, within or outside the organized family unit.

In 'Radosti zhizni' (The Joys of Life; 1995)[16] the first-person female narrator begins her story by contemplating the writer's craft. Soon she moves, however, to the depiction of her grandmother's sister's life. Aunt Tania is widowed early, and her insatiable quest for happiness and sex is at the heart of the story. She is always in search of new romances and new lovers, seeking joyful experiences even in times of tragedy. All other characters and events in the story are there only to illuminate Aunt Tania's endless pursuit of self-gratification.

'U nog lezhashchikh zhenshchin' (At the Feet of Lying Women; 1996)[17] is a novella about the lives of three families of neighbours, presented in the spirit of Soviet *byt* literature. Falsehood, infidelity, and broken families are the norm, rather than the exception. Partners in marriages which appear on the surface to have no problems are going through life together without knowing the truth about each other. At the end of the novella the three women are sick and impaired. The three husbands, in turn, knowing nothing about the past of their wives, look after and cherish them, believing in their devotion and sincerity. The conclusion of the novella is anticlimactic. Nothing significant happens. The three families continue their existence as before: they live a lie.

The title of Shcherbakova's novel *Armiia liubovnikov* (An Army of Lovers; 1998)[18] is the name of a group of singers and musicians. It is also, however, a metaphor referring to the array of lovers and affairs in the life of the heroine, Ol'ga Alekseevna. The novel is mostly narrated in the first person by a nameless friend of Ol'ga, who is some ten years older. Ol'ga marries Kulibin and bears him a daughter, but she is always unfulfilled and continuously seeks new sexual partners. She dreams about a perfect love and an ideal man, but her delusions never materialize. She divorces Kulibin and embarks on a new hunt for an appropriate life partner, taking to bed anyone she comes across, but to no avail. Shcherbakova addresses in the novel the important problem of the personal happiness of the educated middle-class woman in Russia today. She reduces, however, the issue of happiness to sexual passion and satisfaction. While sexual fulfilment is an important component of married life, it is only one aspect of the human relationships indispensable to the attainment of complete personal happiness or family bliss.

Shcherbakova's prose is simple, straightforward, and interesting, but great art it is not. Most of her characters are soon forgotten because they are poorly developed. She deals with issues similar to those discussed in the prose of Iurii Trifonov, but in Trifonov's works the characters are round, the problems are formulated clearly, and the actions of the characters are subjected to psychological scrutiny. Shcherbakova, instead, tells a story in which all human experiences appear to be equal. In fact, the novel in which Ol'ga's sexual affairs form a continuous, monotonous chain comes to an abrupt end only because Ol'ga cannot accept the negative opinion of her friend, the narrator, who doubts the propriety of Ol'ga's involvement with a new, much younger, married partner.

The subject of love, infidelity, and sexuality in literature is eternal. By creating a number of passable narratives appealing to a wide array of readers Shcherbakova utilizes this theme superbly.

Ol'ga Slavnikova

Ol'ga Slavnikova, a prolific prose author and critic, is one of the few new better-known woman writers to appear on the Russian literary scene in the second half of the 1990s. Born in Sverdlovsk, currently Ekaterinburg, and presently residing in Moscow, she is a graduate of the Faculty of Journalism of the Ural State University. Slavnikova's first novel, *Strekoza, uvelichennaia do razmerov sobaki* (A Dragon-Fly, Enlarged to the Size of a Dog),[19] originally published in 1996 in the journal *Ural*, was short-listed for, but not awarded, the 1997 Booker Russian Novel Prize in Literature.

The novel begins with the funeral of Sof'ia Andreevna, a former school teacher. In a flashback, set in the old Soviet Brezhnev days, it relates the story of a dysfunctional family which is composed of only two individuals: Sof'ia Andreevna, the mother, and Katerina Ivanovna, her daughter. Both are unattractive, old-fashioned, and prudish. They share a number of emotional, social, and physical shortcomings and character traits which prevent them from arranging their lives in a meaningful and satisfying fashion. Mother and daughter live together, in a one-room apartment. Despite mutual resentment and annoyance with each other, they appear to be inseparable. 'Mother and daughter never talked about anything serious, but always quarrelled about trifles.' 'The daughter did not love her mother, but mother was the only real thing that she had in her life.'[20]

The mother supports her daughter in all her endeavours. She never criticizes or chastizes her for anything, believing that by refraining from doing so her daughter will appreciate and be forever indebted to her. Unfortunately, despite her mother's dedication the daughter remains detached and aloof. When the old woman becomes seriously ill, Katerina Ivanovna waits impatiently for her demise in order to clear space in the small flat and bring in a prospective husband. Undesirable at thirty-five, Katerina Ivanovna still dreams about a family and possible happiness. That is, however, a delusion. She cannot escape her past, her loneliness, and the image of her dead mother haunts her continuously. This may be an expression of a guilty conscience, but it is more likely the result of an upbringing which did not provide for individual development.

Slavnikova's second novel, *Odin v zerkale* (Alone in the Mirror; 1999),[21] is set in the post-Soviet era. It can be viewed as a literary experiment narrated simultaneously on two levels. The narrator introduces the story of two real people, allegedly acquainted with the author, and later turns them into prototypes for her literary heroes. Thus we are told a real-life story which is fictionalized and transformed into a work of art. The protagonist, Antonov, is a thirty-two-year-old university lecturer. The beautiful seventeen-year-old Vika Ivanova is a failing student. Antonov falls in love with her instantly. At first, he assists Vika with her assignments, then he becomes intimate with her, and finally he marries her. The marriage is a failure. Vika hates her husband and is unfaithful to him. She has an affair with the boss of the commercial enterprise that employs her. Antonov, in turn, is driven to madness from jealousy. The conclusion of the family drama is abrupt. Vika travels with her boss to an out-of-town hideout, and is killed on the way in a head-on car collision.

Despite the fact that the two novels are set in different times and deal with different subjects, there are many similarities between them. The titles of both novels are symbolic. In the first one, the magnified image of the Dragon-Fly, which appears to the dying mother, is a symbol of death, desolation, and destruction. In the second novel the image of the mirror, which recurs time and time again, alludes to the fact that it is there to mask reality, and that in life as in the mirror, everyone has a double. Thus Antonov's relationship with Vika is a fraud. It reflects his desires rather than reality. Vika appears to be here, but she is always evasive and unattainable.

The structures of the two novels are also similar. The first chapter in *Strekoza* deals with the funeral of the mother. In the final chapter the emotional state of the daughter after mother's death is described. In between the tragic saga of the broken family is told, interspersed with a number of digressions in which secondary characters often take over the leading role. Similarly, in *Odin v zerkale* the novel begins with an episode in the concluding days of the Antonov-Vika relationship. In the final pages of the novel Vika is dead, her boss survives the accident, yet Antonov disintegrates mentally. In between, in a flashback, the real and fictitious stories are compared, and the narrative is interspersed with numerous digressions which often distract the reader from the main action.

In 2001 Slavnikova published a new novella, 'Bessmertnyi. Povest' o nastoiashchem cheloveke' (The Immortal: A Tale About a Real Man).[22] The narrative consists of two distinct thematic components which the author attempts, not entirely successfully, to join together. In one part there is the life story of Aleksei Afanas'evich Kharitonov, a decorated war hero and a dedicated worker and family man. Kharitonov, a childless widower, marries Nina Aleksandrovna, who is twenty-five years younger, and adopts her illegitimate daughter Marina. After suffering a stroke Kharitonov is incapacitated and confined for fourteen years to a bed in his room. His wife and daughter try hard to keep him alive, because his veteran's pension is the main source of the family's income. In post-Soviet Russia life is difficult and the family endeavours to protect the old man from the daily barrage of bad news. They create for him an artificial environment, hiding the truth about recent changes in the country, and making him believe that he still lives in Brezhnev's Russia. Nevertheless, Kharitonov is apparently tired of suffering and tries on several occasions to commit suicide. In the end he learns that he lives a lie, and that his daughter has been accused of stealing money from a charitable fund intended for invalids, and he manages to kill himself.

The second part of the novella deals with the election process to the provincial duma. The elections are rigged. Voters are bribed, and they unashamedly collect money from several different candidates at the same time. Marina is hired to assist in the campaign of one candidate, and promised a good job if he is successful. After the elections, however, she is abandoned to fate, without a job and with little hope for the future. The story is a sad irony. Except for Kharitonov, who cannot talk, everyone lies. Marina lies to her mother about money allegedly sent by a nephew who in reality is dead. Marina's husband is unfaithful to his wife and lies to her, while all of them lie to Kharitonov. Moreover, the politician and members of the local administration are also corrupt and liars.

Some critics regard Slavnikova as an optimist, and view her conclusion to the novella in a positive light.[23] But 'Bessmertnyi' provides a depressing picture of the conditions of life in contemporary Russia. Everyone tries to do their best in difficult circumstances, but it is evident from the narrative that honesty and integrity are rare commodities in Russia today.

Stylistically, all three narratives are alike. The language employed is simple, but dense and verbose. Straightforward third-person narration is sprinkled with authorial intrusions. The narrator usually provides the reader with a detailed description of events and human relations, but the portrayal is static. The characters do not act or speak; they are mum. There is not a single dialogue in any of the novels. Moreover, chronology is sometimes confusing, the stories are convoluted, and numerous digressions slow the flow of the narratives. Slavnikova is an independent thinker, able to devise a number of complicated plots, yet her novels lack dramatic intensity. She remains, however, a promising writer. She is not afraid to experiment and innovate, both thematically and stylistically. She understands the female mind well, and she is quite successful in her attempts to untangle complex human relations.

Viktoriia Tokareva

Viktoriia Tokareva (b. 1937) is a professional script writer and a prolific author of short fiction. Her stories are usually interesting and engaging, and her language is compact and witty, with a touch of irony. Most of the narrators and main characters in her stories are female, and the main subject is usually the woman's unfulfilled love. Social and political issues are seldom touched upon in Tokareva's prose. The novella 'Svoia pravda' (One's Own Truth; 2002),[24] however, is different. It is a combination of a family and love story which evolves against the background of the upheaval created by the disintegration of the Soviet Union. The main character, Irina, born, raised, and educated in the city of Baku, is a single mother of two children, abandoned by her Russian husband and deeply in love with the Azeri, Kiamal. Unfortunately, Kiamal is forced by his family to marry a woman of his own faith, but he continues a secret affair with Irina.

The city of Baku is currently the capital of the independent state of Azerbaidzhan, and most Russians are forced to flee from their native places, thus becoming refugees in the Russian Federation. Irina moves to Moscow, and her personal and family life is shattered. She wanders from place to place, from job to job, still dreaming about Kiamal, who uses and abuses her secretly in order not to offend his kin. The difficult fate of Irina is further aggravated by her complicated character. She is an excellent teacher, hard-working and dedicated to her family, but she demands submission from her married children, and tries to rule even those who employ her.

Tokareva's new novella is intense and interesting. Its language is original and expressive, and the psychological delineation of Irina's character is sensitive and to the point. All other characters, unfortunately, are only sketchily drawn and the ending of the novella is inconclusive, leaving the reader guessing about the future fate of Irina and her family.

Tat'iana Tolstaia

Tat'iana Tolstaia (b. 1951), one of the best-known contemporary Russian female prose writers, is a native of Leningrad and a graduate of the Leningrad State University. Her literary debut dates back to 1983, and her first collection of prose, *Na zolotom kryl'tse sideli* (On the Golden Porch), was published in 1987. Most characters in Tolstaia's stories from the 1980s are social misfits or disillusioned dreamers, worn down by the harsh realities of daily existence, and unable to escape the tight grip of their difficult fate. Tolstaia is compassionate and non-committal and she accepts human imperfection. She has no overt ideological or political message, yet under the surface there is a social concern for the underdog and for those who are abused by nature and life. Most important, however, in her early prose is the artful interweaving of fantasy with reality, and her elegant, playful, and musical language, full of striking colours and rich metaphors. In several stories of the early 1990s Tolstaia diverts from her established artistic path and begins to experiment with style and subject matter. The Russian historical past forms the basis of some of her new stories, and most characters in these narratives have real-life prototypes.

In the mid-1990s Tolstaia produced little of substance, but it was well known in the writers' community that she was in the process of writing her first novel. Indeed, in 2000 Tolstaia published the novel *Kys'* (Kys'),[25] which contains a note to the effect that the narrative was written between 1986 and 2000. The year 1986 is ominous in Russian and Soviet history. It was the year of the Chernobyl' nuclear disaster and the second year of Mikhail Gorbachev's rule, when the policies of the so-called *glasnost'* and *perestroika* were introduced. There is no doubt that these events, as well as Tolstaia's experience of living and teaching in the West for several years, prompted and influenced her decision to write *Kys'*.

Kys' is not a conventional realistic novel. It is rather a mixture of fantasy, mythological symbolism, elements of science fiction, *skaz*, anti-utopia, and Russian folklore. It could also be read as a satire and allegory of Russian and Soviet history. The narrative is set in a mythological town which has allegedly survived a big explosion or nuclear disaster, several hundred years ago, and is named after its dictator, Fedor Kuzmich. The characters in the novel are divided into two main groups. To the first belong the old, who managed to survive the explosion and can still remember their distant past. The second group, the majority, is composed of individuals born after the disaster. These individuals have unusual physical attributes. Some characters have tails, others claws, and some are changelings, while many horses in town have human traits. The title of the novel refers to a mythological animal of great power which lives in the vicinity of the town and attacks any individual who appears in sight.

The hero of the narrative, Benedikt, has a tail and is one of those born after the disaster. He becomes friendly with Nikita Ivanovich, an old-timer born before the explosion. Nikita introduces Benedikt to books and reading. But the availability of old books is limited, and all new books are written by none other than Fedor Kuzmich, who plagiarizes everything from some of the old books in his possession. Benedikt falls in love with Olen'ka, the daughter of Kudeiar Kudeiarich, the so-called Chief Sanitarian, who is the watchman over the ideological purity of the people. Soon, Kudeiar decides, with the help of his son-in-law Benedikt, to incite a revolution and abolish the rule of Fedor Kuzmich. Kudeiar assumes power in the name of democracy, but in the end he becomes an autocratic tyrannical dictator much more evil than Kuzmich. The town is renamed Kudeiar, and its inhabitants live under the tight grip of the new dictator's power. Kudeiar keeps his people in the dark and loathes those who seek knowledge. Nikita Ivanovich, and Benedikt, who follows him, long, however, for knowledge, and are in constant search of new old books. For his interest in forbidden books, and for allegedly spreading ideas of which Kudeiar does not approve, Kudeiar orders that Nikita be burnt at the stake. Benedikt tries to save his friend, but to no avail. At the end of the novel Nikita is set on fire, but the fire gets out of control and consumes almost the entire town. Miraculously, Nikita and Benedikt, as well as some other dissidents born before the explosion, manage to survive.

One may wonder whether Tolstaia consciously intends to impart a direct ideological or political message in the novel, but the allusions are on the surface. The conclusion of the narrative points to the fact that major natural disasters, as well as dictatorial oppression, usually create havoc in the personal lives of the people, but rarely eliminate their thirst for knowledge, enlightenment, and freedom. Authoritarian leaders create systems rife with oppression. And while they expose their subjects to torture and darkness, in the end they are consumed by the very flames intended to destroy others.

Tolstaia's first novel, announced long before its appearance, generated exaggerated expectations, and the critical response followed soon after its publication. Some critics hail it as a new classic and encyclopaedia of Russian life, but most others approach it more soberly and bemoan the fact that Tolstaia's new narrative does not come near the artistic level of her early prose. Most important, while in her early stories Tolstaia delved into the minds of her characters, in her novel she observes them from the outside, as objects of irony and derision.[26] Most critics, however, assert, with some reservations, that Tolstaia is still a master of the word, and that her use of language is the only positive aspect of *Kys'*. Thus, for example, after a detailed analysis of all the weak aspects of the narrative, which, in fact, can hardly be referred to as a novel, Alla Latynina concludes that 'Tolstaia does not create any universal model of Russian history, nor does she provide any final solutions to the "eternal questions" ... but the novel presents a masterly created cocktail of anti-utopia, satire, and a parody of science fiction clichés, flavoured with a refined play of language.'[27]

According to Natal'ia Ivanova, on the other hand, *Kys'* 'is not an anti-utopia, but rather a parody of anti-utopia which combines an "intellectual" anti-utopia with Russian folklore, as well as "science fiction" with intense newspaper topical satire, i.e. mass literature with elitist refined prose ... The tension between the grief and anger of the internal message and its figurative rendition turn Tolstaia's novel into a peculiar word in the new Russian prose.'[28] Not everyone, however, is as generous to Tolstaia as Natal'ia Ivanova. Mariia Galina states bluntly that she suspects that *Kys'* 'received super-enthusiastic reviews not in the least because we were finally bestowed with a long expected masterpiece, but rather as the result of a skilfully inculcated interest and the publishers' effective advertisement policy.'[29]

Whatever the artistic merits of Tolstaia's first novel, it is clear that her figurative ornamental language which blends with ease, in a refined manner, elements of Russian folklore, *skaz*, and fantasy, as well as neologisms which relate to life in a modern civilized society, remains the most important positive artistic feature of her new novel. It is also obvious, however, that Tolstaia is not indifferent to the recent past of the Russian people, and she has decided to contribute in *Kys'*, in an artistic fashion, to the ongoing debate about the history of the Russian and Soviet states. Referring to *perestroika* and the end of the so-called Soviet civilization, some even compare life in Russia today to life after an *explosion* of great magnitude.'[30] The question, however, remains whether Tolstaia's use of sarcasm, parody, and farce is an appropriate way to deal with these complex and serious issues.

Liudmila Ulitskaia

Liudmila Ulitskaia (b. 1943), a genetic biologist by profession, is one of the better-known contemporary Russian female prose writers. She was also the first Russian woman to be awarded the prestigious Booker Russian Novel Prize (in 2001) for her book-length narrative *Kazus*

Kukotskogo (The Kukotskii Case; 2000). Ulitskaia's first book of children's stories was published in 1983, but only after the appearance of her novella 'Sonechka' (Sonechka; 1992), which was short-listed for the 1993 Booker Russian Novel Prize, did she become better known in Moscow literary circles as an author of adult prose. Today, Ulitskaia's books are translated into many foreign languages and her novels are just as popular in Russia as they are abroad.

In 1996 Ulitskaia published in *Novyi mir* a narrative titled *Medeia i ee deti. Semeinaia khronika* (Medeia and Her Children: A Family Chronicle).[31] Medeia is a Greek widow, currently living in Crimea, and previously married to a Jewish dentist. In the summer her relatives and friends gather at her house and, although childless, she appears to be the matriarch of the extended clan. Despite the fact that most of her family members intermarry, Medeia attempts to pass on to them their Greek heritage and spirit. The narrative covers a major slice of Soviet life, but most action takes place in the mid-1970s. While Medeia's house is the meeting point where most family members gather, her own role in the narrative is minor. The second half of the novel focuses on the love triangle between Butonov, who is an outsider, and Medeia's nieces, Nika and Masha, with Masha's suicide forming the climax. Masha has been psychologically damaged since childhood. She cannot cope with her love for Butonov and her simultaneous devotion to her husband, and she decides to take her own life.

The language in the novel flows smoothly, and the narrator is a good observer, but the sequence of action is sometimes confusing and there are too many minor, poorly developed, characters in the novel. As stated in the novel's subtitle, the narrative is a family chronicle and in the end, by marrying one of Medeia's kinsman, the narrator becomes a member of the extended clan and family, and a participant in the events.

In the short story 'Zver'' (The Animal; 1998),[32] Ulitskaia explores the state of mind of a young widow who suffers from delusions and hallucinations and is preoccupied with events that transcend her daily reality. Her friends offer a variety of different solutions to help her preserve her sanity, but to no avail. There is no direct message in the story, but there is an intimation that for complete fulfilment something more than dreary daily life experience is required, even if that something is beyond our incidental reality.

As opposed to her other narratives, which are set in the former Soviet Union, the action in Ulitskaia's best-known novella, 'Veselye pokhorony' (The Funeral Party; 1998),[33] takes place in the summer of 1990 in New York. Ulitskaia's two sons and their families live in New York and she spends some time with them every year, thus becoming acquainted with the Russian émigré community in America. On one level Ulitskaia provides a broad picture of life of members of the so-called third wave of Russian emigration. This segment of the novella includes some components of the Soviet *byt* literature of the Brezhnev era, in which hard work and laziness, love and infidelity, dedication and betrayal, go hand in hand. On another level it is the story of Alik, a Russified Jew, a painter and a recent émigré, who is dying from an unspecified illness. Although Alik is a philanderer who leads a bohemian life, no one bears a grudge against him. His inner warmth, his sincerity, and his devotion to his friends compensate for his shortcomings. In life, and even after his death, he helps bring together the scattered representatives of the multinational Soviet diaspora.

After Alik's death his friends gather for the funeral repast and to listen to a tape, recorded while Alik was still alive, in which Alik asks them to have a good time and drink to his memory. Thus, with the help of the dead man, the funeral is turned from a wake into a celebration of life. The life of the Russian émigrés in North America is unstable but dynamic. It is changing under new influences, but also bound by old customs, habits, and associations. The story is narrated in a sketchy manner, and comic episodes alternate with tragic incidents, but Ulitskaia treats her characters with subtlety and understanding. Despite the obvious depravity of the actions of some of them, she does not moralize and tries to see the good in everyone.

Kazus Kukotsogo, Ulitskaia's award-winning novel, was published in *Novyi mir* under the title *Puteshestvie v sed'muiu storonu sveta* (Travel to the Seventh Side of the World; 2000).[34] The first half of the novel deals with the complicated life of Dr Pavel Kukotskii, a teacher, scientist, and professional gynaecologist who spends much of his time investigating the evolution of the body and psyche of the foetus before birth, with the purpose of establishing its relation to the behaviour of people later in their lives. Kukotskii is also a fervent opponent of the official prohibition of abortion in Stalin's Russia, because he believes that it leads to illegal, amateur abortions which may cause injury, and even death. In 1942, in evacuation in Siberia, Kukotskii falls in love with and marries Elena, having previously saved her life in a miscarriage operation. Elena is the mother of two-year-old Tania, and former wife of a man apparently killed in the war. Kukotskii adopts and loves Tania, who finds out much later in life that he is not her biological father. Kukotskii is devoted to his family, his students, and the sciences, but his life is full of tragedy. His wife becomes afflicted by dementia early in life, and the beautiful and bright Tania rebels. She quits medical school, bears a daughter, Zhenia, without clear knowledge of who the father is, and finally dies from an infection during her second out-of-wedlock pregnancy.

The novel consists primarily of a straightforward third-person narrative, with several chapters of Elena's notes written in the first person. In the second half Kukotskii retreats into the background. Tania and her sister Tomochka, another adopted daughter, as well as the Goldberg brothers, the sons of Kukotskii's old colleague, one of whom is the father of Zhenia, are at the centre of the novel. Chronology appears to be a structural device, because there is no climax, only a transition in time and space in which events are selectively described. The fates of Kukotskii and Tania are touching and tragic, but Tania's actions are often contradictory and unexplained, and the conclusion of the novel is not a direct result of the action in the narrative. Ulitskaia captures the atmosphere reigning in the community of genetic scientists in the USSR in the days of Stalin's rule, but she fails to show how it affects the internal lives of those scientists. We learn what happens to the heroes, but remain puzzled as to what motivates their actions.

In 2002 Ulitskaia published the story 'Tsiu-iurikh' (Tsiu-iurikh'–Zurich),[35] which is different from her other prose narratives. The main heroine is Lidia, a single simple woman from Belorussia, presently residing in Moscow, who makes a rational decision to become acquainted with a foreigner in order to change the course of her life. Lidia learns German, approaches a Swiss businessman in Moscow, invites him to her apartment, takes him to bed, and in the end moves to Switzerland, marries the Swiss gentleman and becomes a devoted wife and a successful businesswoman.

The action in the story is set in the days of Soviet rule, when life in the West was idealized, and many Soviet citizens dreamed about a beautiful life abroad. And yet, Lidia's exploits are not very convincing. No self-respecting Russian woman would hunt for a foreigner on the street. That was the domain of prostitutes. Moreover, Martin, the Swiss businessman, is portrayed as a simpleton who falls for a woman he does not know. Ulitskaia paints a broad picture of Soviet life, with particular emphasis on the problem of emigration, but she does not dwell on the psychological aspect of human motivation. She describes the discussions and actions of the characters well, but once again fails to analyse the inclinations that move them.

Most of Ulitskaia's plots, with minor exceptions, deal with the Soviet past and most of her characters are entangled in complicated situations. She claims that while she draws inspiration from her life experience, most of her characters have no real-life prototypes. She says that she is interested in the fate of simple people outside the mainstream of society.[36] Ulitskaia writes in traditional realistic Russian and her prose is compact. Her stories tend to revolve around women with complicated fates, and her focus is usually on her characters. Her plots are absorbing, infused with irony and a touch of sentimentality, and she has a propensity for understatement. Ulitskaia is a compassionate observer. She provides her readers with a view of life, but she does not moralize or interfere in her narratives in the normal course of events.

Svetlana Vasilenko

Svetlana Vasilenko (b. 1956) is an active member of the Moscow liberal writers' association. She is a graduate of the Moscow Literary Institute, and her first published work appeared in 1982. In 1998 Vasilenko published in *Novyi mir* a so-called novel-life *Durochka* (A Little Fool).[37] It is a fantastic tale in the realistic setting of Soviet life, intertwined with stories from Russian folklore and mythology. The novel opens in the late 1950s and concludes in 1962, at the time of the Cuban missile crisis. In between there is a flashback to the 1930s, the time of a famine in Russia, and a story about a little fool, a mute adolescent girl, who apparently has Down's syndrome.

The girl, Ganna, is influenced by religious faith and she represents the positive in the novel. Despite her condition Ganna is able to sing and is possessed of special understanding and spiritual goodness of heart. The main idea of the novel is that strength is not tantamount to goodness, and that goodness can overcome evil. Ganna is in the process of a continuous flight from evil, from those who want to hurt her, including the sadist mistress of the orphanage, the NKVD, and a gang of roving robbers. At one point she has a vision of the Holy Mother and acquires miraculous powers of healing. The conclusion, in which Ganna ascends to heaven, is symbolic. She is pregnant, and gives birth to a new sun and a better future for all children.

Much of the action in the novel is set in Vasilenko's native town, Kapustin Iar, and the emphasis is on the wrongdoings of the leaders of the Soviet regime. The portrayal of life in the Soviet Union of the 1930s is realistic and truthful. Churches are destroyed, priests are imprisoned, and famine rages in southern Russia. On the concluding pages, there is fear of a nuclear encounter with the United States. The beginning and the conclusion of the novel are narrated in the first person by one of the characters; the flashback to the 1930s is told in the third person. The language of the novel is colourful, full of poetic images, but portrayal is not always balanced. In some instances description is too wordy, in others it is too succinct. The novel presents an engaging blend of various motifs, personal and social, religious and secular, political and historical, placed in a setting in which the realistic and fantastic cohabit side by side.

Marina Vishnevetskaia

Marina Vishnevetskaia is a native of the city of Kharkov, in the Ukraine, and a graduate of the faculty of script writing of the Moscow State Institute of Cinematography. After graduating in 1979 she embarked on a career in animation and documentary film. In the early 1990s she began to write prose fiction, and her first story, 'Uvidet' derevo' (To See a Tree),[38] appeared in the 1996 volume of *Znamia*. This first publication was followed by many others, and soon Vishnevetskaia published two collections of prose: *Vyshel mesiats iz tumana* (The Moon Appeared from the Fog) in 1999, and *Uvidet' derevo* in 2000.

Vishnevetskaia's prose is peculiar. Some stories are realistic, others fantastic. Many of her narratives are plotless, without a beginning or an end. Her language is sophisticated but complex. It has a gliding quality, but concentration is required in order to follow the main thrust of the stories. The conflicts in her narratives are ill-defined, but careful reading brings the intended meaning to the fore. In 'Uvidet' derevo'[39] the main character, Sasha, is forty-three years old. Her mother has just died and been cremated. When Sasha goes to the crematorium to pick up the ashes she is told that someone has already taken them away. Ultimately, Sasha discovers that her daughter has taken the ashes to Odessa to scatter them over the Black Sea. That was allegedly her grandmother's wish. Most of the story is composed of racy dialogue between characters we hardly know, which takes place while Sasha tries to find out who has had the temerity to take her mother's ashes.

'Vyshel mesiats iz tumana'[40] apparently contains some elements from the author's personal life. The novella covers a period of some twenty years, and it is originally set in a Ukrainian city. On the concluding pages we encounter the same characters in Moscow. Most of the protagonists are involved in the arts and sciences, and formed a close-knit clan in their youth. Several incidents in the novella move the plot. One is the unsuccessful attempt to form a clandestine organization; the other is an unfulfilled love between two members of the group. Without any introduction, characterization, or explanation Vishnevetskaia presents a slice of Soviet life. The reader is asked, in a sense, to join the group of friends and move along with them without actually being familiar with any of them.

The story 'Arkhitektor zapiataia ne moi' (Architect Comma not Mine)[41] is different. It has a definite plot, and a first-person female narrator. The narrator writes a letter to her younger married sister recounting a casual sexual affair with an older married man during a vacation at a holiday resort. The narrator is upset that she has been taken advantage of by a stranger, but she is also eager to continue the liaison. In 'Nachalo' (Beginning)[42] the mother of the main character becomes ill and crippled. As her illness progresses and her condition worsens she loses weight, and becomes smaller. At one point she becomes so small that her son keeps her in a small box, and is afraid of losing her altogether. In the end the reader is left wondering whether the mother is genuinely ill, or the son mentally unstable.

Vishnevetskaia's plots are inventive and often experimental. Her language is refined and tense, and her portrayal is episodic and impressionistic, but she has the skill to reveal minute elusive nuances of human relations and the extreme state of the human spirit. Vishnevetskaia's stories, however, are intended for the sophisticated reader. Characterization is almost nonexistent, and her narratives are not always easy to follow.

6

The Writers of the Conservative 'Patriotic' Camp

The writers discussed in this chapter are well-known representatives of the so-called Russian conservative patriotic camp. They are grouped together here primarily because of their political and ideological convictions, as well as their membership in the conservative Writers' Union of the Russian Federation. In the days of Soviet rule many of these writers, such as Vasilii Belov, Valentin Rasputin, and Vladimir Lichutin, were associated thematically and spiritually with 'village prose.' Iurii Bondarev, on the other hand, was one of the main proponents of Soviet war prose, while Aleksandr Prokhanov was well known, at that time, for political novels set in foreign countries friendly to the Soviet regime.

Today, the works of these writers remain thematically and stylistically diverse, but most of them are anti-government, anti-liberal, anti-Semitic, anti-Western, and proclaim an allegiance to the Russian Orthodox Church. Their political and ideological views find expression not only in their journalistic writings, but in their prose fiction as well.

Vasilii Belov

Vasilii Belov (b. 1932) is one of the best-known representatives of Soviet 'village prose' of the 1960s and 1970s, and his novella 'Privychnoe delo' (That's How It Is; 1966) has become a classic of Soviet literature. Belov continues to write about the Russian countryside, but his current preoccupation is with political, historical, and ideological issues, rather than imaginative fiction. Belov's recent novel, *Chas shestyi* (The Sixth Hour; 1999),[1] is in the spirit of earlier narratives such as

Kanuny. Khronika kontsa 20–kh godov (Eves: A Chronicle of the Late 1920s; 1976–87) and *God velikogo pereloma. Khronika deviati mesiatsev* (A Year of Great Change: A Chronicle of Nine Months; 1989–91 and 1994), and it deals with the situation in the Russian countryside in the period of collectivization.

The title of the novel is taken from a verse in the New Testament, referring to the approaching death of Christ. The narrative opens with a scene in which one of the protagonists, Evgraf Mironov, is set free from jail in the city of Vologda; he returns to his native village after having served two years for an undefined crime connected with the process of collectivization and the anti-*kulak* campaign. The Russian countryside in the early 1930s was in a state of turmoil. Some peasants have been arrested and exiled, others happily join the new administration, while others still refuse to join the newly formed collective farms and go into hiding. The main subject of the novel is the reaction of the peasants to changes in the old, established way of life imposed by the Soviet regime.

In an afterword to the novel Below asserts that the plot is based on real events which took place in the village of Shibanikha, in the Vologda region. He also alludes to the fact that some characters have real prototypes. It appears, however, that the novel combines fact and fiction, and that much of it is influenced by the author's current political and ideological views. Thus, he criticizes Lenin for his internationalist views and praises Stalin for his Russian nationalism, anti-Semitism, and campaign against the Masons.

As a work of art the novel is a far cry from Belov's early 'village prose' stories. The plot of the novel is diffuse and lacks focus. Individual conflicts are poorly delineated, and in most instances unresolved. Numerous digressions distract the reader from the main course of events. The only positive aspect of the novel is its language. The novel is narrated in the local peasant dialect, and it recreates the atmosphere in remote, provincial Russia in the period under consideration. The mature Belov is still a talented writer, but his obsession with political, ideological, and religious issues interferes with his creative work and has a negative effect on his literary production. Moreover, as the conservative Russian literary scholar, N.M. Fed', suggests, 'the internal discord in Vasilii Belov's creative work intensifies the subjectivity and onesidedness of his interpretation of historical facts and events.'[2] Artistic quality is sacrificed for external and superficial political inferences.

Iurii Bondarev

The Second World War theme was popular in the Soviet Union; this literature attracted a wide range of readers from different population strata, and was supported by the Soviet regime. It glorified the historical past of Russia and the heroism of Soviet soldiers in the war with Nazi Germany, and it instilled in the younger generation a spirit of patriotism and dedication to their Soviet motherland. The political changes in post-war Soviet Russia affected the Second World War literature in both style and substance, but the positive message in these narratives was usually retained.

Iurii Bondarev (b. 1924) is one of the best-known representatives of this prose. As a retired young officer of the Soviet army he published his first war prose in the early 1950s. In the 1970s and 1980s he continued to write about the war, but he juxtaposes battle scenes with the post-war experience of those who have survived the war. He also attempts to examine the private and professional lives of former officers, currently members of the creative intelligentsia. Bondarev, a respected member of the upper echelon of the Soviet literary establishment, was always in the mainstream of official Soviet literature and he always adhered to the ideological and political requirements of the Communist Party and the Soviet regime.

The changes in the Soviet Union connected with the ascent of Mikhail Gorbachev to power, and with *perestroika*, are reflected in Bondarev's narrative *Iskushenie* (Temptation; 1991). This novel is also about the Soviet intelligentsia, but here Bondarev is critical of the Soviet state bureaucracy, the political establishment, and the cultural elite, and he portrays the so-called party-mafia as a group of depraved and power-hungry people without morals or scruples. After the disintegration of the Soviet Union Bondarev became a leading member of the conservative Russian Writers' Union, and despite his advanced age he continues to be active in the writers' community, promoting his new nationalistic and Russian Orthodox views.

In his new novel, *Neprotivlenie* (Non-Resistance; 2000),[3] Bondarev returns, in a sense, to the war theme. The action covers only a few weeks, and takes place in Moscow in 1946, immediately after the Second World War. The main objective of the novel is to portray the political and social situation in the Soviet Union at that time, and to examine the effect of the war on the life of a group of officers and soldiers recently demobilized from the Soviet armed forces. There are few war

scenes in the novel, and most of them appear in the dreams and hallucinations of the hero.

The main character of the novel, the demobilized lieutenant and
commander of a reconnaissance squad, Aleksandr Ushakov, returns to
Moscow after the war and lives with his ailing mother. Without a profession, or any practical life experience, he finds it difficult to adjust to
civilian life. He leads, for a while, an idle existence, and becomes
friendly with a group of young men who are likewise former members
of the Soviet armed forces. Initially, there is no indication that this
group is involved in any criminal activity, but as it turns out its leader,
Arkadii Kiriushkin, is in conflict with a certain Lesik, who is the leader
of a criminal gang. Ushakov unwittingly becomes involved in the confrontation between the two gangs, kills two people with the gun he has
kept from the front, and dies from wounds received in battle.

Aleksandr Ushakov appears to be a decent human being, a good soldier and patriot, and a dedicated son to his ill mother. Fate made possible his survival in the war, but chance exposes him to the unexpected
dangers of civilian existence. He takes a risk and pays with his life,
because he is faithful to the fellowship of former soldiers, Second
World War warriors. Moreover, Ushakov's actions are an expression of
the deeply rooted antagonism between the young officers who have
served their country with distinction and who have just returned from
the front, and the young men who managed to evade army service and
spent the war years in the hinterland.

The title of the novel, *Neprotivlenie*, refers to the religious convictions
and pacifist, non-resistance beliefs of two members of Ushakov's
group. One, El'dar, is a Muslim; the other, Bilibin, is a Christian. The
essence of their faith, however, is not delineated, and Bondarev's occa-
sional philosophical deliberations are shallow and little connected
with the main action. Bondarev's art has changed little since the 1960s.
As in most of his earlier novels, the structure of *Neprotivlenie* is conventional, the plot covers a short period of time, and characterization is
superficial. The novel employs simple, straightforward, third-person
narration, and there is no colourful imagery or figurative speech.

Most important is the picture of the complicated life in the Soviet
Union following the great victory in the Second World War. It appears
that in addition to those killed in the war, an entire generation of
young people who managed to survive has also been lost. The problems posed in the novel are of great social significance, but they are
inadequately explored and treated in a superficial manner. It is obvi-

ous that the Soviet government has failed to provide Ushakov and his colleagues with the necessary assistance required for successful transition from military to civilian existence. And yet Bondarev, who still worships his Soviet past, declines to name the real culprits, and to criticize the Soviet administration for its failure to provide support to those who made the Soviet victory at the front possible.

Bondarev's most recent novel, *Bermudskii treugol'nik* (The Bermuda Triangle; 1999),[4] is set in Moscow in the mid-1990s, and the main character is a representative of the Russian intelligentsia, a painter. Bondarev deals here with political, social, and ethical issues of contemporary Russian life, and he attempts to be topical by addressing the controversial events of 1993, but just as in *Neprotivlenie*, the characters are indistinct, the issues posed are ill-defined, and the treatment of political events is biased.

Vladimir Krupin

Vladimir Krupin (b. 1941) is one of the former so-called *sorokaletnie*, who reached their prime in the late 1970s and 1980s. The works of Krupin, a native of the Viatka region, however, were in the past close in spirit and subject matter to those of 'village prose' writers. In his early stories Krupin idealizes life in the countryside and contrasts its spirituality with the corruption of city life. But in the days of *perestroika*, and in the early post-Soviet years, Krupin became an outspoken critic of the new order of things in Russia, and an ardent proponent of Russian nationalism and Orthodoxy.

In the mid-1990s, at the behest of the new Russian leadership, the intellectual elite embarked on an effort to devise a new national idea to fill the vacuum created by the repudiation of Marxism-Leninism. According to Krupin this is a fruitless endeavour, because Russia already has a national idea: Orthodoxy and nationalistic Russianness. Hence, Krupin became a vociferous advocate of these ideas and a political supporter of the official opposition to the government. He ceased to write fiction, limited his writing to first-person narratives with a clear religious message,[5] and worked for seven years as a teacher in the Moscow Spiritual Academy.

In the novella 'Liubi menia, kak ia tebia' (Love Me, as I Love You; 1998),[6] the first-person narrator is a graduate student in a Moscow Institute, the objective of which is to devise an appropriate ideology for the period of transition to democracy in Russia. The purpose of the narrator's dissertation is to invent a system which will help to combine the efforts of different branches of the sciences to create an idea which will assist in the revival of Russia, and he is sent to St Petersburg to participate in a conference of theologians. There, unexpectedly, he falls in love with a Russian woman who attacks a foreign Baptist preacher from the podium. The narrator's love is obviously prompted by his identification with the ideas expressed by the woman, rather than by her beauty.

The story is narrated on two levels. There is the romantic, yet platonic, love affair between two individuals who live in two different cities, an infatuation which unfortunately ends in tragedy, with the death of the woman. She has a sick heart and cannot withstand the emotional stress of her love. On another level, there is the operation of the Moscow Institute and the views of the narrator's supervisor, who declares 'that there is not, and will not be, any new idea for the period of democracy [in Russia]. The Russian idea is the same as it has always been, it is orthodoxy. Russia will have no other idea.'[7]

In addition to the national and religious concerns of the intelligentsia, the reader is informed about the activities of political organizations working to assume power in Russia. One such formation, named 'Vlast' russkim' (Power to Russians), advocates racial purity and refuses to accept members of mixed marriages. Its aim is first to take power, and only later to make Orthodoxy the ruling state idea. According to 'Vlast' russkim' only Orthodox Russians are good, all others are damned. It is not long before the Institute is closed, and both the narrator and his supervisor remain without jobs.

Krupin's ideological position is not new. It is, in a sense, a form of racial religious fundamentalism which draws modern civilization back into the dark ages. His prose, however, is even more dangerous than his ideas. Krupin's nationalistic and chauvinistic notions are expressed in a colourful language, full of irony and comic intonations, and the unsophisticated reader could be easily influenced by its preposterous message.

Vladimir Lichutin

Vladimir Lichutin is another former 'village prose' writer who is presently a member of the conservative 'patriotic' camp and an outspoken advocate of its nationalistic agenda. His recent novel, *Miledi Rotman* (Milady Rotman; 2001),[8] was received by the critics with a dose of scepticism, and it failed to satisfy the expectations even of those who share Lichutin's ideological views. Milady Rotman is the wife of Ivan Zhukov, a Moscow journalist and a native of the village of Zhukovka, who decides to convert to Judaism. He assumes the name of Rotman, and returns to his native village. The only logical motivation for Zhukov's action is his belief that Jews are clever, self-reliant, and guided by self-interest, and that they will help him in case of need. Unfortunately, Zhukov's conversion does little to improve his life. He is in all probability impotent, and his wife, who craves a child, is impregnated by a local Russian artist, Bratilov. She bears a son who subsequently is regarded by Zhukov as his own child. In the end, Rotman-Zhukov perishes accidentally in 1993, on his way to Moscow to assist in the defence of the mutineers who have barricaded themselves in the Russian parliament.

The narrative is monotonous, boring, and generates no real tension. The plot is poorly devised, and the language is archaic. In fact, except for the squabbles in the Rotman family, there is little action. Mariia Remizova suggests in her review of the novel that Lichutin has an allegorical subtext and a symbolic message, namely that Zhukov has assumed the Jewish sin, and is initially condemned by the author to perdition. Moreover, the fate of Zhukov's alleged son is to parallel the destiny of Christ.[9] Nikolai Pereiaslov, on the other hand, asserts that Lichutin, one of the most national Russian writers, is so distraught by the current plight of the Russian people that he impels Zhukov to embrace Judaism as a means of escape. Unfortunately, according to Pereiaslov, Zhukov's conversion 'is ineffective and ruinous, because the national idea of another nation is unacceptable and useless to the Russian people.'[10]

Whatever the ideological objectives of Lichutin's recent novel, artistically it has many shortcomings. Characterization is inadequate, and there is no psychological substantiation of the characters' actions. Moreover, the dramatic collisions and external intrigue are poorly defined, and the intended message, if any, is difficult to unravel.

Aleksandr Prokhanov

One of the best-known current ideological opponents of the government, Aleksandr Prokhanov (b. 1938), is both an inveterate politician and a prolific writer. In the 1980s he worked as a Soviet journalist in Afghanistan, Kampuchea, Mozambique, and Nicaragua and he writes novels set in these countries. He denounces the American government and way of life; supports the Soviet invasion of Afghanistan, and deliberates upon the global competition between alleged American imperialism and the 'progressive' revolutionary forces led by the Soviet Union.

With the ascent of Mikhail Gorbachev and the subsequent dissolution of the Soviet state, Prokhanov joined hands with the most extreme pro-communist and nationalistic forces in Russia and became the editor of the weekly *Den'*, the mouthpiece of the 'patriotic' and nationalistic opposition. Prokhanov and *Den'* supported the failed August 1991 anti-government coup, and, in the post-Soviet era he called for the overthrow of President Yeltsin's government and the establishment of a dictatorial regime in Russia. Eventually, the publication of *Den'* was banned, but it was soon replaced by *Zavtra*, also edited by Prokhanov, an equally vitriolic anti-government newspaper. The prose fiction of Prokhanov in the late 1980s and early 1990s is undistinguished, and his novels of that period combine journalism, politics, and art.

By the mid-1990s the situation in Russia stabilized to some degree, and Yeltsin's grip on power strengthened, but Prokhanov's opposition to those in charge did not wane, and he continued his anti-government campaign in the press as well as in his fiction. Three long novels published between 1998 and 2001 exemplify the areas of his political interest, and Prokhanov is apparently the only well-known contemporary Russian author to write about the Russian debacle in Chechnia. Prokhanov is still able to produce well-written narratives, but he readily sacrifices artistic quality for journalistic effect, and he includes poorly developed sections for solely ideological and political reasons. The emphasis on politics in Prokhanov's recent novels may indicate that his creative skills are in the process of decline.

Prokhanov's novel *Chechenskii bliuz* (The Chechen Blues; 1998)[11] is set simultaneously in two locations, Moscow and Chechnia. In Moscow the protagonist is Iakov Berner, a successful banker and entrepreneur, while in Chechnia the main character is the Russian company commander, Captain Kudriavtsev. Berner is a greedy and cunning operator who circulates in the company of corrupt high state and business officials and is acquainted with many military leaders. He owns property and business interests all over Russia, including Chechnia, and he manipulates official Russian political decisions to suit his personal economic needs. Berner pretends to be a Russian patriot, but his real interest is protecting his oil business, which he owns jointly with a childhood friend, Varshatskii. In the end Berner has Varshatskii murdered and becomes the sole proprietor of the Chechen oil enterprise.

Kudriavtsev, in contrast, is a simple Russian officer, serving in the Caucasus, who is lured into a trap by the treacherous Chechens and wounded in combat. Kudriavtsev refuses, however, to surrender and manages to survive his unexpected confrontation with the enemy. In the final chapter of the novel Kudriavtsev is back in his native village, in the region of Smolensk, in Russia. His relatives, descendants of an old Russian priestly family, conduct church services in support of the Russian victory in Chechnia, and for the life and health of their native son – Kudriavtsev.

The names given to most protagonists in this novel deceive no one. It is clear that in the character of Berner Prokhanov satirizes the Russian tycoon Boris Berezovskii. The general who hates Berner but seeks his financial support in the forthcoming presidential election campaign is none other than General Aleksandr Lebed,' Yeltsin's rival in the struggle for the seat in the Kremlin. Prokhanov does not spare the demoralized Russian military leaders either. He blames them for the military losses in Chechnia and decries the fact that, instead of being concerned with the fate of Russian soldiers serving under them, the Russian generals are preoccupied with issues of promotion, enrichment, or simply having a good time. It is suggested, however, that the main culprits responsible for all of Russia's troubles are the Jews. Only once is it hinted that Berner is a Jew, but his Jewish-sounding name and those of his business associates make it obvious.

Prokhanov juxtaposes the selfless patriotism of Kudriavtsev, who is ready to sacrifice his life in order to save Russia's honour, with the behaviour of Berner, who sacrifices Russia, and Russian lives, in order to make money and gain power. The contrast between the two characters is sometimes stretched to the extreme. In one instance Berner rapes a female journalist who comes to interview him. Kudriavtsev, on the other hand, initially refuses the advances of a single Russian woman he encounters in a house in Grozny, where he and several other Russian soldiers have barricaded themselves.

The novel is a straightforward third-person narrative, interspersed with some dialogue and political invectives. The main focus is not on the inner world of human experience, but rather on the political, military, and business activity of the main characters. The divide between good and evil in the novel is always clear. Those who reflect the author's personal views are always portrayed positively, while those

representing his political and ideological adversaries are always perverse and destructive. In Prokhanov's Soviet novels most negative
characters are enemies of the Soviet state: foreigners, spies, or traitors.
In his recent novels they are usually members of the Russian ruling
elite, or Russian citizens who are not ethnic Russians.

Artistically, the novel is no masterpiece. Not a single protagonist
receives adequate artistic treatment. Even the heroes are depicted only
episodically and in a one-sided manner which highlights only those
character traits and actions which satisfy the political objectives of the
author. The ideological message in the novel is clear, and art is sacrificed for political effect.

Prokhanov's next novel, *Krasno-korichnevyi roman* (The Red-Brown
Novel; 1999),[12] is similar in spirit but different in substance. An introductory note states that this is 'a book about the national uprising of
1993 ... It is a text book of contemporary history, and the gospel of Russian patriotism. It is a combat instruction for all those who are strug-
gling for the freedom and independence of the Motherland.' The
narrative combines fact and fiction. At the centre of the plot are the
Moscow events of 1993. At first, anti-government demonstrators attack
the Moscow television station in Ostankino in an attempt to take
power in the capital. In response, government forces which support
President Boris Yeltsin attack the Supreme Soviet, which is occupied by
Yeltsin's enemies under the leadership of the Supreme Soviet Chairman Ruslan Khasbulatov and Vice-President Aleksandr Rutskoi.

Most historical figures, in particular those who currently occupy
official positions in Russia's political life, appear under their real
names. Most leaders of opposition groups, however, are given fictitious ones. The plot turns on the character and fate of the retired colonel Khlop'ianov. He has just returned to Moscow from a tour of duty
which included service and fighting in Afghanistan, in the contested
region of Nagorno Karabakh between Armenia and Azerbaidzhan, as
well as in the Dnestr region in the southwestern part of the USSR.
Khlop'ianov, who abhors the recent changes in Russia, is ready to join
the opposition forces to the government. In Moscow he meets the journalist Klokotov, with whom he was acquainted in Afghanistan. It is
clear that Prokhanov himself is the prototype for the character of
Klokotov. Klokotov introduces Khlop'ianov to leaders of a number of
anti-government opposition groups. Khlop'ianov, a former reconnaissance and intelligence officer in the Soviet Army, in turn, offers his
services to the opposition.

A major part of the novel is taken up by the description of Khlop'ianov's meetings with various leaders of opposition groups. He meets, among others, with the leaders of the communists, monarchists, and national-fascists, as well as with a former KGB general, a Red Army general, the leader of the Cossacks, and representatives of the Russian Orthodox Church. The general picture of the opposition that transpires from Khlop'ianov's impressions is confusing. The opposition is disorganized and splintered into many small warring factions with different agendas. It has no joint leadership or unified vision for the future of Russia. It is united only by a deep hatred of the existing regime and a desire to overthrow it. Most opposition leaders are interested in Khlop'ianov's plan, which envisages the creation of a special intelligence and security service. And yet, no one is ready to accept his offer. Some opposition groups are still in the process of organizing and have no clear notion of their future actions. Others are simply suspicious of this stranger who, though introduced by the respected Klokotov, has appeared from nowhere, and who, before being taken into their confidence, would have to be thoroughly checked out.

When Khlop'ianov attempts to join the opposition he accidentally encounters in Moscow another acquaintance from Afghanistan, Colonel Karetnyi. Karetnyi, who is presently active in the Russian state security organs, manages to recruit the unsuspecting Khlop'ianov to act in the capacity of a double agent. Khlop'ianov agrees because he wants to learn as much as possible about the government's plot and to report his findings to the opposition. In the end, however, Khlop'ianov is outwitted by Karetnyi and his cohorts, who doubt his honesty and murder him. Similarly, Klokotov is killed during the skirmish at the Ostankino television station. The most important protagonists in the narrative have been removed from the scene, bringing the novel to its logical conclusion.

Colonel Khlop'ianov is supposed to personify the positive qualities of those who oppose the current government, and to illustrate the superiority of the Soviet past over the current corrupt regime. Unfortunately, Khlop'ianov is not a strong character. He becomes involved in a political charade, the rules of which he fails to comprehend, and he is not endowed with the character traits required for the task he has undertaken. He is indecisive, he constantly vacillates, and he has no definite vision of the future. He is unable to arrange even his personal life properly. He appears to be in love with Katia, a single, idealistic woman, but he fails to appreciate her devotion, and in the end he abandons her.

It is possible to draw a parallel between the author of the novel and his hero. Both are negative thinkers who have nothing positive to offer. This problem haunts the leaders of the Russian opposition as well. They have no clear vision for a better future for Russia, just a desperate desire for a return to the past. Prokhanov's vague appeal for the creation of a '"Russian civilization" which will be a synthesis of communist earthly construction with a religious burst into the unknown universe,'[13] is nothing but a call to create in Russia a new version of the old communist utopia.

The novel combines elements of a detective story, a love story, and a political narrative with details of Russia's recent history, but none of the themes broached is fully developed. Moreover, the novel lacks compositional unity. There are too many abrupt digressions, unimportant details, and irrelevant subplots, and far too much political diatribe. Prokhanov's communist fervour, displayed in his earlier novels of the Soviet period has been replaced with religious zeal. The struggle between the current regime and the so-called patriotic opposition is always portrayed as a conflict between good and evil. The overriding emphasis on the political aspects of reality may satisfy the needs of a political pamphlet, but it is hardly sufficient for the creation of an artistically viable work of prose.

Prokhanov's next novel, *Idushchie v nochi* (Those Walking in the Night; 2001),[14] is in many ways similar to *Chechenskii bliuz*, but it is also different. Parts of the novel are reminiscent of Soviet Second World War prose narratives, while other episodes deal with current political affairs. Where *Chechenskii bliuz* is set in the time of the first Russian offensive in Grozny, in 1994, the action in *Idushchie v nochi* takes place during the second assault on the city in 1999. Vladimir Putin is already in charge of Russian government affairs, and is getting ready to replace Yeltsin in the top Kremlin position. The novel covers several days in the life of the main characters, and it provides a realistic picture of the Chechen-Russian conflict, as it is perceived by most members of the two warring factions. Chapters devoted to the life and battles of a Russian platoon, commanded by Lieutenant Pushkov, alternate with chapters dealing with the activities of the Russian military command in Chechnia. The work of Colonel Pushkov, the head of the reconnaissance staff, and the father of the platoon commander, is contrasted with the actions of the simple soldiers under the command of the latter's son. Separate sections of the novel are set in the camp of the Chechen fighters and focus on Shamil' Basaev, the leader of the Chechen insurgent army.

The Russian soldiers are patriotic. They hate the Chechens, and their main objective is to capture Grozny and destroy the enemy. But they are also human and they want to live. In one instance two Russian soldiers are taken prisoner by the Chechens. One of them, Sergeant Klychkov, is strong, brave, and fearless in battle, but when he is imprisoned and condemned by the Chechens to die, he breaks down. He begs his captors not to kill him, and agrees to convert to Islam and join the Chechen fighters. In order to prove his sincerity to his jailors he agrees to shoot at the barricade behind which his Russian colleagues are hiding. The other prisoner, the soldier Zvonarev, although physically weak, is strong in spirit. He is a deeply religious man who hopes one day to join the Russian priesthood. He does not distinguish himself in his army service, but when he is put to the real test he stands up to his torturers. He refuses to disclose army secrets, because, as he says, he took an oath. Moreover, he refuses to convert to Islam to save his life, and is ready to face destiny without regrets. The Chechens murder him on the spot. This episode in the novel is reminiscent of the well-known Soviet Second World War novella, 'Sotnikov,' by the Belorussian writer Vasil' Bykov, in which two Soviet partisans are taken prisoner by the Nazis. The one who is bold and physically strong breaks down emotionally and saves his life by agreeing to join the pro-Nazi police; the other, sick and weak in body, is morally firm. He does not succumb to temptation and sacrifices his life rather than becoming a traitor.

The first part of *Idushchie v nochi*, which deals with the predicament of ordinary soldiers, is interesting and absorbing. The second part, however, in which Prokhanov tries to develop the main conflict, is obscure and confusing. An offer of safe passage from Grozny is made to the Chechen leader Shamil' Basaev by a certain magnate in Moscow, who allegedly has good relations with the Chechens and supports Basaev because he has important business interests in Chechnia. By getting safely out of Grozny Basaev could save his army, and the Russians could declare victory. A similar offer of safe passage is made to Basaev by Colonel Pushkov. He pretends to be a Russian officer willing to sell the secret for money. Basaev is suspicious, but in the end he agrees to the offer and pays the money. The shrewd Basaev, however, demands that Colonel Pushkov come along for the trip. The Russian command mines the alleged path to safety, trapping Basaev and his men. Most of the Chechens are killed in the ambush, although Basaev himself survives. Colonel Pushkov pays with his life for his bold exploit, and his son, Lieutenant Pushkov, loses his life a day earlier in direct combat.

A secondary character, the Moscow painter Litkin, appears only sporadically, but artistically he is probably the most fully developed character. He has been hired by a French studio to videotape the events in Chechnia and produce a film about the heroic struggle of the Chechen people for their independence, with particular emphasis on the exploits of Basaev. Prokhanov treats Litkin with contempt, but he captures the urge of the artist to penetrate the minds and souls of the subjects he photographs. Litkin risks his life in order to videotape scenes of affliction, mortal suffering, and death. He is everywhere, on the battlefield and in Basaev's camp as well as among the Russians. He manages to produce a tape of great artistic and historic value, but does not live to reap the rewards of his labour. Litkin is killed by a Russian officer who apparently mistakes him for a Chechen.

Up to the last chapter most of the novel reads as an ordinary war story set in contemporary Russia. The final chapter, however, is written in a different tone. Prokhanov returns to his political invectives and his well-known anti-Semitism. The setting is now a Moscow *dacha*. The host of the open house party is the converted-to-Christianity Jewish tycoon, Parusinskii. Those present are members of the Russian political, economic, and artistic elite, and Vladimir Putin is among them. It appears that the magnate and Parusinskii are one and the same person, and that the prototype for both of them is none other than Boris Berezovskii, who allegedly wants to save Basaev and his army in order to protect his personal economic and business interests in Chechnia. In order to denigrate Berezovskii, who has also converted to Christianity, Prokhanov questions the sincerity of Parusinskii's conversion. He concocts a story according to which the latter is allegedly behind a plan to create a Russian-Jewish state, Khazaria, on the territory presently occupied by Russia. 'Jewish genius, Jewish bold thought, and ability to organize, and the Russian resources, Russian ability to self-sacrifice for a great purpose,'[15] are to provide the foundation for this mythological state.

Idushchie v nochi, which was nominated (by Iurii Bondarev), for but not awarded, the Russian 2001 best-seller prize, is better constructed and more focused than his earlier novels. The plot is inventive, and most of the narrative flows smoothly. A failure, however, to delineate clearly the main conflict in the novel, and the constant intrusion of political and ideological diatribes lower its artistic value.

There is no doubt that the main objective of Prokhanov's recent novels is to discredit Yeltsin and the Russian government and to enhance the stature of those who oppose it. One theme, however, permeates all aspects of Prokhanov's plots: Judophobia and anti-Semitism. Jews are Prokhanov's scapegoats, and they are blamed for all of Russia's ills. Prokhanov's hatred of the Jews has no bounds. It is stressed throughout *Krasno-korichnevyi roman*, leading to the falsification of actual events. Prokhanov invents the figure of a mythical Israeli sniper who allegedly comes to Moscow to assist the Russian government in its fight against the opposition. He also claims that Jews are behind the anti-patriotic atrocities instigated by the Yeltsin regime. Aleksandr Tsipko, a columnist for *Literaturnaia gazeta*, suggests that Prokhanov 'is certainly a talented writer, and I do not doubt the patriotic motives of his creative work, nevertheless, it is difficult not to see that everything that comes out from under his pen is burdened by some kind of lifelessness, by some gloominess of his soul ... In every patriotic undertaking, in each text, created in the name of the Russian Party he mixes in a spoon of Judophobia, as if purposely trying to combine Russian patriotism with anti-Semitism ... The patriotism [of Prokhanov] which refers to Communism as a notion with a capital letter ... presumes the moral castration of the soul, and the freeze of ethical feeling.'[16] It is well known that procommunism and anti-Semitism are the main components of the political program and propaganda methods of the 'patriotic' left in Russia today. The patriot Prokhanov and the pro-communist opposition fail, however, to denounce the shortcomings of the former Soviet system and to censure the atrocities of the Soviet regime.

The change in leadership in Russia and the ascension of Vladimir Putin to power have affected the subject matter and composition of Prokhanov's most recent prose. His new novel, *Gospodin Geksogen* (Mister Hexogen),[17] published early in 2002 and awarded the Russian best-seller prize, shocked the Moscow intelligentsia, especially since Prokhanov promptly donated the prize money to the defence of Eduard Limonov, who is incarcerated for alleged politically motivated criminal activity.

In this novel Prokhanov attempts to combine realistic description of recent Russian political life with a fantastic detective plot. Most characters in *Gospodin Geksogen* have real-life prototypes, and any reader familiar with Russia's current events has no difficulty in identifying them. There is, of course, a certain slant in the presentation of factual material, which reflects Prokhanov's political and ideological views. The novel is characterized by a sarcastic tone and a scurrilous attack on members of the Russian state administration who, although they appear under invented names, are instantly recognizable. The Little

God or Moron is none other than President Boris Yeltsin, and his daughter is portrayed as a nymphomaniac and a whore.

In the beginning of the novel the main objective of the secret plot organized by a clique of former KGB generals appears to be to install the so-called Chosen One, or Putin, in the position of Head of State. The real goal, however, becomes clear somewhat later. With the help of intrigue, provocation, and violent means the clique intends to establish their rule worldwide. In the meantime, in order to instigate a new offensive in Chechnia, they blow up an apartment block in Moscow and blame the Chechens for this atrocious crime.

The main character of the novel is the former Soviet intelligence general Belosel'tsev, who is unwittingly recruited into the clique of conspirators but refuses to cooperate once he learns the real objectives of the group. The character of Belosel'tsev is reminiscent of that of Colonel Khlop'ianov from *Krasno-korichnevyi roman*. Both are Russian patriots. Both reminisce about their Soviet glorious past, and their escapades in various Third World countries. Both, however, are indecisive, lack vision, are duped by others, and go down in defeat.

Prokhanov's new novel has agitated and disturbed the Russian reading public. It demystifies the workings of former members of the Soviet security apparatus; it reveals their Stalinist nostalgia and their attempt to turn back the clock of history; and it again reveals Prokhanov's pronounced anti-Semitism. The novel can be read as a satire, lampoon, or phantasmagoric account of recent Russian history, but it is not a great work of art. *Gospodin Geksogen* is topical, it may even be interesting and thought provoking, but the characters are poorly developed, their ideas are not articulated clearly, and the conclusion does not resolve the conflict. Prokhanov is a prolific and talented writer, but he usually sacrifices artistry for political effect, and he tries to act the role of missionary and visionary at the same time. His ideas, however, are nothing more than a morbid and confusing combination of communism and Russian Orthodoxy. Prokhanov declares that he intends to write seven novels about the fate of the former red empire. He sees this task as a mission from God.[18] It is clear, however, that unless he learns to separate his political, ideological, and nationalistic interests from his creative concerns he will never realize his full artistic potential.

Valentin Rasputin

Valentin Rasputin (b. 1937), one of the best Russian writers of the

Soviet era, is still in the news, but in most instances not because of his recent artistic achievements. With the ascent of Gorbachev to power in the mid-1980s, and the abolition of state censorship, Rasputin's creative talent diminished. In the 1970s there was always harmony between the form and substance of his prose, and the narrator seldom interfered with the smooth flow of the narrative. The language of Rasputin in that era is compact, precise, and has a stern poetic quality. It contains traces of Russian folklore, and most characters can be distinguished by the local Siberian dialect they speak. In his most important work of the period, 'Proshchanie s Materoi' (Farewell to Matera; 1976), Rasputin addresses the conflict between the individual and the impersonal collective state. He defends the external environment, the internal fabric of life of the Siberian peasant, and the spiritual values associated with this life. Moreover, he decries the forced urbanization and the imposition of technological progress and Western civilization. Rasputin's novella 'Pozhar' (The Fire), published in 1985, is artistically much poorer than his earlier prose. There is a certain incompleteness in this narrative, a lack of unity between image and idea, and journalism intrudes into the artistic text.

In the mid-1980s Rasputin abandoned creative writing and became involved in politcs. At one point, he was nominated by Mikhail Gorbachev and became active in the President's Advisory Committee. Soon, however, Rasputin joined hands with the most reactionary elements in the Soviet state, and he supported the August 1991 anti-Gorbachev coup. After the disintegration of the Soviet Union Rasputin emerged as one of the most vociferous spokesmen of the Russian conservative nationalistic camp, and an ardent supporter of the pan-Slavist Orthodox cause.

In 1995 Rasputin went to the Serbian enclave in Bosnia, where he spoke in support of the Serbian and Slavic cause and advocated taking United Nations peace keepers as hostages. He compared the situation of the Bosnian Serbs with the Russian predicament in Chechnia and exclaimed that Russia also 'needs today a victory, any victory.'[19] Moreover, Rasputin declared 'in *Pravda* (Truth) that all Croatians and Bosnians are traitors to Orthodox Christianity, and that the aim of the dark international forces is to destroy Orthodox states, first Serbia, then Russia, and later the Ukraine ...'[20] In 1996 Rasputin visited Belorussia, announced his support for the anti-democratic totalitarian regime of President Aleksandr Lukashenko, and attacked the progressive writer Vasil' Bykov for his opposition to the Lukashenko dictatorship.[21] Rasputin spoke out against globalization and the mechanical integration with the West, and asserted that he is convinced that Russia can be secure only when it is ruled by a strong authoritarian government.[22]

Although Rasputin often had difficulties publishing his manuscripts in Brezhnev's Russia, and 'Proshchanie s Materoi' appeared in print only after the intervention of highly placed admirers, Rasputin now idealizes the Soviet past and finds little positive in contemporary Russia. He declares, 'in the past literature occupied an important place in society. Art, albeit in a somewhat deformed manner, was the pride of the authorities. The government was interested in, and provided considerable support, for its development. Literature could not replace the Church, but it fulfilled one of its functions, namely it nurtured the spirit and enriched life.'[23]

According to Rasputin, the decade-long interruption in his artistic literary activity, and his involvement in politics and journalism, has logical reasons. He asserts that with the appearance of 'Pozhar' he reached a dead end in his creative work. As a so-called *derevenshchik*, or proponent of 'village prose,' he had nothing more to say on the subject. The theme had exhausted itself. Hence, Rasputin asserts, he engaged in journalism, intending to use his considerable prestige to influence the reading public. Today, Rasputin declares 'this period is over, because there is no need any more to explain anything to anyone about what is happening'[24] in Russia. That does not mean, of course, that Rasputin abandoned his engagement in political affairs; it indicates only his return, in the mid-1990s, to creative writing.

A decade of creative silence has had little effect on Rasputin's artistic interests, the setting of his stories, or the essence of his prose. As before, the action in most of his narratives takes place in remote Siberia, and the main characters are old peasant women with difficult lives. The artistic quality of his recent prose, however, is much below the level reached in his pre-*perestroika* narratives. The story 'Zhenskii razgovor' (Women Talk; 1995)[25] is presented in the form of a dialogue between an elderly peasant woman, Natal'ia, and her sixteen-year-old granddaughter, Vika. The teenage girl is brought by her father to the countryside to recover after an abortion. Rasputin returns in this story to his old themes and original artistic means. He contrasts the old, good village life of Natal'ia with the degeneration, permissiveness, and lack of morals of Vika and her city friends. Natal'ia's Siberian dialect is juxtaposed with Vika's city parlance, and the old woman's life story is related in detail. We learn, however, nothing about Vika's past, or about the effect of the pregnancy on her state of mind. It appears that while hydro-electric stations have been constructed, villages flooded, and people resettled, there is still not enough electricity to serve those who need it. Indeed, the life of the Siberian peasant appears to be more difficult than ever before.

In the next story, 'Po-sosedski' (Neighbourly; 1995),[26] Rasputin sketches an episode of village life. Two neighbours are involved in a dispute about empty vodka bottles thrown across the fence dividing their property. The story may be funny, but it lacks focus and the conflict is never resolved. Rasputin's main objective is to compare the current difficult situation in the country with the allegedly better Soviet past. He emphasizes that today there is less order, less employment, and more pollution than before. Moreover, salaries are not paid, and the government in Moscow is useless.

The story 'V tu zhe zemliu ...' (Into the Same Earth; 1995)[27] is in a similar vein. Pasha, a peasant woman from Siberia, is caught up by the Soviet construction euphoria and moves to the city to seek a better life. Her elderly mother comes to visit Pasha, becomes ills, and dies. Pasha is faced with a dilemma. Without the so-called *propiska*, or residence permit, and without an official death certificate, which is difficult to procure for a non-resident in the city, it is impossible to obtain a burial plot in the city cemetery. Pasha decides to avoid dealing with the local authorities, and to save money, by burying her mother without permission in the nearby forest. Rasputin implies that funerals and the burial process are now in the hands of unscrupulous operators who abuse the bereaved and demand money for the privilege of a dignified burial. The imagery in this story is grim, and everything is presented in a negative light. Most people are mean and greedy and they cheat. There is a feeble indication of a return to religion, but it seems an escape from the current difficult reality, and an attempt to replace the former ideological haze with something emotionally more satisfying rather than a sincere return to faith. The language employed in the story is little different from that found in Rasputin's early prose, but the conflict here is social rather than personal, and the narrative lacks dramatic tension.

'Nezhdanno-negadanno' (Unexpected and Unsurmised; 1997)[28] is another tale of social depravity in contemporary Russia. A six-year-old orphan girl is kidnapped by a gang of thugs. She is placed on a city street to beg for alms and required to give any money received to her bosses. This is a tragic story about someone too young and helpless to take care of herself, who is abused by the dark forces of society. Rasputin's criticism of the social ills in contemporary Russia is presented, however, in journalistic form. There is no character development or psychological investigation, and the Soviet past is idealized.

In 1998 Rasputin published 'Novaia professiia' (New Profession).[29] It is the first narrative by Rasputin set in the city in which there are no peasant characters. The protagonist, Alesha Korenev, is a faint-hearted, thirty-five-year-old, twice-divorced, formerly well-known mathematician and physicist. After the disintegration of the Soviet Union, he is without a job, or his own abode, and makes a meagre living by delivering speeches at weddings of the new rich, but witless Russians, pretending to be a relative of the brides. Korenev contemplates the current predicament of many Russians inadequately prepared by their Soviet past for the new conditions of contemporary Russia. It appears, however, that the system, rather than the individual, is responsible for everyone's happiness. Thus, the irresolute and ineffectual Korenev, who drifts aimlessly and fails to take charge of his life, is absolved of any responsibility for his own destiny. As in most of Rasputin's recent stories, the narrative flows smoothly and the language is metaphoric. The development of the main character, however, is sacrificed to the elaboration of a social cause. Hence, we learn about the protagonists' actions but know little about his perception of his personal drama.

Rasputin's story 'Izba' (Peasant House; 1999)[30] can be read as a continuation of 'Proshchanie s Materoi.' We encounter here the same language and imagery, similar problems and characters. Villages are flooded, nature is ravaged, and a way of life is destroyed. The main character, the single peasant woman, Agafiia, is hard-working, ascetic, and determined. With the help of a neighbour she moves her house from the village that is to be flooded into the new settlement, and single-handedly rebuilds it. After her death the house stands empty for a while, and those who eventually move in meet with bad luck and are forced to abandon their new home. It is implied that the spirit of Agafiia haunts the house, and thus, at least symbolically, that it is wrong to uproot people, abuse nature, and destroy a way of life.

Despite Rasputin's assertion that the village theme has exhausted itself, and that he has nothing new to add to it, he returns, time and again, to his old subject. Rasputin, after all, knows little about anything but Siberian peasant life, and he appears to have had a hard time adjusting to the political, economic, and social changes in Russia. In a recent conversation with Iurii Vigor', Rasputin declared bluntly that 'he does not understand the current strange life. He is puzzled by designations such as offshore zones, monitoring, or integration process in the market.'[31]

Rasputin's recent prose retains some of its former artistic merit. The writer has an acute eye for detail, he is sensitive to the natural environment, he uses symbolic devices judiciously, and his language is colourful and precise. His subjects and conflicts, however, reverberate like an old record, and pessimism and negativism overshadow all his narratives. Rasputin's lack of faith in the new Russia affects even his choice of imagery, and the inanimate peasant hut, in 'Izba,' replaces the Russian peasant as a symbol of the continuity of the old Russian spirit.

Rasputin's political stance and his art are routinely attacked by liberal critics, but even some conservative scholars find it difficult to accept the decline in the artistic quality of his works and his contentious ideological propositions. After censuring Rasputin's prose, N.M. Fed' asserts that 'Valentin Rasputin is a man of duplicity, hyperbola, and impulsive thinking.'[32] Rasputin appears to have lost his way in the complicated labyrinth of political and literary life in contemporary Russia.

7

The Mystery Novel Writers

The conventional detective story is a narrative in which a mystery, often involving murder, is unravelled by a detective. There is usually a seemingly perfect crime; a suspect who, from the circumstantial evidence, appears to be guilty but is later proven innocent; a policeman, or another representative of the administration of justice, who questions the detective's course of action; and a denouement in which it becomes clear who killed whom, how, and why. The author of the detective novel invites, in a way, the reader to match wits with the central character, as both the reader and the detective uncover clues leading to the culprit. The truth in the story is thus revealed gradually.

In the Soviet days, when literary production was determined by Communist Party policy and ideology, and the Soviet Union aspired to become a country in which criminal activity was a thing of the past, the market for ordinary detective stories was limited. The political detective novel, however, was different. This genre served the political and ideological objectives of the state, and it received wide acclaim. A case in point are the novels of Iulian Semenov (1931–93), who described the covert activities of intelligence services during the Second World War, and the post-war confrontation between the CIA and the Soviet security forces. Semenov's best-known hero was the Soviet double agent Isaev-Shtirlits who, concealing his true identity and objectives, managed to infiltrate the Nazi headquarters. The content of the Soviet political detective story was determined by political considerations, and its aim was to attract the attention of the reader primarily through identification with the heroic feats of the protagonist. The action in the novel moved quickly, the language was dry and often stylistically deficient, and little attention was devoted to the emotional or psychological state of the heroes.

In the new conditions of the post-Soviet market economy, in which publication policy is determined not by party policy, but rather by public demand, the detective novel occupies an important position. It satisfies the needs of many readers who regard literature as a form of entertainment, and who are tired of both serious literature and their difficult lives. Moreover, since in the 1990s many authors shied away from writing traditional psychological novels about contemporary life, the detective novel has replaced, in a sense, that literature. It portrays current Russian reality in which crime, racketeering, and murder are commonplace. Anyone who wants to find out about the current situation in Russia watches television and reads newspapers, but he or she also reads detective fiction.

The first authors to produce detective or mystery novels in contemporary Russia were people employed by, or connected with, the police and state security forces. Currently, however, criminal stories and the so-called *boeviki*, or violent action thrillers, are often written by literary scholars, serious fiction writers, and other intellectual professionals. Today, some of these people have been forced to abandon their former principles and high standards to produce a literature of limited artistic value, in order to make a living.

Suspense, which plays on the reader's curiosity, is one of the main narrative devices of detective fiction. The plot, in which important information is usually withheld, takes hold of the reader's attention, making it difficult for him or her to put the book down. In the end, however, the reader may experience a certain disappointment, because in order to solve the conflict both heroes and villains often resort to the same violent means. Moreover, in pulp literature, including the detective story, most heroes are concerned with their personal interests and well-being, and they usually survive, while in 'serious' narratives the hero is most often preoccupied with the social good and is defeated in the struggle to attain it.

By the mid-1990s the contents of the Russian detective novel gradually began to change. Many authors started to diversify their plots by including discussion of problems of social significance, as well as issues of a personal nature and family life. Some authors even suggest that today 'nobody writes detective stories ... Authors produce rather criminal novels. The main question in these works is not "who" ... but rather what will be the end of it.'[1] Any narrative in which criminal or illegal activity is described is frequently regarded as a detective story. In this sense Dostoevskii's novels can be viewed as criminal stories, but with the significant difference that in his works artistic merit is not sacrificed. Moreover, in the classical novel the crime usually provides a motive for the investigation of the human predicament and the study of the human psyche. In most current detective novels character traits, ideas, and social issues are seldom touched upon, and in the rare instances in which they are, the discussion is superficial and lacks depth. In any event, it appears that the genre of the detective novel is currently being diluted.

Among the best-known contemporary Russian writers of detective stories are Aleksandra Marinina, Boris Akunin, Polina Dashkova, Dar'ia Dontsova, Daniil Koretskii, and a few others. All of them deal with the criminal world, but each draws his or her material from different sources, which are often determined by personal experience.

Aleksandra Marinina

Aleksandra Marinina (a pseudonym used by Marina Alekseeva) is a forty-five-year-old Moscow resident who spent close to twenty years of her life serving in the Soviet and Russian police, and in the security forces of the Ministry of Internal Affairs, where she reached the military rank of lieutenant-colonel. Her first novel was published in 1991 and since then she has produced more than twenty narratives which focus on criminal and police activity. Her novels have sold millions of copies, and they have been translated into many foreign languages. Most of her plots involve the police investigator Nastia Kamenskaia, a woman in her mid-thirties whose prototype is often the author herself. Kamenskaia's husband, Aleksei Chistiakov, a scholar-mathematician, also appears in many of the novels. Most of Marinina's narratives have a complicated structure. They attract a wide readership because, in addition to the depiction of individual heinous crimes, they also reveal the activities of the Russian mafia and its connection with the Russian police. Moreover, they expose the corruption in the Russian security forces and the Russian administration of justice.

In *Ne meshaite palachu* (Do Not Interfere with the Executioner; 1998),[2] Anastasiia Kamenskaia holds the rank of major in the Moscow police. In the opening chapter of the novel she is on her way to the city of Samara to retrieve the criminal Pavel Sauliuk. Sauliuk, a former KGB major, is incriminated in a number of major offences, and he is to be a witness for the prosecution in the trial of General Minaev, who is accused of many terrible crimes. Kamenskaia's task is to deliver Sauliuk, who is allegedly wanted by members of a criminal gang who fear that he may disclose damaging information, safely to Moscow. In the end, Minaev's complicity with the mafia and his involvement in murder is established, but Sauliuk fails to appear in court and instead commits suicide.

The narrative has several only slightly related plot lines, and the many subplots do not converge. The secondary characters are poorly developed and disappear unnoticed. Marinina continually tries to complicate the story by creating new mysteries and puzzles which often convolute the narrative and confuse the reader. Many small conflicts in the novel, in particular those which relate to the complicity of representatives of the government with the criminal underground, are interesting in themselves, and they may be true to life. Some of them, however, appear to be artificial, and are created with the sole purpose of stimulating the readers' interest. In sum, the narrative is uneven. Some parts flow smoothly, while others are verbose and difficult to follow. There are too many generalities, allusions, and hints, but little substantial evidence, even in reference to the main crime.

Marinina's more recent novel, *Sed'maia zhertva* (The Seventh Victim; 1999),[3] is different in structure and has some stylistic innovations. Kamenskaia is now a lieutenant-colonel in the Moscow Department of Criminal Investigation. Her antagonist in the novel is the murderer Kazakov, an intellectual and a scholar who, in order to satisfy a mystical urge, kills six innocent people. The victims allegedly personify six deadly sins. Kazakov is convinced that life is senseless, because it results only in suffering. He believes that he himself personifies the seventh deadly sin, and he intends to kill himself, to become the seventh victim.

The narrative begins with an open-mike town hall television broadcast, conducted on one of Moscow's central streets. The subject of the program is 'Women in Unusual Professions.' Kamenskaia and a colleague, police investigator Tat'iana Obraztsova, are the guests. The plot is set in motion by the appearance on the street of an individual who carries a poster with a question directed to the two policewomen. It reads: 'If you are so smart, guess where you will face your own death?' Kamenskaia views the poster as a threat to her personal life, and the investigation starts immediately. In the meantime, innocent people are murdered daily. Kamenskaia eventually uncovers the murderous scheme, drawing her suppositions from a film she has seen in which a maniac kills six people who allegedly personify different deadly sins. Unfortunately, Marinina's deliberations about life and death, and her incursions into the psycho-philosophical reasons for the murders, are shallow and simplistic. In addition, Marinina interferes with the basic tenets of the detective novel, which require that the identity of the murderer be uncovered gradually, and revealed only at the very end of the story. The novel is constructed in such a manner that the life story of the murderer and the process of investigation are presented concurrently, in alternating chapters. The mystery of the crime is solved only in the end of the novel, but allusions to the murderer are present from the very beginning.

The structure of this novel is cumbersome. Many short chapters with different characters in them, as well as subplots which are often little connected to the main plot, follow each other. Different, often minor, characters in the novel tell their own life stories in the first person, alternating with the omniscient narrator who attempts unsuccessfully to connect all the loose ends. At the end of the novel the reader is relieved not only because he has finally learned the 'who' and 'why,' but also because the drawn-out narrative was becoming tedious to read.

Marinina is today one of the best-known Russian detective novel writers, yet that apparently does not satisfy her ambitions. She 'considers herself a psychological writer who is primarily interested in depicting the ups and downs of everyday life. "It is only after I've done that," she says, "that I invent the crime story to tie it all together."' According to Marinina, 'there are great writers in Russia today who cannot write anything of interest to ordinary readers because they were taught to write something immortal, for the future. So today, few people are reading them.' Instead, she says, 'I offer them hope, and I don't have a message to deliver.'[4] One may wonder what kind of hope transpires from Marinina's crime-infested narratives. Her melodramatic novels may intrigue, excite, and even teach readers about the dangers of daily existence in Russia today, but they can hardly infuse them with optimism.

In 2001 Marinina changed the course of her creative production somewhat, indicating that she aspires to be known as a writer of serious prose. In her recent two-volume novel, *Tot, kto znaet* (The One Who Knows; 2001),[5] Marinina describes the life of the Soviet intelligentsia in the years between 1965 and 1999. The novel has a new cast of characters, and police investigator Nastia Kamenskaia is nowhere to be found. Before its publication the new novel was advertised as a significant masterpiece. According to a review in *Knizhnoe obozrenie*,[6] the plot structure, characterization, form, and language of the novel are all of the highest quality. Moreover, it is claimed that this novel deserves a place among the recognized classics of the Russian literary psychological genre. Unfortunately, the review in question tells us more about Russian marketing techniques than about the artistic quality of Marinina's latest novel. In fact, the language employed differs little from the language in her detective novels, and the portrayal of family, social, and professional life lacks psychological insight and truthfulness. Instead of turning into an artistic investigation of the human psyche the novel degenerates into melodrama. More than mere literary skill is required to produce a masterpiece. Vastly more important is the presence of creative talent, which in this case is apparently lacking.

Boris Akunin

Boris Akunin (a pseudonym of Grigorii Chkhartishvili), a well-known intellectual, scholar, translator, and editor, is one of the most popular contemporary Russian authors of detective novels. Akunin's narratives, however, are different from those by Marinina, and they belong to a different literary genre. Marinina writes detective fiction which is set in contemporary Russia and deals with ingenuous criminal and police activity. Most of Akunin's novels, on the other hand, are set in tsarist Russia, and the action usually takes place in upper-class nineteenth-century society. This seemingly highly respectacle social environment is in fact rife with corruption and social decay.

Akunin attempts to combine elements of the modern adventure story with those of the classical mystery and detective novel. He also makes use of postmodern approaches to the material covered, and he includes elements of classical literature. Akunin's plots are intertextual. They blend unimpeded treatment of historical facts, cultural digressions, literary play, stylization, and a language reminiscent of that employed in nineteenth-century Russian classics. Akunin's novels are constructed according to the accepted model of a detective story, at the root of which are mystery and suspense. They differ, however, from most other current detective narratives, because they appeal not only to the mass readership but to the intelligent reader as well.

In Akunin's first novel, *Azazel'* (Azazel'; 1998),[7] the hero, Erast Petrovich Fandorin, is a lowly clerk in the Russian criminal investigation police. By virtue of his ingenuity and acumen he advances professionally, reaches high office in the tsarist state bureaucracy, and becomes a diplomat. His character, however, is somewhat artificial. Fandorin is a psychological introvert, and it is difficult to identify with him. He is too pragmatic, always aloof, and we know little about his past. Fandorin appears in novel after novel, but recently Akunin began a new series of detective narratives in which the hero, Pelageia, is a nun.

Azazel' opens in 1876, in Moscow, with the unexpected suicide of a young rich nobleman. This death is followed by the murder of another member of high society. It soon becomes clear that a clandestine international organization is operating in Russia, its membership composed of former graduates of special boarding schools run by a charitable foundation under the leadership of a certain English baroness. The name of this organization is 'Azazel',' and its objective is to take over and rule the world. Members of 'Azazel'' are ready to murder anyone in their way, performing, at the same time, useful charitable work to disguise their true purpose. Fandorin plays an important role in uncovering this secret plot and he is rapidly promoted to high office. He moves to the capital in St Petersburg and is about to marry the daughter of a prominent government official. The members of 'Azazel',' however, decide to punish Fandorin, and they send a wedding 'gift' full of explosives which blows up in the hands of the bride on the day of the wedding.

Akunin nicely captures the language of the time and the milieu in which the action is set, but the conflict is artificially constructed and does not lead to any logical conclusion. The final scene of the bride's murder is not very convincing, and it is apparently introduced with the purpose of ending the saga. After reading the novel the intelligent reader may be left with a feeling of emptiness, but even the unsophisticated reader, after momentary excitement, may wonder whether the story has any roots in real life.

Statskii sovetnik (Councillor of the State; 2000)[8] is political detective fiction. Most of the action takes place in Moscow in 1891. Anti-tsarist revolutionaries murder a number of highly placed tsarist officials. The government's secret political police and gendarmery in turn wage war against the terrorists. Prince Pozharskii, a protégé of the tsar who aspires to become governor of Moscow, is a provocateur who arranges for the murder of his political opponents in the administration. These murders are attributed to the revolutionary anarchists, and as public apprehension and the need to fight the terrorists grow, so does the power and influence of Pozharskii. State Councillor Fandorin, an official in charge of special assignments attached to the governor of Moscow, is instrumental in uncovering the hidden plot. Fandorin reports to St Petersburg about Pozharskii's duplicity, but the damaging information is ignored. In the end, Pozharskii is blown up together with some revolutionaries, while Fandorin is offered the post of deputy governor and head of the Moscow police. He refuses to accept these positions, however, and resigns from the service to become a civilian.

The character of Fandorin is idealized in this novel. He is ethically superior to the average bureaucrat and refuses to become part of the corrupt administration. It may appear to the unsuspecting reader that the author's sympathy lies with the terrorists rather than the corrupt tsarist regime. Since the novel is set in pre-revolutionary tsarist Russia some readers may interpret it as a perversion of history, in which the corruption and abuses of tsarist rule in Russia are covered up. Others, however, may assume that the idealization of the tsarist official, Fandorin, proves that no historical interpretation is intended. In most classical detective novels the policeman, or the investigating officer, is usually successful and the culprit is apprehended. Here the ending is inconclusive, and there is no clear victor. Both Pozharskii and the head of the revolutionary cell are dead, and Fandorin abandons ship.

At the centre of Akunin's next novel, *Koronatsiia, ili poslednii iz Romanovykh* (Coronation, or the Last Romanov; 2000)[9] is the fate of Russia and the Romanov dynasty. Most members of the tsarist family are portrayed as self-absorbed cowards, rogues, or homosexuals. It is thus not surprising that the novel has been greeted by many, in particular those who currently support the tenets of the Russian Orthodox Church, with disdain, especially since it was awarded, some believe undeservedly, the 'Anti-Booker Prize' for literature for the year 2000. Thus, for example, the well-known Russian writer Aleksei Varlamov writes in *Literaturnaia gazeta* that 'Koronatsiia is a libellous lampoon on the Romanov family, and first of all the Emperor Nikolai Aleksandrovich ... Being familiar with the fate of the last Russian tsar, only a stranger to our culture could jeer, and speak ironically, and with depravity about his loneliness and religiosity ... Canonized by the Russian Orthodox Church he [the tsar] is no longer subject to human and writers' judgement.'[10] The tsarist past is clearly still a sensitive subject in Russia, and there is still no uniformity in the interpretation of Russian history. Assessments of the Russian past made by members of the liberal writers' community are vastly different from the views expressed by those who belong to the Russian 'patriotic' camp, or who have become fervently religious.

Akunin's *Lefiatan* (Leviathan; 2001)[11] is different from his other novels. The crime is committed in 1878 in Paris, and most of the characters are not Russian. A dozen people, mainly servants of a British lord, are poisoned, and a valuable statuette of a Hindu goddess is stolen. The main culprit appears to be a first-class passenger on the liner 'Leviathan,' which is sailing from Europe to Asia. The French police commissar, Gosh, is assigned the task of solving the case and he joins the first-class passengers on the liner. Fandorin, too, is travelling first class from Constantinople to Calcutta, on his way to a diplomatic posting in Japan.

The novel is constructed in an innovative manner. Each of the passengers tells his or her story not by means of dialogue, but rather with the help of self-analysis and self-exploration expressed in letters and diaries. The letters or diary notes are based on conjecture rather than facts and serve to confuse the issue rather than to clarify it. This method of narration heightens the suspense and complicates the plot. The reader is soon unable to untangle the web of events. Gosh and several other travellers are eventually murdered, and Fandorin, who has been a secondary character, becomes the hero. He uncovers the plot and saves the life of an innocent passenger suspected by Gosh.

Akunin, the unconventional detective storyteller, employs a variety of thematic approaches, polished language, and various artistic means in order to appeal to a wide-ranging audience, especially to the intelligent reader. Many educated Russians assume that it is beneath their dignity to read Marinina, but reading Akunin is different; he is an intellectual.

Polina Dashkova

Polina Dashkova is another popular writer of detective novels. She is a graduate of the Moscow Literary Institute, where she originally studied poetry. Her first detective novel was published in 1996. Despite the fact that her narratives are unwieldy and her plots contrived and convoluted, she has many fans. Dashkova prides herself on the fact that 'Gorbachev has said that in his difficult moments he opens [a book by] Dashkova, which helps him to cope.'[12] Dashkova claims that 'today many writers are too much concerned with their own personalities, with self-expression.' She, however, is mostly interested in her readers. Lacking experience of work in the police or the security apparatus, she relies heavily on thorough research, consultation, and invention. Her objective in her novels is not only to uncover the crime, but also to educate the reader, and most of her stories have a positive ending.[13]

At the centre of the plot of *Efirnoe vremia* (Broadcasting Time; 2000)[14] is the hunt for a famous diamond named 'Pavel.' The diamond eventually falls into the hands of a gangster, but in the process many individuals are murdered. Criminal activity takes place on a variety of levels, and among those involved are highly placed Russian bureaucrats and police officers. Subplots and digressions, and a lack of focus, occasionally make it difficult to follow the main course of the story.

Zolotoi pesok (Gold Sand; 2000)[15] is set in the early 1990s in post-Gorbachev Russia. A secret gold mine, somewhere in Siberia, is jointly controlled by the governor of the region, Rusov, and members of a criminal gang. The workforce in the mine is composed of Muscovites, members of a special sect. They are brainwashed into believing that eventually they will be transported into a special world where there is absolute freedom, and where they will be able to devote their lives to serve those they are taught to obey. In the mine, however, they are exploited, abused, and killed. The plot is uncovered with the help of a writer invited to produce a book hailing the achievements of Rusov, and in the end Rusov is forced by one of the gangsters to commit suicide. The contrived story manages to sustain an atmosphere of suspense, but it is clear that many characters and scenes are introduced with the sole purpose of mystifying the reader and prolonging the action.

Daniil Koretskii

Another author of detective novels, Daniil Koretskii, is a legal scholar and a department head at the school of advanced studies of the Soviet Ministry of Interior Affairs, in the city of Rostov. He is also a member of the Writers Union. His *Oper po prozvishchu 'Starik'* (The Detective Nicknamed 'Old Man'; 1998)[16] incorporates the novella 'Zaderzhanie' (Arrest) and the novel *Smiagchaiushchie obstoiatel'stva* (Mitigating Circumstances). At the centre of 'Zaderzhanie' is the conflict between the detective, Major Sizov, nicknamed 'Starik,' and the head of the department of criminal investigation, Lieutenant-Colonel Mishuev. On the surface both are involved in solving the murder of several police officers. In reality, Mishuev tries to confuse the issue in order to disguise his lack of moral stamina and his professional inability to lead the investigation. The story is set in Soviet times, and it illustrates convincingly that those who know how to manipulate the system and curry favour with their superiors usually advance in the service.

Smiagchaiushchie obstoiatel'stva has two little-connected plot lines. In the first, the hero, the retired Sizov, solves a serious crime, while the careerist Mishuev tries to take credit for it. In the second, an unsuccessful love affair which leads to a murder is described. Where 'Zaderzhanie' is well constructed and possesses a certain intensity, *Smiagchaiushchie obstoiatel'stva* turns little by little from a detective novel into a poorly developed love story.

Koretskii's narratives are different from most current detective novels. Crimes are mentioned only in passing, and attention is focused instead on description and analysis of the work of the department of criminal investigation, and the relationships among its associates in the process of their work. Sizov, of course, is a positive hero. He is professional and humble. A Second World War veteran, he failed to receive the education required for advancement, but he is dedicated and experienced and always ready to assist those in need.

By the end of the 1990s the new Russian detective novel had gained for itself a sizable niche in the Russian book market. The artistic quality of these novels is in most instances poor and their authors pay little attention to characterization, language, or style. With the demise of traditional serious prose, however, detective novels provide the unsophisticated reader with engaging stories which portray not only the activities in the Russian criminal world, but the other side of contemporary Russian life and society as well.

8
The New Names of 1995–2002

All of the writers discussed in this chapter are in their thirties and forties, and most did not become well known until the second half of the 1990s. Some, like Sergei Gandlevskii and Nikolai Kononov, were established poets, but their first successful attempts in prose were made in the late nineties. Others published some insignificant prose before 1995, but their early works received little critical attention. Ol'ga Slavnikova and Marina Vishnevetskaia also belong to this group of new prose writers, but their works have already been discussed in the chapter on women writers.

The prose of these new writers is diverse in style and subject matter. Some, like Anton Utkin, produce stylized, nineteenth-century realistic prose. Others, like Kononov, employ ornate and expressive poetic language. Gandlevskii's novella is narrated in confessional style, while Oleg Pavlov's realistic prose is rooted in his personal, mostly military, experience. It remains to be seen whether these new writers will be able to improve the artistic quality of their literary production and diversify their creative output.

Andrei Dmitriev

The first stories by Andrei Dmitriev (b. 1956) were published in the mid-1980s, but only with the appearance of his novellas 'Voskoboev i Elizaveta' (Voskoboev and Elizaveta; 1992) and 'Povorot reki' (The Turn of the River; 1995)[1] did he become better known in Russian literary circles.

The action in 'Povorot reki' takes place in a boarding school, located out of town, for children ill with tuberculosis. One of the pupils,

Smirnov, is seriously ill, but his father arrives with a police warrant to take him away. The elder Smirnov assumes that if the boy is at home his wife, who allegedly wants to leave her husband, will stay with the family. Snetkov, the physician-in-chief of the boarding school, refuses to yield. He knows that at home, without proper medical care, the child's life will be in danger, and he decides to hide the boy in a hut not far from the school. There the young Smirnov dreams and has delusions which take him into an imagined fantastic world. In a digression, there is a story with religious overtones. We are told about a former monastery in the vicinity of the school where there are paintings with alleged miraculous powers.

The setting of 'Povorot reki' is realistic but the narrative blends reality and fantasy. There is a constant transition from one realm into another, and from one time sequence to another. The story is narrated on several different levels. Each character is different, but all are simple people and human. Much attention is devoted to description of the external world, but there is little detail about the traits of individual characters. The story ends inconclusively. Dmitriev tends towards understatement; he does not moralize, and lets the reader draw his own inferences. A river near the boarding school, referred to in the title, symbolizes changes looming in the not-too-distant future. The fate of the boarding school is in question, and it will probably have to move to a new location. Similarly, the young Smirnov's future is uncertain. The fantastic episodes in the story hint at the fluctuations between the predictable and unpredictable in human life.

'Doroga obratno' (The Road Back; 2001)[2] is set in the region of Pskov, in post–Second World War Soviet Russia. The main character, Mariia Pavlovna, is the only one with whom we become familiar. She is a nannie in the household of the first-person narrator who, as a mature individual, reminisces about his early childhood. Mariia is a simple, illiterate, peasant woman. She wants to live a good life, but she is always seduced by evil forces, and by those who use and abuse her. Too weak to withstand the allure of freedom, alcohol, and sex, she often gives in to temptation, getting unintentionally into trouble. Paradoxically, the destiny of this illiterate woman is intertwined with a literary theme, namely the commemoration of A.S. Pushkin's birthday. Mariia is sent by her employers to run some errands in town. She encounters some old acquaintances and takes off with them, without notifying her employers, to Pushkinskie Gory, where the young Pushkin lived with his nannie, to celebrate Pushkin day. In the end, they all get drunk, and Mariia is abandoned by her alleged friends without money or transportation. She is forced to walk over 100 kilometres to Pskov, all by herself.

The story is told in laconic language by first- and third-person narrators. It is rich in metaphor and detailed description of nature, but without a trace of fantasy, embellishment, or the grotesque. The symbolism in the story is implied in the fate and predicament of the heroine. Dmitriev presents a story of an individual who, through no fault of her own, is forced to suffer. Mariia is by nature a good woman, but her difficult life does not equip her with the necessary tools to resist temptation. Dmitriev is an interesting writer. His plots are inventive and his language is simple, but his prose is intended for the intelligent reader. His aim is to tell touching stories about ordinary people who find themselves in pathetic situations.

Sergei Gandlevskii

'Trepanatsiia cherepa. Istoriia bolezni' (Trepanation of the Skull: A Medical Case History; 1995)[3] was the first significant work of prose by the well-known Russian poet Sergei Gandlevskii (b. 1952). The narrative, which was awarded the 'Little Booker Prize' in 1996 for the best debut in prose, is not a medical case history as the subtitle suggests. It is rather a confessional autobiographical sketch with three distinct thematic threads. The author's medical condition, which results in brain surgery, and the successful removal of a benign tumour, prompts his musings about issues of life and death in the expectation of surgery, but this is only one part of the narrative. The other two parts explore his family roots and history, and the author's reminiscences about his relationship with some of his friends, most of them Russian poets, writers, and artists, in the 1970s and 1980s.

Many of the author's close friends, including Bakhit Kenzheev, Mikhail Aizenberg, Timur Kibirov, Lev Rubinshtein, and Semen Faibisovich, among others, are today well-known personalities in the Russian arts community. Gandlevskii recounts their meetings, parties, and drinking bouts, as well as life in pre-Gorbachev Russia. This part of the narrative may be of special interest to students of Russian poetry and Soviet society, and it provides a personal, insightful commentary on the literary and social history of the late Soviet era. Only those, however, who are familiar with the Soviet cultural milieu will follow with ease the main thrust of the story. A multitude of names are mentioned, characters appear and disappear without being properly developed, and the issues of the day are not thoroughly examined.

The author's family story, however, is straightforward. He is the product of a mixed marriage; his mother is Russian and his father Jewish. His mother comes from a family of Russian priests, and she makes sure that her son is baptized in the Russian Orthodox tradition. Hence, Gandlevskii regards himself as a Russian Christian and wears a cross. His situation, however, highlights the sensitive issue of mixed marriages in Russia today. Most Russian nationalists refuse to accept into their fold Christian progeny of mixed marriages in which one partner comes from a non-Slavic background. Gandlevskii is furious, and he does not even try to hide his resentment.

The first-person narrator's illness, and his imminent surgery, are mentioned, from time to time, throughout the narrative. Only in the end, however, when the narrator is already in hospital for the operation, does it become the main subject. The story concludes with the author's philosophical ruminations about life and death, and about the fact that the brain operation offers only a temporary reprieve. All people are mortal, and everyone dies. In the final paragraph the narrator poses a simple question: 'What do I want?' The answer that follows demonstrates that the illness and fear of death have humbled him. His expectations of life are moderate. All he wants is to retain his job at the journal *Inostrannaia literatura* (Foreign Literature), and to master the English language, so that he can become a good professional editor. He wants to save some money to buy a comfortable three- or four-room apartment. He wants to die instantly, because he is afraid of pain. Most of all, he wants his children to grow up to be decent young people. If his wife dies first, he wants that there should be no bickering among the children about splitting the family property.

Gandlevskii's prose is lucid, and the narrative flows smoothly, occasionally in the form of stream of consciousness, but there is also considerable use of slang and colloquialisms. The structure of the narrative is disjointed, and there is no chronological sequence to the presentation of material. Despite the fact that one of the subjects is health, life, and death, there is no special intensity to the narrative. The author tells his story in a prosaic, down-to-earth manner. Most important is, perhaps, the atmosphere created, and the author's originality and sincerity. There is no attempt to shock, to show off, or to impress the reader, just an endeavour to open the heart. Consequently, Gandlevskii's memoirs have been well-received. Boris Ekimov, the well-known Russian writer, comments that 'Trepanatsiia cherepa' 'appears to be nothing special, the history of one's own life, some kitchen staff, but this is an honest and sincere book.'[4]

In 2002 Gandlevskii published a new novel, *NRZB* (NRZB),[5] which is similar in substance to his first prose narrative, but different in structure, style, and composition. *NRZB* is narrated alternately in the third person and by the first-person protagonist, the poet Lev Krivorotov. The action alternates between the early 1970s and contemporary Russia. In the 1970s, when the hero and his colleagues are in their early twenties, it centres on the activity of an anti-Soviet semi-clandestine poetic studio, and some fleeting love affairs and intrigues among members of this group. Most attention in this part of the novel is devoted to the poet Chigrashov, allegedly a living classic, who perishes at the young age of thirty-seven. Thirty years later Krivorotov is a literary scholar and a specialist in the poetry of Chigrashov, and a family man in poor health. Much of the material in this novel appears to have been drawn from the author's own experience.

The prose in the novel is poetic, but the sketches of its characters and events are episodic and impressionistic. The plot consists of two slices of life, existing independently of each other, and many characters from the first chronological sequence disappear from sight in the second part of the narrative. Although it has many parallels with 'Trepanatsiia cherepa,' Gandlevskii's recent novel is more inquisitive and sincere, and it deals with real life and real people, rather than with artificially constructed conflicts and poorly explored or motivated love affairs. *NRZB* was short-listed for the Booker Russian Novel Prize, and was nominated for the Russian State Prize in Literature for 2002 and several other literary competitions as well. The narrative, however, is more properly designated a novella, rather than a novel. It is too short for an extended prose narrative, it pays little attention to psychological character study, and it covers a small range of serious life experiences. The subject matter is nonetheless interesting, relevant, and true to life.

The title of the novel apparently refers to the Russian *nerazborchivo*,[6] a proofreader's typographical mark which can mean difficult to decipher, unravel, or interpret. It may be intended to imply that much in the life of the heroes is irrational, unexplained, and difficult to fathom. But nothing is hidden in this novel. The narrator, an aspiring poet, appears to be a failure, his best friend, Nikitin, who betrays him, turns out to be a KGB agent. It has been suggested that Krivorotov was created in the image of Iurii Trifonov's male characters, most of whom are dreamers and losers in real life.[7] There are indeed parallels in the novel with the Soviet city prose of the 1970s, but, as opposed to Trifonov novellas, in Gandlevskii's narrative women are treated superficially. Gandlevskii is a talented writer, and his most recent novel is topical, energetic, and advances positive liberal ideals, but it also lacks depth and psychological analysis.

Nikolai Kononov

Nikolai Kononov, a St Petersburg poet and author of several collections of poetry, recently ventured into the domain of prose and produced a novel entitled *Pokhorony kuznechika* (The Funeral of a Grasshopper; 2000),[8] selected for the 2000 Booker Russian Novel Prize shortlist. Like the prose of most poets, Kononov's novel has a number of poetic traits. The language is figurative, lyrical, and metaphoric, and the prose is charged with emotional nuances and inflections. Even the construction of the novel has poetic features, and it is clear that the author is more concerned with his poetic reveries than with the reaction of his readers.

Pokhorony kuznechika is a first-person narrative in which the adult narrator, with the unusual name Ganemid–Gania, reminisces about his childhood and youth, with particular emphasis on several important events in his life. One short episode deals with the death of a grasshopper mortally wounded by a wasp. The boy is overwhelmed with love for the grasshopper. He keeps the dead insect in a box, still believing that it is alive. Later he buries the grasshopper, but refuses to accept the actuality of death. As a child, he is simply unable to accept the finality and inevitability of death. The second episode, which occupies most of the novel, is connected with the last few days in the life, and the death, of his maternal grandmother. Gania is outraged by the fact that his mother is tired of looking after the sick old woman and would rather his grandmother die as soon as possible. As a child Gania fails to understand that the dying process is not only a burden for those who take care of the sick, but that those who are ill also suffer, and that many welcome death as an end to their suffering.

The novel lacks any special intrigue or chronological portrayal. Similarly, we learn very little about the characters introduced, including the narrator. Instead, the author provides the reader with an array of complex observations of high intensity, and minute realistic detail of daily life experience. This, in turn, leads to psychological investigation, self-analysis, and self-exploration. External detail is always the starting point for sensitive deliberations about the internal state of the human mind. The novel explores distinctions between actuality and the perception of reality, and how these change with the passing of time. At one point, together with his mother, the boy sorts the pictures of his deceased grandmother. He comes across a photo of her nude young body, and his fondness for her becomes invigorated with new strength. He cannot accept the fact that she is no more, and he is subdued by his inability to fathom the secret of death. The mature narrator's attachment to, and the image of, his grandmother haunt him all his life.

The nude picture of the grandmother is not the only image in the book with sexual overtones. In fact, the few short digressions in the novel, which have no connection with the history and fate of grandmother, are of a peculiar sexual nature. As a child Gania observes through a neighbour's window, but fails to understand properly, the act of what is presumed to be oral sex. Later in his life Gania has homosexual relations with a former schoolmate, an encounter which is also described in detail. The inclusion of such scenes remains unexplained and the author may merely be attempting to expose the reader to a wide range of human experiences. The title of the novel relates little to its main subject, and the death of the grasshopper serves only as an introduction to grandmother's ordeal, which ends with her death. The child's adoration of the picture with the grandmother's naked body, and the narrator's obsession with sexual imagery, may indicate the latter's morbid consciousness, as well as nostalgia for his youthful past.

There is no question that Kononov is a talented writer. But while his language is ornate and expressive, his prose is not always easy to follow. Some sentences are terse and eloquent, others are as long as a whole chapter. Some of his pictures are vivid and his ideas transparent, others are obscure and hazy. In sum, the prose of Kononov, which is infused with elements of poetry, is not perfect yet, but the author is certainly on the right track.

Dmitrii Lipskerov

Dmitrii Lipskerov (b. 1964) is one of the newest writers to appear on the Russian literary scene. A graduate of a drama college in Moscow, he first tried his hand at writing plays. He published his first novel, *Sorok let Chanchzhoe* (Forty Years of Chanchzhoe), in 1996.[9] The novel is set in a mythical town located somewhere in the eastern regions of Russia. The history of the town covers no more than forty years, and its inhabitants appear from nowhere, and disappear into thin air. In one instance the city is overrun by hordes of chickens. By constructing a food-producing factory the residents of Chanchzhoe manage to turn disadvantage to advantage, but not for long. Soon they become afflicted by a so-called chicken disease and begin to grow feathers, just like chickens. Regarding this development as a curse, people slaughter the chickens and abandon town. In general terms the novel can be read as a satire of nineteenth-century Russian society, but in many instances the actions of the residents of Chanchzhoe reflect the behaviour of Russians today. Corruption, infidelity, crime, superstition, and hatred are rife.

Lipskerov's *Poslednii son razuma* (The Last Dream of Reason; 2000)[10] is similar in vein. It combines elements of contemporary Russian life with fantastic episodes in which humans become changelings and assume the role of fish, birds, or cockroaches. The plot has a realistic underpinning and some scenes provide a truthful reflection of the state of affairs in Russia today, while the love story of two Tartar youngsters appears to have tragic dimensions. The shifts from one narrative mode to another, however, are abrupt, and some scenes are so bizarre that it soon becomes clear that the whole story is a product of the author's whimsy.

Lipskerov certainly has a vivid imagination. His novels are inventive, interesting, well constructed, and infused with humour. They combine myth and reality, detective stories and fantasy, as well as erotic scenes with tender lyricism. The few intellectual discussions in his novels, however, have little depth, and the solutions offered to the problems posed are simplistic. Moreover, in order to simplify the course of action the author often removes some of his most important characters by having them murdered or perish unexpectedly. The subjects of Lipskerov's narratives also determine their language. It is simple, straightforward, with some superfluous detail; despite some plot complications, the stories are easy to follow. Critical reception of Lipskerov's novels varies. Some critics regard him as a Russian Kafka, but many others do not take his narratives seriously. Lipskerov's creative talent is still in the process of developing, and it is too early to predict the course of his artistic evolution.

Oleg Pavlov

Born in 1970 in Moscow, Oleg Pavlov is one of the youngest contemporary Russian prose writers. He is a prolific author of prose fiction narratives, as well as of literary criticism, and he is one of those who create in the spirit of Russian traditional realism. Pavlov opposes postmodern innovation and asserts that 'post-modernism, as well as socialist realism, are nurtured by falsehood and lies. Our existence today, just as under Soviet rule, is wrapped in lies. Russia lives its own life, while literature exists ... in some other space.'[11] Pavlov first attempted to write poetry, but met with little success. Soon, however, he turned to prose and in 1990 he was admitted to the Moscow Literary Institute. In the same year he published his first stories. With the appearance of *Kazennaia skazka* (An Official Tale; 1994),[12] which was short-listed for the 1995 Booker Russian Novel Prize, Pavlov suddenly became well known in Moscow literary circles. *Kazennaia skazka*, and most of the narratives that followed, are deeply rooted in Pavlov's personal experience, in particular his army service. In 1988, at the age of eighteen, Pavlov was conscripted and enlisted for two years in a military detachment of the Soviet Ministry of the Interior. The duty of the soldiers was to guard and convoy Soviet prisoners incarcerated in labour camps in Central Asia.

The novel *Delo Matiushina* (The Case of Matiushin; 1997)[13] has two parts. One deals with Matiushin's family background, the other with his army duties. Originally, Matiushin is recognized as unfit for military service; after numerous demands and entreaties, however, he is finally accepted and sent to serve in Central Asia. He is assigned there to various duties, including guarding the so-called Zone, the area where labour camps are located. Pavlov's description of life in the Zone is shocking. Degradation, anger, loneliness, and a nightmarish existence involving drugs, alcohol, homosexual advances, and physical and mental abuse by superiors permeate daily life. Matiushin is exposed to all of the evils of life in the Zone, but he is physically strong and does not easily submit. After a fight he is injured, and placed in a military infirmary for a while. There he views life in the Zone from a somewhat different perspective. In one instance, Matiushin takes money from a prisoner to buy vodka for him. Matiushin, however, drinks the vodka himself and kills the prisoner. When questioned by the authorities he declares that the convict tried to escape. Matiushin is suspected of foul play, but some of his superiors defend him. There is an unwritten rule in the Zone that a guard who kills a convict who tries to escape is demobilized and sent home. At the end of the novel we see Matiushin back home, at the local cemetery, visiting the grave of his father, a former colonel in the Soviet army, who has recently died.

The plot of *Delo Matiushina*, which is set in the early 1980s, is complicated and the conflicts are poorly defined. The language is straightforward and metaphoric, but full of slang and military jargon. The
general picture is grim, and at times grotesque. Everything is painted
in dark colours. There is little positive in Matiushin's family life, or in
his army experience. The ultimate message of the novel remains
obscure, but one suspects that the author absolves Matiushin from
blame for the murder of the convict. It appears that the terror to which
the soldier was subjected during his days of service justifies his violent
behaviour. The possible conclusion is that both the prisoners and those
who guard them are so dehumanized by the conditions of their life
that they are equally guilty.

In 1998 Pavlov published in *Oktiabr'* a sequence of stories entitled
'Rasskazy iz *Stepnoi knigi*' (Stories from the Book of the Steppe)[14] which
were eventually included in *Stepnaia kniga*, published in St Petersburg
the same year. The atmosphere and the setting of the stories is similar
to those of Pavlov's earlier narratives, but there are some differences as
well. The emphasis in many stories is on the portrayal of the natural
environment. Most Soviet labour camps are located in remote areas of
the far north or in Central Asia, because escape from these areas is
almost impossible. The steppe is like a desert with no end in sight, and
both the prisoners and their guards are trapped in this ocean of grass
and sand. Pavlov renders the pervading sense of seclusion, and the
fear which the steppe inspires, well. He exposes the insignificance of
human life when contrasted with the grandeur of nature, and the
frailty of humans when they are unexpectedly confronted with the
impossible task of coping with the elements.

In these arduous conditions each prisoner, soldier, and officer must
fend for himself. Most, including those in command, are unhappy and
depressed, and it is fruitless to expect compassion or understanding
for others from them. In order to survive one has to be strong, fight
back, or try to adapt, which usually entails suffering and constant
humiliation. The masses hate those who are smart and educated and
only by keeping a low profile is it possible to survive. There are occasions when positive human instincts come to the fore, but they are
soon suppressed. Thus, in the story 'Velikaia step'' (The Great Steppe)
the officer in charge fails to shoot a prisoner who seemingly tries to
escape. The convict apparently merely wants to tease the officer,
because both are well aware that there is no chance of escape in the
steppe, and they are not far from the camp anyway. Yet later the officer

has a guilty conscience and hates himself for this momentary weakness, for failing to aim his gun directly at the convict. It is clear that duty and instinctive goodness are not always compatible, and that service in the steppe deprives the individual of instinctive compassion, which usually values human life above the need to comply with inhuman and cruel laws.

In another series of stories about army life, *Karagandinskie deviatiny, ili Povest' poslednikh dnei* (Karaganda Commemorations, or a Tale of the Last Days; 2001),[15] which was awarded the 2002 Booker Russian Novel Prize, Pavlov recounts a number of episodes from life in a military infirmary, and in 'V bezbozhnykh pereulkakh' (In the Godless Alleys; 2001)[16] he ventures into his family past. Pavlov is a good observer and storyteller. His language is expressive and often ornate. Some stories have a definite plot line, and are structured chronologically. Others consist solely of a brief description of a single episode in a difficult life. The life that Pavlov portrays is usually grim. Most of his characters are angry young men, humiliated, lonely, and with little compassion for suffering fellow humans. Pavlov's mode of presentation creates some narrative complications. Characterization in most instances is superficial, and the central conflicts are often poorly delineated. Hence, the message which emerges from his novellas is a cumulative expression of negativism.

Pavlov acknowledges the influence of some writers on his creative output, and asserts that Andrei Platonov is his spiritual mentor. Aleksandr Solzhenitsyn and Iurii Koval', on the other hand, introduced him to prose about difficult camp life, but also taught him to love life.[17] Most of Pavlov's prose is based on fact, and it is only occasionally interspersed with fiction. Moreover, most of it is autobiographical. Hence, it is difficult to judge Pavlov's imaginative potential, and whether he will be able to successfully diversify his literary production in the future.

Anton Utkin

Anton Utkin (b. 1967) is a graduate of the Faculty of History of the Moscow State University, and an aspiring young writer who works in the tradition of Russian conventional realism. His first published work, the novel *Khorovod* (The Round-Dance; 1996),[18] is set in early nineteenth-century Russia and written in a language and style resembling closely that of the Pushkin era. The first-person, nameless narrator is a member of the nobility. He serves for a while in the Caucasus with his friend, the cornet Nevrev, who is of lower birth. The relationship of the narrator with Nevrev forms one of the main plot lines in the novel; the other centres on the fate of the prince, the narrator's uncle, and his allegedly illegitimate son.

The structure of this novel, in which elements of surprise play an important role, is original, but it is not conducive to a deeper understanding of what moves the characters. The events in the novel are not acted out. We learn about them instead from stories related by secondary characters, people encountered accidentally by the protagonist, as if with the sole purpose of passing on the information to the narrator. There are many melodramatic episodes, such as duels, elopements, and infidelity, but normal family life is never described. The characters of both the narrator and Nevrev are reminiscent of the proverbial Russian nineteenth-century superfluous man. Nevrev contemplates life and is distraught because he is poor and of low rank, while the narrator is disheartened because his life has no meaning and he cannot find any positive outlet for his energies. In the end Nevrev is killed, and the narrator, abandoned by his wife, takes care of Nevrev's widowed sister's children. This is certainly a noble deed, but apparently one performed out of boredom rather than altruism.

The title, *Khorovod*, is apparently symbolic. The characters move in circles, without having accomplished anything momentous in their lives, either as individuals or as members of the social environment. Utkin's first novel can be regarded as a relative success. He proves himself to be a good storyteller and manages splendidly to reconstruct the literary language and style of the 1830s, but he is not yet a great novelist. To become one he would have to diversify his narrative techniques and master better the art of characterization and psychological analysis.

Utkin's novella, 'Svad'ba za Bugom' (A Wedding on the Other Side of the Bug; 1997),[19] is similarly written in the language of the first half of the nineteenth century, but the substance of the story is related to the art of Gogol' rather than to that of Pushkin. It includes images from the Russian mythological and demoniac world, just as Gogol' does in his stories. *Samouchka* (Self-Taught),[20] a novel published in the following year, is different from Utkin's earlier works in both style and substance. The action takes place in the 1990s, in post-Soviet Russia. One of the heroes, Pavel Razuvaev, is a businessman who becomes rich. His brother delivers medication from southern Russia, and Pavel sells it at a substantial profit. The drugs appear to have narcotic potency, and the entire business is suspect. Pavel is a simple, uneducated man. He engages Petr, a journalist and a friend from the days of army service, to educate and introduce him to the world of culture in the city. Pavel is a decent fellow and he treats people well. He leaves to Petr, in his will, a house somewhere in the Krasnoiarsk region. Unfortunately, there is no place today in the rapacious Russian business environment for an honourable individual. Hence, Pavel's brother is murdered, and Pavel himself soon perishes in a car explosion.

The novel is narrated in the first person by Petr, the journalist. The conflict described is realistic and mirrors the shady side of current Soviet business ventures. The language flows smoothly and, as in Utkin's earlier narratives, it reflects the vernacular of the time period in which the action takes place. Utkin's artistic portrayal, however, is still inadequate. He fails to capture the development of human relationships, or to reveal the motives guiding his characters.

Andrei Volos

Andrei Volos (b. 1955) is another contemporary Russian writer of the younger generation who produces fiction in the spirit of Russian traditional realistic prose. A geophysicist by profession, Volos was born in Dushanbe, the capital of the former Soviet Tadzhik republic, presently the principle city of independent Tadzhikistan. Today, Volos resides in Moscow. The appearance of his first book, entitled *Khurramabad* (Khurramabad; 2000),[21] which includes several of his earlier stories, previously published in *Novyi mir* and *Znamia*, caught the eye of the critics. The city of Khurramabad, where most of the action is set, is a fictitious name for Volos's native city. *Khurramabad* is not a novel, but rather a collection of stories, each with a different plot and a different set of characters. All of the stories, however, share a certain thematic unity and time frame.

Most action in the narrative takes place in the early 1990s, just after the collapse of the Soviet empire and the dissolution of the USSR. Separate stories deal with the fate of different Russian individuals, most of whom are born in Tadzhikistan, or live there most of their lives. Now they are forced to abandon their homes and flee into Russia, where their future is uncertain. The young leave eagerly, still hoping for a better future in their ethnic motherland. Many old Russians, however, are insecure, in doubt, and prefer to stay. They have nowhere to go, and little hope for the future. The disintegration of the Soviet Union leads to disarray. Families are broken up, relationships destroyed, and property acquired during the years of hard work is ravaged. Volos provides a distressing picture of the transition from Soviet rule to Tadzhik independence. It is accompanied by social strife, tribal and gang warfare, abuse of power, corruption, and simple criminal activity. Most of the victims are Russians, but many Tadzhiks also oppose the chaotic and criminal state of affairs, and are nostalgic about their peaceful Soviet past. Some Tadzhiks even contemplate abandoning their native land in search of a more satisfying and peaceful life in Russia. In reality, there is no positive future for the refugees anywhere. The Russians, hated in Tadzhikistan, are hardly welcome in their ethnic motherland.

In a way *Khurramabad* addresses one of the major problems of Russian national policy of the nineteenth and twentieth centuries. Tsarist military expansion resulted in the conquest of Central Asia and the Caucasus and the incorporation of these regions into the Russian Empire. After the revolution of 1917 the Soviet state 'liberated' these subjugated nationalities by creating allegedly independent Soviet republics. It provided them with national languages, and local native bureaucracies. The government and the Central Communist Party Committee of Tadzhikistan, however, were always tightly controlled by Moscow, and by its local non-Tadzhik representatives. The Tadzhiks resented this control, but were forced to submit and keep quiet. Deep in their hearts, however, they regarded the outsiders as oppressors rather than liberators. Most Tadzhiks hated the Russians and refused to accept them as equals. This situation is well portrayed in several stories which deal with the notion of *'svoi-chuzhoi,'* our own versus the stranger.

In the story *'Svoi'* (Our Own)[22] Volos provides a tragic account of a futile attempt by his Russian hero to escape his past and be accepted by his Tadzhik neighbours and colleagues as one of their own. The Muscovite Sergei Makushin falls in love with Tadzhikistan, its nature and people. He forsakes his Moscow roots, abandons his family, and moves to Tadzhikistan. He masters the language, marries a local Tadzhik woman, and tries hard to be recognized as *'svoi'* among the local Tadzhiks. With time, Makushin becomes convinced that he is successful in this endeavour. But this is a delusion. In reality, he is never able to understand the mentality of the locals or their inherent resentment of Russian superiority and rule. Makushin accepts in good faith the superficial and insincere friendship of some Tadzhiks without real-izing that to them he remains a stranger. As soon as Soviet rule is abolished Makushin realizes that his attempt to assimilate has been a wasted effort. He loses a good job and the alleged respect of his acquaintances and colleagues and is ultimately attacked and murdered by a gang of nationalistic thugs.

Makushin's predicament reflects the personal tragedies of close to twenty million ethnic Russians who were scattered all over the USSR in the Soviet days. Many of them still reside in the newly created independent states, formerly Soviet Union republics. In the ten years since the disintegration of the USSR 8.6 million ethnic Russians have returned from the former Soviet republics to the Russian Federation. Most of them, however, face many new obstacles and have a hard time creating a satisfying life for themselves in the difficult economic conditions of post-Soviet Russia. The fate of those who remain in the Central Asian former Soviet republics is complicated and unpredictable. They are treated there today as second-class citizens.

Unlike most of these stories, which are set in Tadzhikistan, the epilogue, which consists of the story 'Zavrazh'e' (Zavrazh'e),[23] is set in Russia. Zavrazh'e is the name of a small town located in the region of Kaluga, in central Russia, in which Russian refugees have settled just four years ago. Most of them are highly educated professional people, unable to obtain residence permits in major urban centres or to secure employment in their specialties. They are forced to accept agricultural and menial jobs in order to make a living. Hard work bears fruit and the newcomers establish themselves firmly. The local peasants, however, most of whom are loafers and alcoholics, are jealous and hate the diligent newcomers. The new settlers disturb, in a sense, their idle life style, and the locals want to get rid of them. Just as in Tadzhikistan, where the Russians have always been viewed as strangers, so also here, in central Russia, ethnic Russian refugees are regarded as *'chuzhie'* – strangers and intruders into a long-established pattern of indolent life. In fact, Lobachev, the protagonist of 'Zavrazh'e,' a refugee from Tadzhikistan, is denounced to the local authorities by a neighbour and accused of setting a fire in a nearby house. The incrimination is, of course, false, but only chance saves Lobachev's skin.

Khurramabad is a topical narrative dealing with some of the burning issues of post-Soviet reality. Seventy years of Soviet rule have done little to change the Tadzhik mentality. Instead, it has cultivated among the Russians and other citizens of the former Soviet Union a lack of compassion and a cold, unresponsive attitude to those in need. The loosely connected stories in *Khurramabad* may lack a single dramatic focus, but Volos knows the milieu he describes well, and he manages to provide the reader with a sense of urgency, and to make a subtle call for help and understanding from those who have never been forced to abandon their homes and who accept their peace and good fortune as a God-given right. The stories in *Khurramabad* touched the jury members of the 1998 Anti-Booker Prize to the point that, despite the fact that only parts of the narrative had been published, and the collection as a whole was only available in manuscript form, they awarded Volos the prize.

The style of Volos's novel, *Nedvizhimost'* (Real Estate; 2001),[24] is similar to that of *Khurramabad*, but the location, characters, and plot are completely different. Most of the action is set in bustling, dreary Moscow, and most protagonists are ordinary Moscow residents. The novel introduces the reader to the chaotic world of residential real estate transactions in Moscow today. In the Soviet times all real estate belonged to the state, and only members of the elite could afford private or cooperative dwellings. In the process of post-Soviet privatization most residents of communal dwellings have become owners and are now able to sell, buy, or exchange their apartments. The current Russian system of private apartment ownership, however, is vastly different from that existing in North America, and real estate transactions are often subject to corruption, fraud, and crime. Moreover, the Russian financial system lacks stability, and buyers and sellers of real estate are always in danger of losing their money.

The main character of the novel, the real estate agent Sergei Kapyrin, is also the first-person narrator. He is apparently a recent arrival to Moscow, and still lives in rented quarters. Kapyrin has a hard time making ends meet. He is divorced, and his aged parents live in poverty somewhere in the outlying regions of the former Soviet Union. Kapyrin tries hard to help them by sending food parcels. Another close relative, Pavel, lives in the provinces and is also in trouble. Pavel is sick and has a broken family, and Kapyrin is forced to borrow money in order to bribe a police investigator and save him from jail after a fatal car accident. While Kapyrin is a dedicated family man and a decent human being, his life is not easy. He is under constant pressure to repay the loan he has taken out in order to save Pavel, and it is difficult to make a living in Moscow by selling low-priced residential real estate.

The narrative alternates between chapters dealing with Kapyrin's family story and the description of his real estate transactions. The reader is exposed to an array of Moscow residents, of different ages and different social standing, who for different reasons are forced to move. Volos attempts to describe the psychological state of those who are under pressure of moving, but his art is descriptive rather than analytic, and many questions posed in the novel remain unanswered. We also learn about the peculiarities and hidden aspects of the real estate business in Moscow. Most real estate deals discussed in the novel, however, never come to fruition, and since the novel lacks a single intrigue the conclusion is anti-climactic.

Volos clearly has creative talent. He is a good observer and he writes about things he knows well. His prose is simple and straightforward, and his subjects are sufficiently topical to attract the contemporary reader. He employs a number of literary devices, such as internal monologue, reminiscences, letters, lyrical digressions, changing narrators, and much dialogue. His narratives, however, lack focus and the intellectual discussions lack depth. Except for the narrator himself, who often ventures into self-analysis, the portrayal of most characters remains superficial. We may know what they say, even what they think, but we hardly learn who they are, or what motivates them.

Conclusion

The end of the twentieth century was marked by the change of political leadership in Russia, and some attempts of economic reform, but there was no improvement in the living standards of the majority of Russian citizens. The introduction of a market economy and the privatization of state property led to social polarization and the creation of two classes of 'new Russians': the minority who became rich, and the majority who turned into paupers. The transition from communist rule to democracy has been an agonizing process, characterized by economic instability, ideological squabbles, the re-evaluation of old values, and the search for new ideals and beliefs to fill the vacuum created by the demise of Marxist-Leninist ideology.

Literature continues to reflect, in some measure, the political and social situation in the country, but the influence of writers on public opinion and social policy is minimal. The difficult economic situation affects both writers and readers. The position of writers in Russia has deteriorated, in the last decade, to the point that they cannot support their families by writing serious literature. Most readers have also become destitute and have no money to buy books, the price of which continues to rise. Moreover, members of the new Russian middle class, who still can afford to buy books, are tired of mediocre serious novels, and opt to spend their money on detective and mystery novels, or thrillers. Little by little Russian literature has degenerated from a source of education and enlightenment into one of entertainment and recreation. This has caused a decline in the published editions of the so-called thick literary journals and editions of serious novels. Most titles published in Russia today appear in small editions, and more than a third of all titles published are printed in editions of less than 500 copies.

The Russian writers' community is split into two ideologically distinct antagonistic camps, and instead of working together to regain some of their former influence and prestige, the writers are at daggers drawn. Those belonging to the conservative 'patriotic' camp are nationalistic, pro-Slavic, anti-Western, and remain faithful to the Russian historical heritage and the Russian Orthodox Church. The liberal writers also adhere to old Russian cultural values, but they are democratic, pro-Western, and support freedom of expression, human rights, and political reforms.

In practical terms, the contemporary Russian literary scene is paradoxical. On the one hand, there is a great deal of literary activity in the country, while on the other, the artistic quality of literary production is declining. Literary activity in Russia finds expression today in, and is fostered by, the appearance of a number of new, small publishing houses; the publication of new literary journals and almanacs, particularly in the provinces; the appearance of many new aspiring authors; the establishment of a number of literary prizes to reward writers for their creative accomplishments; and the institution of a number of flourishing literary sites on the Internet. Unfortunately, all of these developments have contributed little to the artistic level of literary production. In fact, the artistic quality of most Russian works of prose published on the threshold of the new millennium does not reach the level of the best novels published earlier in the century. Not a single work of prose produced in the last decade of the twentieth century will become a classic, and not a single new author whose works appeared in print in the same period demonstrates any prodigious talent.

There are several unrelated phenomena which negatively affect the quality of contemporary Russian literature. The creative output of most established old and mature writers, who are now in their sixties and seventies, has slowed down. Some, like Andrei Bitov, write little and are content with their established reputations. Others, like Valentin Rasputin, cannot adjust their creative and ideological impulses to reflect the new realities in Russia. Still others, like Aleksandr Prokhanov, sacrifice artistic quality for political and ideological effect.

Most writers who appeared on the literary scene in the last decade have a hard time making a living and are under constant economic pressure. Since many are forced to work in the capacity of editors, reviewers, or journalists, their novels are hastily produced, and they have little time to hone their skills. Consequently, most current prose is descriptive rather than analytical, there is no emphasis on psychological investigation, and characterization tends to be inadequate. The treatment of serious ideas is superficial, and theoretical discussion lacks depth. Moreover, many young authors, such as Oleg Ermakov or Oleg Pavlov, rely heavily on their personal experience rather than imagination, limiting the scope of their creative activity. Some talented authors, such as Viktor Pelevin and Tat'iana Tolstaia, use their imaginative faculties well and produce interesting narratives. Unfortunately, in their novels substance, atmosphere, and sincerity are often sacrificed and their ideas lack depth. The artistic quality of contemporary Russian prose is also perverted by the business practices of publishers and book-sellers, by the pressure of sponsors, and by political and ideological considerations.

The future development of Russian literature will depend, to a large extent, on the general economic, political, and social situation in the country. Even today, however, the Russian literary scene remains vibrant, and there is hope for the future. Literary activity in provincial Russia is more apparent now than in the days of Soviet rule, and women are more prominent in Russian literature than ever before. Besides, among the multitude of new writers who publish in print and on the Internet, a new, natural genius may appear who will set new standards and serve as an example for the younger generation.

Notes

1. Russian Literature and Society on the Threshold of the New Millenium

1 According to the Annual Corruption Index released by the German watch-dog group Transparency International, Russia tied for eleventh worst place out of ninety-one countries included in the survey. See *Globe and Mail* (Toronto), 14 July 2001, B6.
2 *New York Times*, 24 March 2002, 2 yne.
3 *Literaturnaia gazeta*, 14–20 July 1999, 9.
4 Ibid., 26–30 November 1999, 9.
5 Ibid.
6 Ibid., 30 January–5 February 2002, 7.
7 Ibid., 10–16 April 2002, 11.
8 *New York Times*, 31 October 1999, 5y.
9 *Literaturnaia gazeta*, 20–6 March 2002, 8.
10 *Novyi mir*, 1999, no. 4, 3–43.
11 N.L. Leiderman and M.N. Lipovetskii, *Sovremennaia russkaia literatura: Kniga 3: V kontse veka (1986–1990-e gody)* (Moscow 2001).
12 *Russkaia postmodernistskaia literatura* (Moscow 1999).
13 *Novyi mir*, 1996, nos. 9–11.
14 Leiderman and Lipovetskii, *Sovremennaia russkaia literatura: Kniga 3*, 99.
15 Roza Glintershchik, *Sovremennye russkie pisateli – postmodernisty* (Kaunas 2000), 219–59.
16 *Prazdnik starukh* (Vologda 1998).
17 *Akh, Flamenko* (Moscow 1998).
18 *Moskva*, 1998, no. 9, 45.
19 *Literaturnaia gazeta*, 19–25 February 2003, 7.
20 Ibid., 29 May–4 June, 2002, 2.

21 Mikhail Nenashev, 'Otluchat' li Rossian ot knigi?,' *Literaturnaia gazeta,* 22–9 May 2002, 3.
22 *Literaturnaia gazeta,* 16 September 1998, 10.
23 *Knizhnoe obozrenie,* 11 March 2002, 12Pro4.
24 *Literaturnaia gazeta,* 12 August 1998, 9.
25 Ibid., 3–9 October 2001, 2.

2. The Seniors' Prose

1 *Znamia,* 1994, no. 12, 9–109.
2 Ibid., 48.
3 Ibid.
4 *Literaturnaia gazeta,* 11 January 1995, 5.
5 *Novyi mir,* 1996, no. 3, 218.
6 *Literaturnaia gazeta,* 25 January 1995, 5.
7 Ibid., 8 October 1997, 10.
8 *Znamia,* 1995, no. 4, 3–113.
9 *Novyi mir,* 1996, no. 8, 3–51.
10 Ibid., 1998, no. 5, 3–58, no. 6, 3–91.
11 *Znamia,* 2001, no. 1, 21–43.
12 1996, no. 5, 6–66, no. 6, 144–68.
13 *Literaturnoe segodnia. O russkoi proze. 90-e* (Moscow 1998), 13.
14 *Novyi mir,* 2000, no. 6, 7–91.
15 *Znamia,* 1999, no. 9, 3–33.
16 *Sofichka. Povesti i rasskazy* (Moscow 1997).
17 *Znamia,* 1997, no. 9, 7–34.
18 *Novyi mir,* 1998, no. 4, 3–78.
19 *Znamia,* 2001, no. 1, 68–76.
20 Fazil' Iskander, *Antalogiia satiry i iumora Rossii XX veka* (Moscow 2001), 7.
21 *Druzhba narodov,* 1995, no. 7, 5–58, no. 8, 43–17.
22 *Novyi mir,* 1996, no. 6, 3–25.
23 Ibid., 1998, no. 9, 47–125, no. 10, 93–153.
24 Ibid., 1999, no. 3, 3–29.
25 Ibid., 1999, no. 3, 30–55.
26 *Znamia,* 1994, no. 4, 3–71, no. 5, 6–49.
27 *Literaturnaia gazeta,* 21–7 February 2001, 10–11.
28 Ibid.
29 Mikhail Lobanov, 'Liberal'nye tsennosti,' *Molodaia gvardiia,* 1996, no. 4, 244. Quoted from V. Bogomolov, *Svobodnaia mysl',* 1995, no. 7.

30 *Sovremennaia russkaia literatura. Kniga 3. V kontse veka (1986–1990-e gody)* (Moscow 2001), 80.
31 Ibid.
32 *Literaturnoe segodnia. O russkoi proze. 90-e* (Moscow 1998), 89.

3. The Mature Generation

1   *Moskva*, 1998, no. 11, 3–79, no. 12, 3–88.
2   Ibid., 1999, no. 10, 3–82.
3   *Novyi mir*, 1996, no. 2, 3–15.
4   Ibid., 1998, no. 10, 103–10.
5   Ibid., 1998, no. 10, 111–14.
6   Ibid., 1999, no. 4, 4–43.
7   *Literaturnaia gazeta*, 27 August 1997, 10.
8   Ibid.
9   Moscow 1998.
10 Moscow 1999.
11 A. Vandenko, *Novoe russkoe slovo*, 9–10 May 1998, 32.
12 Moscow 1999.
13 *Entsiklopediia russkoi dushi*, 235.
14 'Russkii Bog,' *Druzhba narodov*, 1966, no. 12, 187.
15 *Volchii pasport* (Moscow 1998), 434.
16 *Globe and Mail*, 13 May 1995, C8.
17 Anatolii Kim, 'Moe proshloe,' *Oktiabr'*, 1998, no. 2, 3–82.
18 1995, no. 2, 9–55, no. 3, 59–112.
19 *Literaturnoe segodnia, O russkoi proze. 90-e* (Moscow 1998), 197.
20 *Literaturnaia gazeta*, 19 April 1995, 4.
21 *Novyi mir*, 1998, no. 10, 3–71.
22 Ibid., 2001, no. 11, 12–71, no. 12, 13–78.
23 'Moe proshloe,' *Oktiabr'*, 1998, no. 4, 103–4.
24 *Znamia*, 2000, no. 7, 50–66.
25 *Literaturnaia gazeta*, 28 January–5 February 2003, 16.
26 *Znamia*, 2000, no. 7, 66–75.
27 *Neva*, 2001, no. 1, 7–122.
28 Eduard Limonov, *Sobranie sochinenii v trekh tomakh*, vol. 3 (Moscow 1998), 7–282.
29 Ibid., 423–639.
30 Ibid., 283–422.
31 St Petersburg 2000.

188   Notes to pages 72–94

32 *Literaturnaia gazeta,* 4–10 July 2001, 3.
33 Ibid., 12–18 September 2001, 3.
34 *Novyi mir,* no. 4, 3–19.
35 *Znamia,* 1996, no. 1, 209.
36 1998, no. 1, 5–106, no. 2, 32–96, no. 3, 69–137, no. 4, 53–116.
37 'On the Page and on the Snow: Vladimir Makanin's *Andergraund, ili Geroi nashego vremeni,' Slavonic and East European Review,* vol. 79, no. 3 (July 2001), 456.
38 *Znamia,* 2000, no. 2, 195.
39 2000, no. 4, 7–35.
40 *Novyi mir,* 2001, no. 10, 7–20.

4. The New Writers of the *Perestroika* Era

1 Originally published in *Znamia,* 1996, no. 8, 6–97. Republished in book form in *Skoree iabloko, chem ptitsa* (Moscow 2000), 6–180.
2 *Literaturnoe segodnia. O russkoi proze. 90-e* (Moscow 1998), 71.
3 *Literaturnaia gazeta,* 1 April 1998, 11.
4 *Znamia,* 1997, no. 1, 8–49, no. 2, 106–57.
5 Moscow 1998.
6 *Oktiabr',* 1998, no. 11, 101–25.
7 *Novyi mir,* 2000, no. 5, 7–44.
8 Ibid., 1999, no. 1, 11–76, and no. 2, 14–59.
9 Ibid., 2002, no. 7, 110–19.
10 *Znamia,* 1997, no. 8, 10–88.
11 Ibid., 1998, no. 2, 100–35.
12 Ibid., 1999, no. 9, 75–118.
13 Moscow 1995.
14 Aleksandr Kabakov, *Schitaetsia pobeg* (Moscow 2001), 7–184.
15 Ibid., 347–402.
16 *Kontinent,* 1996, no. 1, 88–153.
17 *Znamia,* 2000, no. 9, 76–86.
18 *Novyi mir,* 2000, no. 7, 14–73, no. 8, 109–41.
19 Ibid., 2001, no. 9, 11–71, no. 10, 24–80.
20 Ibid., 2001, no. 9, 48–50.
21 *Znamia,* 1996, no. 4, 27–121, no. 5, 23–114.
22 Ibid., no. 5, 100.
23 Moscow 1999.
24 *Generation 'P'* (Moscow 1999), 5.
25 Ibid.

26 *Novyi mir,* 1999, no. 8, 107–17.
27 *New York Times Magazine,* 23 January 2000, 22.
28 *Znamia,* 1999, no. 12, 204–7.
29 *Sovremennye russkie pisateli-postmodernisty. Ocherki noveishei russkoi literatury* (Kaunas 2000), 135.
30 *Sovremennaia russkaia literatura. Kniga3. V kontse veka (1986–1990-e gody)* (Moscow 2001), 66.
31 *New York Times Book Review,* 10 March 2002, 17.
32 Moscow 1997.
33 *Znamia,* 2002, no. 8, 111–22.
34 Moscow 1999.
35 *Znamia,* 1999, no. 10, 9–99, no. 11, 55–126, no. 12, 46–97.
36 Aleksandr Shchuplov, *Literaturnaia gazeta,* 26 February-4 March 2003, 16.
37 *Znamia,* 2001, no. 3, 209.
38 *Novyi mir,* 1999, no. 6, 3–101.
39 *Vladimir Sorokin* (Moscow 1992), 120.
40 Moscow 1999.
41 *Literaturnaia gazeta,* 7–13 August 2002, 3.
42 Moscow 2001.
43 Viacheslav Kuritsyn, *Russkii literaturnyi post-modernism* (Moscow 2000), 115.
44 Ibid., 114.
45 *Literaturnaia gazeta,* 18 November 1998, 10.
46 *Nezavisimaia gazeta* (Moscow), 3 April 1994, 7.
47 *Literaturnaia gazeta,* 29 August–4 September 2001, 5.
48 Moscow 1995.
49 *Literaturnaia gazeta,* 14 August 1996, 4.
50 *Oktiabr',* 1995, no. 2, 3–84.
51 *Novyi mir,* 1995, no. 7, 3–50.
52 *Moskva,* 1996, no. 12, 3–21.
53 *Oktiabr',* 1997, no. 3, 3–60, no. 4, 61-117.
54 *Novyi mir,* 2000, no. 10, 7–66, no. 11, 85–128.

5. Women Writers

1 *Novyi mir,* 1995, no. 8, 49–92, no. 9, 62–99.
2 *Znamia,* 2002, no. 6, 6–69.
3 *Oktiabr',* 2002, no. 7, 86–128.
4 Ibid., 2002, no. 3, 123–6.
5 *Novyi mir,* 1997, no. 1, 7–71, no. 2, 3–78.
6 *Literaturnaia gazeta,* 1 April 1998, 10.

7 *Novyi mir*, 1999, no. 10, 9–66, no. 11, 13–66.

8 *Druzhba narodov*, 1996, no. 12, 37–43.

9 Ibid., 43–8.

10 Ibid., 48–51.

11 *Znamia*, 2000, no. 10, 68–76.

12 Ibid., 76–82.

13 Ibid., 82–6.

14 Ibid., 89–92.

15 Ibid., 93–6.

16 *Novyi mir*, 1995, no. 3, 27–44.

17 Ibid., 1996, no. 1, 3–40.

18 Ibid., 1998, no. 2, 3–64, no. 3, 21–73.

19 Moscow 1999.

20 *Strekoza, uvelichennaia do razmerov sobaki*, 137–8.

21 *Novyi mir*, 1999, no. 12, 11–110. Republished in Moscow in book form in 2000.

22 *Oktiabr'*, 2001, no. 6, 3–104.

23 Evgenii Ermolin, *Novyi mir*, 2001, no. 11, 82–6.

24 *Novyi mir*, 2002, no. 9, 65–112.

25 Moscow 2000.

26 Karen Stepanian, *Znamia*, 2001, no. 3, 217.

27 *Literaturnaia gazeta*, 22–8 November 2000, 10.

28 *Znamia*, 2001, no. 3, 221.

29 *Literaturnaia gazeta*, 10–16 April 2002, 7.

30 Nikolai Pereiaslov, 'Zhizn' posle Vzryva,' in ibid., 24–30 October 2001, 7.

31 *Novyi mir*, 1996, no. 3, 3–46, no. 4, 7–79.

32 Ibid., 1998, no. 4, 98–106.

33 Moscow 1998.

34 *Novyi mir*, 2000, no. 8, 12–105, no. 9, 11–104.

35 Ibid., 2002, no. 2, 86–102.

36 *Literaturnaia gazeta*, 20 September 1995, 3.

37 *Novyi mir*, 1998, no. 11, 9–73.

38 1996, no. 9, 105–23.

39 *Vyshel mesiats iz tumana* (Moscow 1999), 87–116.

40 Ibid., 117–99.

41 Ibid., 41–54.

42 Ibid., 55–86.

6. The Writers of the Conservative 'Patriotic' Camp

1 Moscow 1999.

2 N.M. Fed', *Opavshie list'ia. Russkaia literatura kontsa XX veka* (Moscow 2000), 95.
3 Moscow 2000. Originally published in 1995.
4 *Nash sovremennik*, 1999, no. 11, 3–81, no. 12, 3–62.
5 *Literaturnaia gazeta*, 12–18 December 2001, 7.
6 *Moskva*, 1998, no. 9, 63–106.
7 Ibid., 102.
8 *Nash sovremennik*, 2001, no. 3, 3–84, no. 4, 107–60, no. 5, 38–92, no. 6, 145–86.
9 *Novyi mir*, 2001, no. 11, 186–8.
10 *Literaturnaia gazeta*, 20–6 February 2002, 7.
11 *Nash sovremennik*, 1998, no. 8, 3–52, no. 9, 120–202.
12 Moscow 1999.
13 *Krasno-korichnevyi roman*, 426.
14 *Nash sovremennik*, 2001, no. 1, 17–92, no. 2, 40–104.
15 Ibid., no. 2, 97.
16 *Literaturnaia gazeta*, 5–11 September 2001, 1–3.
17 Moscow 2002.
18 Interview with A. Prokhanov, *Literaturnaia gazeta*, 19–25 June 2002, 7.
19 Ibid., 12 July 1995, 11.
20 Ibid., 23 August 1995, 14.
21 Ibid., 26 June 1996, 10.
22 Ibid., 10–16 April 2002, 11.
23 *Iunost'*, 1997, no. 3, 4–9.
24 Ibid.
25 *Moskva*, 1995, no. 7, 3–10.
26 Ibid., 10–22.
27 *Nash sovremennik*, 1995, no. 8, 3–21.
28 Ibid., 1997, no. 5, 7–28.
29 Ibid., 1998, no. 7, 3–23.
30 Ibid., 1999, no. 1, 3–20.
31 *Literaturnaia gazeta*, 31 July–6 August 2002, 7.
32 Fed', *Opavshie list'ia*, 73.

7. The Mystery Novel Writers

1 Viktor Pronin, 'Detektivy nikto ne pishet,' *Literaturnaia gazeta*, 11–19 February 2002, 12.
2 Moscow 1998.
3 Moscow 1999.
4 Sandra Martin, *Globe and Mail*, 22 July 2000, D4.
5 Moscow 2001.

6 30 May 2001, 10.
7 Moscow 1998.
8 Moscow 2000.
9 Moscow 2000.
10 'Sterilizator,' 17–23 January 2001, 10.
11 Moscow 2001.
12 *Literaturnaia gazeta*, 28 June-4 July 2000, 11.
13 Ibid.
14 Moscow 2000.
15 Moscow 2000.
16 Moscow 1998.

8. The New Names of 1995–2002

1 *Znamia*, 1995, no. 8, 129–61.
2 Ibid., 2001, no. 1, 81–106.
3 Ibid., 1995, no. 1, 99–151.
4 *Literaturnaia gazeta*, 27 August 1997, 10.
5 *Znamia*, 2002, no. 1, 5–84.
6 See ibid., 69.
7 Valerii Shubinskii, *Znamia*, 2002, no. 9, 210–12.
8 St Petersburg 2000.
9 *Novyi mir*, 1996, no. 7, 3–91, no. 8, 58–129.
10 Moscow 2000.
11 *Literaturnaia gazeta*, 14 August 1996, 4.
12 *Novyi mir*, 1994, no. 7, 8–85.
13 *Oktiabr'*, 1997, no. 1, 3–43, no. 2, 33–76.
14 Ibid., 1998, no. 2, 88–120, no. 9, 54–63.
15 *Oktiabr'*, 2001, no. 8, 3–73.
16 Ibid., 2001, no. 1, 3–54.
17 Oleg Pavlov, *Stepnaia kniga* (St Petersburg 1998), 6–7.
18 *Novyi mir*, 1996, no. 9, 3–60, no. 10, 28–114, no. 11, 21–81.
19 Ibid., 1997, no. 8, 73–98.
20 Ibid., 1998, no. 12, 4–109.
21 Moscow 2000.
22 Originally published in *Znamia*, 1996, no. 5, 122–38.
23 Originally published in *Znamia*, 1997, no. 7, 38–56.
24 Moscow 2001.

Bibliography

The list of suggested background reading includes several Russian and Western histories of literature, as well as other important publications dealing with different aspects of Soviet and contemporary Russian literary theory and practice. Particular emphasis is placed on the period of *perestroika* and the post-Soviet era. The list of contemporary Russian prose includes works by authors residing in Russia, and published in Russia between 1995 and 2002. It does not include detective and mystery novels, or pulp fiction. The list of Russian prose in English translation also includes works published before 1995 but only recently translated into English.

Background Reading

Arkhangel'skii, Aleksandr. *U paradnogo pod"ezda: literatura i kulturnye situatsii perioda glasnosti, 1987–1990*. Moscow, 1991.

Bocharov, Anatolii. *Literatura i vremia*. Moscow, 1988.

Brown, Deming. *Soviet Russian Literature Since Stalin*. New York, 1978.

– *The Last Years of Soviet Russian Literature: Prose Fiction 1975–1991*. New York, 1993.

Brown, Edward J. *Russian Literature Since the Revolution*. Cambridge, MA, 1982.

Clowes, Edith W. *Russian Experimental Fiction. Resisting Ideology After Utopia*. Princeton, 1993.

Epshtein, Mikhail N. *After the Future. The Paradoxes of Postmodernism and Contemporary Russian Culture*. Amherst, MA, 1995.

– *Postmodern v Rossii: Literatura i teoriia*. Moscow, 2000.

Fed', N.M. *Opavshie list'ia. Russkaia literatura kontsa XX veka*. Moscow, 2000.

Glintershchik, Roza. *Sovremennye russkie pisateli-postmodernisty. Ocherki noveishei russkoi literatury*. Kaunas, 2000.

Graham, Shelagh D. *New Directions in Soviet Literature.* New York, 1992.

Leiderman, N.L., and M.N. Lipovetskii. *Sovremennaia russkaia literatura.* 3 vols. Moscow, 2001.

Lilly, Ian K. and Henrietta Mondry, eds. *Russian Literature in Transition.* Nottingham, 1999.

Kuritsyn, Viacheslav. *Russki literaturnyi postmodernism.* Moscow, 2000.

Laird, Sally. *Voices of Russian Literature: Interviews with Ten Contemporary Writers.* New York, 1999.

Lipovetskii, Mark. *Russian Postmodernist Fiction: Dialogue with Chaos.* Armonk, NY, 1999.

McMillin, Arnold B., ed. *Reconstructing the Canon: Russian Writing in the 1980s.* Amsterdam, 2000.

Nemzer, Andrei. *Literaturnoe segodnia. O russkoi proze. 90–e.* Moscow, 1998.

Olcott, Anthony. *Russian Pulp: The Detektiv and the Russian Way of Crime.* London, 2001.

Parthe, Kathleen. *Russian Village Prose: The Radiant Past.* Princeton, 1992.

Peterson, Nadya L. *Subversive Imaginations. Fantastic Prose and the End of Soviet Literature, 1970s–1990s.* Boulder, CO, 1997.

Shneidman, N.N. *Soviet Literature in the 1980s: Decade of Transition.* Toronto, 1989.

– *Russian Literature 1988–1994: The End of an Era.* Toronto, 1995.

Skoropanova, I.S. *Russkaia postmodernistskaia literatura.* Moscow, 1999.

Russian Prose Fiction, 1995–2002

Aitmatov, Chingiz. *Tavro Kassandry. /Iz eresei XX veka/* (The Brand of Cassandra) (From the Heresies of the XXth Century). 1994.

Astaf'ev, Viktor. 'Tak khochetsia zhit'' (What a Desire to Live). 1995.

– 'Oberton' (Overtone). 1996.

– 'Veselyi soldat' (The Happy Soldier). 1998.

– 'Trofeinaia pushka' (A Trophy Cannon). 2001.

– 'Zhestokie romansy' (Cruel Romances). 2001.

Azol'skii, Anatolii. *Kletka* (Cage). 1996.

– *Monakhi* (Monks). 2000.

– *Diversant* (Saboteur). 2002.

Baklanov, Grigorii. 'Moi general' (My General). 1999.

Belov, Vasilii. *Chas shestyi* (The Sixth Hour). 1999.

Bondarev, Iurii. *Neprotivlenie* (Non-Resistance). 2000.

– *Bermudskii treugol'nik* (The Bermuda Triangle). 1999.

Borodin, Leonid. *Triki, ili khronika zlobnykh dnei* (The Three 'K's, or the Chronicle of the Wicked Days). 1998.

- 'Povest' o liubvi, podvigakh i prestupleniiakh starshiny Nefedova' (A Tale About the Love, Exploits, and Crimes of Sergeant-Major Nefedov). 1999.

Borodynia, Aleksandr. *Besy* (Devils). 1997.

Buida, Iurii. *Ermo* (Ermo). 1996.

- *Boris i Gleb* (Boris and Gleb). 1997.
- *Prusskaia nevesta* (The Prussian Bride). 1998.
- 'Summa odinochestva' (The Sum of Loneliness). 1998.
- 'U koshki deviat' smertei. Povest' v rasskazakh' (The Cat Has Nine Deaths: A Narrative in Stories). 2000.

Butov, Mikhail. *Svoboda* (Freedom). 1999.

- 'V kar'ere' (In the Quarry). 2002.

Dmitriev, Andrei. 'Povorot reki' (The Turn of the River). 1995.

- 'Doroga obratno' (The Road Back). 2001.

Ekimov, Boris. 'Fetisych' (Fetisych). 1996.

- 'Vozvrashchenie' (The Return). 1998.
- 'V stepi' (In the Steppe). 1998.
- 'Pinochet' (Pinochet). 1999.

Ermakov, Oleg. *Svirel' vselennoi* (The Reed-Pipe of the Universe). 1997–9.

Erofeev, Viktor. *Piat' rek zhizni (roman reka)* (Five Rivers of Life [A Novel River]). 1998.

- *Entsiklopediia russkoi dushi. Roman entsiklopediia* (The Encyclopaedia of the Russian Soul: A Novel with an Encyclopaedia). 1999.
- *Muzhchiny* (Men). 1999.

Evtushenko, Evgenii. *Volchii pasport* (Blacklisted Passport). 1998.

Gandlevskii, Sergei. 'Trepanatsiia cherepa. Istoriia bolezni' (Trepanation of the Skull: A Medical Case History). 1995.

- *NRZB* (NRZB). 2002.

Gorlanova, Nina. *Nel'zia, mozhno, nel'zia. Roman-monolog* (Impossible, Possible, Impossible: A Novel Monologue). 2002.

Gorlanova, Nina, and Viacheslav Bukur. *Roman vospitaniia* (A Novel About Education). 1995.

- 'Afrorossianka' (Afro-Russian). 2002.
- 'Storozhevye zapiski' (A Janitor's Notes). 2002.

Iskander, Fazil'. 'Sofichka' (Sofichka). 1997.

- 'Poet' (Poet). 1998.
- 'Kozy i Shekspir' (The Goats and Shakespeare). 2001.
- 'Dumaiushchii o Rossii i amerikanets' (One Thinking About Russia and an American). 1997.
- 'Son o Boge i d'iavole' (A Dream About God and the Devil), 2002.

Kabakov, Aleksandr. *Poslednii geroi* (The Last Hero). 1995.

- *Schitaetsia pobeg* (It Is Considered an Escape). 2001.

Kaledin, Sergei. 'Takhana merkazit' (Central Station). 1996.

Kharitonov, Mark. *Vozvrashchenie niotkuda* (The Return from Nowhere). 1995.

Kim, Anatolii. *Onliriia* (Onliriia). 1995.

- 'Moe proshloe' (My Past). 1998.
- 'Stena. Povest' nevidimok' (The Wall: A Story of Invisible Beings). 1998.
- *Ostrov Iony* (The Island of Jonah). 2001.

Kononov, Nikolai. *Pokhorony kuznechika* (The Funeral of the Grasshopper).
    2000.

Krupin, Vladimir. 'Liubi menia, kak ia tebia' (Love Me, as I Love You). 1998.

Kuraev, Mikhail. 'Razreshite proiavit' zrelost' (Please, Permit to Display
    Maturity). 2000.

Kurchatkin, Anatoliii. 'Schast'e Veniamina L.' (The Luck of Benjamin L.). 2000.

- 'Sfinks' (Sphinx). 2000.
- *Amazonka* (The Amazon). 2002.

Lichutin, Vladimir. *Miledi Rotman* (Milady Rotman). 2001.

Limonov, Eduard. *Palach* (The Executioner). 1998.

- *Smert' sovremennykh geroev* (The Death of Contemporary Heroes). 1998.
- *316, punkt 'V'* (316, Point 'V'). 1998.
- *Kniga mertvykh* (The Book of the Dead). 2000.
- *V plenu u mertvetsov* (Imprisoned by the Dead). 2002.

Lipskerov, Dmitrii. *Sorok let Chanchzhoe* (Forty Years of Chanchzhoe). 1996.

- *Poslednii son razuma* (The Last Dream of Reason). 2000.

Makanin, Vladimir. 'Kavkazskii plennyi' (A Captive in the Caucasus). 1995.

- *Andergraund, ili Geroi nashego vremeni* (Underground, or the Hero of Our
    Times). 1998.
- 'Bukva 'A'.' (Letter 'A'). 2000.
- 'Odnodnevnaia voina' (One-Day War). 2001.

Mamleev, Iurii. *Chernoe zerkalo* (Black Mirror: Collection of Prose). 1999.

Melikhov, Aleksandr. *Roman s prostatitom* (A Novel with a Prostate). 1997.

- *Nam tselyi mir chuzhbina* (We Are Strangers in the Whole World). 2000.
- *Liubov' k otecheskim grobam* (The Love of Paternal Graves). 2001.

Morozov, Aleksandr. 'Chuzhie pis'ma' (Someone Else's Letters). 1997.

Palei, Marina. *Mesto rozhdeniia vetra* (The Wind's Birth Place). 1998.

Pavlov, Oleg. *Delo Matiushina* (The Case of Matiushin). 1997.

- *Stepnaia kniga* (Book of the Steppe). 1998.
- *Karagandinskie deviatiny, ili Povest' poslednikh dnei* (Karaganda Commemora-
    tions, or a Tale of the Last Days). 2001.
- 'V bezbozhnykh pereulkakh' (In the Godless Alleys). 2001.

Pelevin, Viktor. *Chapaev i Pustota* (Chapaev and Void). 1996.

- *Generation 'P'* (Generation 'P'). 1999.

Petrushevskaia, Liudmila. 'Belye doma' (White Houses). 1996.
- 'Laila i Mara' (Laila and Mara). 1996.
- 'Mladshii brat' (The Younger Brother). 1996.
- 'Dom s fontanom' (The House with a Fountain). 2000.
- 'Dva boga' (Two Gods). 2000.
- 'Naidi menia, son' (Find Me, Sleep). 2000.
- 'Zapadnia' (A Trap). 2000.
- 'Detskii prazdnik' (Children's Holiday). 2000.
P'etsukh, Viacheslav. *Gosudarstvennoe ditia* (The Child of the State). 1997.
- 'Kryzhovnik' (Gooseberries). 2002.
Polianskaia, Irina. *Prokhozhdenie teni* (The Passing of a Shadow). 1997.
- *Chitaiushchaia voda* (The Reading Water). 1999.
- *Gorizont sobytii* (The Horizon of Events). 2002.
Popov, Evgenii. *Podlinnaia istoriia 'zelenykh muzykantov'* (The True History of the 'Green Musicians'). 1999.
Prokhanov, Aleksandr. *Chechenskii bliuz* (The Chechen Blues). 1998.
- *Krasno-korichnevyi roman* (The Red-Brown Novel). 1999.
- *Idushchie v nochi* (Those Walking in the Night). 2001.
- *Gospodin Geksogen* (Mister Hexogen). 2002.
Rasputin, Valentin. 'Po-sosedki' (Neighbourly). 1995.
- 'V tu zhe zemliu ...' (Into the Same Earth). 1995.
- 'Zhenskii razgovor' (Women Talk). 1995.
- 'Nezhdanno-negadanno' (Unexpected and Unsurmised). 1997.
- 'Novaia professiia' (New Profession). 1998.
- 'Izba' (Peasant House). 1999.
Sergeev, Andrei. *Al'bom dlia marok. Kollektsia liudei, veshchei, slov i otnoshenii (1936–1956)* (Stamp Album: A Collection of People, Things, Words and Relationships [1936–1956]). 1995.
Shcherbakova, Galina. 'Radosti zhizni' (The Joys of Life). 1995.
- 'U nog lezhashchikh zhenshchin' (At the Feet of Lying Women). 1996.
- *Armiia liubovnikov* (An Army of Lovers). 1998.
Shishkin, Mikhail. *Vziatie Izmaila* (The Conquest of Izmail). 1999.
Slapovskii, Aleksei. *Den' deneg* (The Day of Money). 1999.
Slavnikova, Ol'ga. *Strekoza, uvelichennaia do razmerov sobaki* (A Dragon-Fly, Enlarged to the Size of a Dog). 1996.
- *Odin v zerkale* (Alone in the Mirror). 1999.
- 'Bessmertnyi. Povest' o nastoiashchem cheloveke' (The Immortal: A Tale About a Real Man). 2001.
Solzhenitsyn, Aleksandr. 'Na izlomakh. Dvuchastnyi rasskaz' (On the Splinters: A Story of Two Components). 1996.

– 'Adlig Shvenkitten' (Adlig Shvenkitten). 1999.
– 'Zhelabugskie vyselki. Dvuchastnyi rasskaz' (The Zhelabug Settlements: A Story of Two Components). 1999.
Sorokin, Vladimir. *Tridtsataia liubov' Mariny* (The Thirtieth Love of Marina). 1995.
– *Goluboe salo* (Blue Lard). 1999.
– *Pir* (Feast). 2001.
Terekhov, Aleksandr. *Krysoboi* (Exterminators). 1995.
Tokareva, Viktoriia. 'Svoia pravda' (One's Own Truth). 2002.
Tolstaia, Tat'iana. *Kys'* (Kys'). 2000.
Ulitskaia, Liudmila. 'Veselye pokhorony' (The Funeral Party). 1998.
– *Medeia i ee deti. Semeinaia Khronika* (Medeia and Her Children: A Family Chronicle). 1996.
– 'Zver' (The Animal). 1998.
– *Kazus Kukotskogo* (The Kukotskii Case). 2000.
– 'Tsiu-iurikh' (Tsiu-iurich-Zurich). 2002.
Utkin, Anton. *Khorovod* (The Round-Dance). 1996.
– 'Svad'ba za Bugom' (A Wedding on the Other Side of the Bug). 1997.
– *Samouchka* (Self-Taught). 1998.
Varlamov, Aleksei. *Lokh* (Moron). 1995.
– 'Rozhdenie' (Birth). 1995.
– 'Gora' (Hill). 1996.
– *Zatonuvshii kovcheg* (The Sunken Ark). 1997.
– *Kupavna* (Kupavna). 2000.
Vasilenko, Svetlana. *Durochka* (A Little Fool). 1998.
Vishnevetskaia, Marina. 'Uvidet' derevo' (To See a Tree). 1996.
– *Vyshel mesiats iz tumana* (The Moon Appeared from the Fog). 1999.
Vladimov, Georgii. *General i ego armiia* (The General and His Army). 1994.
Volos, Andrei. *Khurramabad* (Khurramabad). 2000.
– *Nedvizhimost'* (Real Estate). 2001.

Russian Writers in English Translation

Aleshkovsky, Peter. *Skunk: A Life*. Trans. by Arch Tait. Moscow, 1997.
Bakin, Dmitry. *Reasons for Living*. Trans. Andrew Bromfield. London, New York, 2002.
Bitov, Andrei. *The Monkey Link: A Pilgrimage Novel*. Trans. Susan Brownsberger. New York, 1995.
Buida, Iurii. *The Zero Train*. Trans. Oliver Ready. London, 2001.
– *The Prussian Bride*. Trans. Oliver Ready. London, 2002.

Dombrovsky, Yuri. *The Faculty of Useless Knowledge.* Trans. A.G. Myers. New York, 1996.

Erofeyev, Victor, and Andrew Reynolds, eds. *The Penguin Book of New Russian Writing.* New York, 1995.

Goscilo, Helena, ed. *Lives in Transit: A Collection of Recent Russian Women's Writing.* Dana Point, CA, 1995.

Iskander, Fazil'. *The Old House Under the Cypress Tree.* Trans. Jan Butler. London, 1996.

Kagal, Ayesha, and Natasha Perova, eds. *Present Imperfect: Stories by Russian Women.* Boulder, CO, 1996.

Kharitonov, Mark. *Lines of Fate: A Novel.* Trans. Helena Goscilo. New York, 1996.

Khvoshchinskaia, Nadezhda. *The Boarding School* Girl. Trans. Karen Rosnek. Evanston, IL. 2000.

Makanin, Vladimir. *Baize-Covered Table with Decanter.* Trans. Arch Tait. London, 1995.

– *Escape Hatch and The Long Road Ahead.* Trans. Ann Szporluk. Ann Arbor, Mich. 1996.

– *The Loss: A Novella and Two Short Stories.* Trans. Byron Lindsey. Evanston, IL. 1998.

Pelevin, Viktor. *The Life of Insects.* Trans. Andrew Bromfield. London, 1996.

– *The Blue Lantern and Other Stories.* Trans. Andrew Bromfield. New York, 1997.

– *A Werewolf Problem in Central Russia and Other Stories.* Translated by Andrew Bromfield. New York, 1998.

– *The Clay Machine-Gun.* Trans. Andrew Bromfield. London, 1999.

– *Buddah's Little Finger.* Trans. Andrew Bromfield. New York, 2000.

– *Homo Zapiens.* Trans. Andrew Bromfield, New York, 2002.

Petrushevskaia, Liudmila. *Immortal Love.* Trans. Sally Laird. London, 1995.

Rasputin, Valentin. *Siberia, Siberia.* Trans. Margaret Winchell and Gerald Mikkelson. Evanston, IL, 1996.

Sadur, Nina. *Witch's Tears and Other Stories.* Trans. Cathy Porter. London, 1997.

Tolstaya, Tatyana. *Pushkin's Children.* Trans. Jamey Gambrell. Boston, 2003.

– *The Slynx.* Trans. Jamey Gambrell. Boston, 2003.

Ulitskaya, Ludmila. *The Funeral Party.* Trans. Cathy Porter. London, 1999.

– *Medea and Her Children.* Trans. Arch Tait. New York, 2001.

Vasilenko, Svetlana. *Shamara and Other Stories.* Trans. Andrew Bromfield, Helena Goscilo, et al. Evanston, IL, 2000.

Verbitskaya, Anastasya. *Keys to Happiness.* Trans. Beth Holmgren and Helena Goscilo. Bloomington, Ind. 1999.

Volos, Andrei. *Hurramabad.* Trans. Arch Tait. Chicago, 2001.

Index

Ageev, Aleksandr, 19
Aitmatov, Chingiz, vii, 29, 34; 'Belyi parakhod' (The White Steamship), 30, 33; *Plakha* (Execution Block), 30; 'Proshchai, Gul'sary!' (Farewell, Gul'sary!), 30, 33; *Tavro Kassandry* (The Brand of Cassandra), 30–4
Aizenberg, Mikhail, 167
Aksenov, Vasilii, viii, 60
Akunin, Boris, 18, 156, 159–62; *Azazel'* (Azazel'), 160; *Koronatsiia, ili poslednii iz Romanovykh* (Coronation, or the Last Romanov), 161; *Lefiatan* (Leviathan), 162; *Statskii sovetnik* (Councillor of the State), 160–1
Amnesty International, 48
Anan'ev, Anatolii, 11, 29
Anashkevich, Marina, 111
Andropov, Iurii, 48, 101
Anninskii, Lev, 19
Anti-Booker Prize, 161, 180
Arkhangel'skii, Aleksandr, 19
Astaf'ev, Viktor, viii, 11, 21–2, 29, 34–7; *Do budushchei vesny* (Until Next Spring), 34; 'Oberton' (Overtone), 35; *Pechal'nyi detektiv* (A Sad Detective Story), 34; *Poslednii srok* (The Last Respects), 34; *Prokliaty i ubity* (The Cursed and the Slain), 34; 'Tak khochetsia zhit'' (What a Desire to Live), 35; 'Trofeinaia pushka' (A Trophy Cannon), 36; *Tsar'-ryba* (Queen Fish), 34; 'Veselyi soldat' (The Happy Soldier), 36; 'Zhestokie romansy' (Cruel Romances), 36
avant-garde, 16
Azol'skii, Anatolii, viii, 21, 37–9; *Kletka* (Cage), 21, 37; *Monakhi* (Monks), 38

Babaevskii, Semen, 60
Baklanov, Grigorii, 11, 22, 29, 39–40; 'Moi general' (My General), 39
Basaev, Shamil', 144–6
Basinskii, Pavel, 19, 95–6, 106
Bavil'skii, Dmitrii, 19
Belov, Vasilii, 6–7, 9, 11, 13, 133; *Chas shestyi* (The Sixth Hour), 133–4; *God velikogo pereloma. Khronika deviati mesiatsev* (The Year of Great Change: A Chronicle of Nine

Months), 134; *Kanuny. Khronika kontsa 20-kh godov* (Eves: A Chronicle of the Late 1920s), 134; 'Privychnoe delo' (That's How It Is), 133–4
Belyi, Andrei, Prize, 22
Bezrodnyi, Mikhail, 22
Bibikhin, Vladimir, 22
Bitov, Andrei, 6, 11, 16, 22, 183
Bogomolov, V., 50
Bolshevik, 43, 47
Bondarenko, Vladimir, 7
Bondarev, Iurii, 6, 11, 29, 133, 135, 146; *Bermudskii treugol'nik* (The Bermuda Triangle), 137; *Iskushenie* (Temptation), 135; *Neprotivlenie* (Non-Resistance), 135–7
Booker Russian Novel Prize, vii, 15, 20, 21, 37, 44, 48, 73, 81, 83, 92, 95, 99–100, 113, 120, 126–7, 169–70, 173, 175
Borodin, Leonid, 7, 23, 52–5; 'Povest' o liubvi, podvigakh i prestupleniakh starshiny Nefedova' (A Tale About the Love, Exploits, and Crimes of Sergeant-Major Nefedov), 54–5; 'Povest' strannogo vremeni' (The Story of a Strange Time), 53; *Triki, ili khronika zlobnykh dnei* (The Three 'K's, or the Chronicle of the Wicked Days), 53–5; 'Vstrecha' (The Meeting), 53
Brezhnev, Leonid, 13, 37, 41, 63, 76, 78, 98, 108, 120, 122, 128, 150
Brodskii, Iosif, 44, 63
Buida, Iurii, viii, 16, 80–3, 105; *Boris i Gleb* (Boris and Gleb), 82; 'Don-Domino' (The Zero Train), 81; *Ermo* (Ermo), 81–2; *Prusskaia nevesta* (The Prussian Bride), 82;

'Shkola russkogo rasskaza' (The School of the Russian Story), 83; 'Summa odinochestva' (The Sum of Loneliness), 82–3; 'U koshki deviat' smertei. Povest' v rasskazakh' (The Cat Has Nine Deaths: A Narrative in Stories), 83
Bukur, Viacheslav, 112–13; 'Afrorossiianka' (Afro-Russian), 113; *Roman vospitaniia* (A Novel About Education), 112; 'Storozhevye zapiski' (A Janitor's Notes), 112
Bulgakov, Mikhail, 60, 82
Bunin, Ivan, 81
Butov, Mikhail, viii, 12, 16, 21, 80, 83–5; *Svoboda* (Freedom), 21, 83–5; 'V kar'ere' (In the Quarry), 84–5
Bykov, Dmitrii, 19, 105
Bykov, Vasil', 145, 149; 'Sotnikov' (Sotnikov), 145
Byron, Lord, 41
byt (everyday city life), 14, 18, 117–18, 128

Chapaev, Dmitrii, 93–5
Chernichenko, Iurii, 8
Chikin, Valentin, 10
Chuprinin, Sergei, 19
communism, 4, 31, 47, 147–8; Communist Party, 3, 6, 10, 29, 44, 103, 135, 154, 178; communist ideology, 9; communist regime, 18, 47, 50; communist rule, 182; pro-communist, 140
conceptualism, 16, 103; conceptualist art, 102–3

Dante, 81
Dashkova, Polina, 18, 111, 156, 162–3;

Efirnoe vremia (Broadcasting Time), 163; *Zolotoi pesok* (Gold Sand), 163

Davydov, Iurii, 11

Den' i noch' (Day and Night), Krasnoiarsk, 26

Den' literature (The Day of Literature), Moscow, 7

Dmitriev, Andrei, ix, 12, 16, 165–7; 'Doroga obratno' (The Road Back), 166–7; 'Povorot reki' (The Turn of the River), 165–6; 'Voskoboev i Elizaveta' (Voskoboev and Elizaveta), 165

Don (Don), Rostov, 26

Dontsova, Dar'ia, 18, 111, 156

Dostoevskii, Fedor, 34, 156

Druzhba narodov (Friendship of Peoples), 27

Ekimov, Boris, viii, 14, 22, 55–8, 168; 'Fetisych'' (Fetisych'), 55–6; 'Ocherki nashikh dnei' (Sketches of Our Days), 58; 'Pinochet' (Pinochet), 14, 57; 'Vozvrashchenie' (The Return), 56; 'V stepi' (In the Steppe), 56–7; 'Zhiteiskie melochi' (Everyday Stories), 58

Ermakov, Oleg, 12–13, 80, 85–6, 184; *Svirel' vselennoi* (The Reed-Pipe of the Universe), 85–6; *Znak zveria* (Sign of the Beast), 85

Erofeev, Viktor, 6, 52, 58–62; *Entsiklopediia russkoi dushi. Roman entsiklopediia* (The Encyclopaedia of the Russian Soul: A Novel with an Encyclopaedia), 60–1; *Muzhchiny* (Men), 59–60; *Piat' rek zhizni* (Five Rivers of Life), 59; 'Pominki po sovetskoi literature' (A Funeral Feast for Soviet Literature), 58; 'Popugaichik' (Parakeet), 58; *Russkaia krasavitsa* (Russian Beauty), 58

Evseev, Boris, 32

Evtushenko, Evgenii, 6, 8, 15, 60, 62–4, 112; *Iagodnye mesta* (Wild Berries), 62; *Ne umirai prezhde smerti* (Don't Die Before Your Death), 62; *Volchii pasport* (Blacklisted Passport), 62–4

Faibisovich, Semen, 167

Gabyshev, Leonid, 80

Galina, Mariia, 126

Galkovskii, Dmitrii, 16

Gandlevskii, Sergei, ix, 12, 15, 21, 112, 165, 167–70; *NRZB* (NRZB), 21, 169–70; 'Trepanatsiia cherepa' (Trepanation of the Skull), 21, 167–9

Gasparov, Mikhail, 21

Gavrilov, Anatolii, 11

Gershtein, Emma, 22

Gestapo, 37–8

Girshovich, Leonid, viii

glasnost', 3, 34, 86, 124

Glintershchik, Roza, 17, 95

Goldshtein, Aleksandr, 21

Golyshev, V.P., 22

Gorbachev, Mikhail, 3, 30, 34, 44, 48, 53, 62, 75–6, 80, 87, 90, 106, 124, 135, 140, 149, 162; post-Gorbachev, 163; pre-Gorbachev, 167

Gorlanova, Nina, 15, 17, 111–13; 'Afrorossiianka' (Afro-Russian), 113; *Nel'zia, mozhno, nel'zia. Roman-monolog* (Possible, Impossible, Possible: A Novel Monologue), 112; *Roman vospitaniia* (A Novel About

Education), 112; 'Storozhevye
  zapiski' (A Janitor's Notes), 112
Gorenshtein, Fridrikh, 11
Grani (Borders), 48
Granin, Daniil, 22
Grekova, I., 11
Grigor'ev, Apollon, Prize, 22

Hitler, Adolf, 49, 104

Iskander, Fazil', 40–2; 'Dumaiush-
  chii o Rossii i amerikanets' (One
  Thinking About Russia and an
  American), 41; 'Kozy i Shekspir'
  (The Goats and Shakespeare), 42;
  'Poet' (Poet), 41; *Sandro iz Chegema*
  (Sandro of Chegem), 40; 'Sofichka'
  (Sofichka), 40
Ivanchenko, Aleksandr, 12, 80
Ivanova, Natal'ia, 19, 126
Izvestiia (News), 19

Kabakov, Aleksandr, 12, 86–9; 'Den'
  iz zhizni gluptsa' (A Day in the
  Life of a Fool), 88; *Nevozvrash-
  chenets* (No Return), 87; *Poslednii
  geroi* (The Last Hero), 87, 89; *Pozd-
  nii gost'. Istoriia neudachi* (The Late
  Guest: A History of Failure), 88
Kafka, Franz, 172
Kaledin, Sergei, 12, 80, 89–90; 'Pop
  i rabotnik' (The Priest and the
  Worker), 89; 'Smirennoe kladbish-
  che' (The Humble Cemetery), 89;
  'Stroibat' (Construction Battalion),
  89; 'Takhana merkazit' (Central
  Station), 89–90
Kennedy, Jacqueline, 63
Kennedy, Robert, 63
Kenzheev, Bakhit, 167

Khasbulatov, Ruslan, 142
Khrushchev, Nikita, 104
Kibirov, Timur, 167
Kim, Anatolii, viii, 11, 64–8; *Onliriia*
  (Onliriia), 65–6, 68; *Ostrov Iony*
  (The Island of Jonah), 67–8; 'Stena.
  Povest' nevidimok' (The Wall: A
  Story of Invisible Beings), 66–7
Kireev, Ruslan, 11
Knizhnoe obozrenie (Review of Books),
  159
Koksheneva, Kapitolina, 9
Komsomol (Young Communist
  League), 14, 44, 98
Kononov, Nikolai, 12, 27, 165, 170–1;
  Pokhorony kuznechika (The Funeral
  of a Grasshopper), 170–1
Kontinent (Continent), 27
Koretskii, Daniil, 156, 163–4; *Oper po
  prozvishchu 'Starik'* (The Detective
  Nicknamed 'Old Man'), 163;
  Smiagchaiushchie obstoiatel'stva
  (Mitigating Circumstances), 163–4;
  'Zaderzhanie' (Arrest), 163–4
Korkin, Vladimir, 32–3
Kornilov, Vladimir, 11
Korolev, Andrei, 11
Kostyrko, Sergei, 19, 27
Koval', Iurii, 175
Kuraev, Mikhail, 11, 22, 80, 90–1;
  'Razreshite proiavit' zrelost''
  (Please, Permit to Display Matu-
  rity), 90–1
Krupin, Vladimir, 6, 11, 137–8; 'Liubi
  menia, kak ia tebia' (Love Me, as I
  Love You), 137–8
Kurchatkin, Anatolii, 11, 68–70; *Ama-
  zonka* (The Amazon), 69–70;
  'Schast'e Veniamina L.' (The Luck
  of Benjamin L.), 68–9; 'Sfinks'

(Sphinx), 69; 'Zapiski ekstremista' (Notes of an Extremist), 68
Kuritsyn, Viacheslav, 19, 27, 105
Kuz'min, Dmitrii, 27
Kuzminskii, Boris, 27
Kuznetsov, Sergei, 27

Latynina, Alla, 18, 126
Lavrin, Aleksandr, 11
Lebed', General Aleksandr, 141
Leiderman, N.L., 17, 50, 96
Lenin, Vladimir, 134
Lermontov, Mikhail, 60
Lichutin, Vladimir, 6, 133, 138–9; *Miledi Rotman* (Milady Rotman), 138–9
Limonov, Eduard, viii, 9, 52, 70–2, 147; *316, punkt 'V'* (316, Point 'V'), 71; *Kniga mertvykh* (The Book of the Dead), 72; *Palach* (The Executioner), 70–1; *Smert' sovremennykh geroev* (The Death of Contemporary Heroes), 71
Lipovetskii, M.N., 17, 50, 96
Lipskerov, Dmitrii, ix, 12, 171–2; *Poslednii son razuma* (The Last Dream of Reason), 172; *Sorok let Chanchzhoe* (Forty Years of Chanchzhoe), 171–2
Lisnianskaia, Inna, 22
Literaturnaia gazeta (Literary Gazette), 7–8, 25, 96, 147, 161
Literaturnaia Rossiia (Literary Russia), 6, 8
'Little Booker' Prize, 21, 22, 92, 167
Lobanov, Mikhail, 49–50
Lukashenko, Aleksandr, 149

Makanin, Vladimir, viii, 6, 17, 20, 22, 72–9; *Andergraund, ili Geroi nashego vremeni* (Underground, or the Hero of Our Times), 74–8; 'Bukva "A"' (Letter 'A'), 78; 'Kavkazskii plennyi' (A Captive in the Caucasus), 73–4; 'Odnodnevnaia voina' (One-Day War), 78–9; *Priamaia liniia* (The Straight Line), 72; 'Stol pokrytyi suknom i s grafinom poseredine' (Cloth-Covered Table with Carafe in the Middle), 20, 73
Maksimov, Vladimir, 45
Marinina, Aleksandra, 18, 111, 156–9, 162; *Ne meshaite palachu* (Do Not Interfere with the Executioner), 156–7; *Sed'maia zhertva* (The Seventh Victim), 157–8; *Tot, kto znaet* (The One Who Knows), 158–9
Marquez, Gabriel Garcia, 63
Marxism-Leninism, 90–1, 137, 182; Marxist ideology, 9
Melikhov, Aleksandr, 80, 91–2, 112; *Izgnanie iz Edema: ispoved' evreia* (The Exile from Eden: The Confession of a Jew), 91; *Liubov' k otecheskim grobam* (The Love of Paternal Graves), 91–2; *Nam tselyi mir chuzhbina* (We Are Strangers in the Whole World), 91; *Roman s prostatitom* (A Novel with a Prostate), 91
Metropol' (Metropol'), 58, 98
Mikhalkov, Sergei, 8
Milosovic, Slobodan, 22
Molodaia gvardiia (Young Guard), 6, 25
Molotov, Viacheslav, 60
Morozov, Aleksandr, 21; 'Chuzhie pis'ma' (Someone Else's Letters), 21
Moskva (Moscow), 7, 25, 53

Nabokov, Vladimir, 81
Narbikova, Valeriia, 11, 12, 17, 80
Nash sovremennik (Our Contemporary), 6
National Bestseller Prize, 22, 146–7
Nemzer, Andrei, 19, 38, 50, 65, 82, 95
Neva (Neva), 25
Nevskii, Aleksandr, Prize, 22
Nosov, Evgenii, 11
Novikov, Vl. 19
Novyi mir (New World), 11, 21, 25, 27, 37, 45, 48, 65, 73, 78, 83, 95, 112, 115, 127–8, 130, 177

Okean (Ocean), Vladivostok, 26
Oktiabr' (October), 11, 25, 27
Okudzhava, Bulat, 20; *Uprazdnennyi teatr* (The Closed-Down Theatre), 20

Palei, Marina, 12, 27
Pasternak, Boris, 43, 63, 82
Pavlov, Maksim, 95
Pavlov, Oleg, 7, 12, 19, 74, 165, 172–5, 184; *Delo Matiushina* (The Case of Matiushin), 173–4; *Karagandinskie deviatiny* (Karaganda Commemorations), 21, 175; 'Rasskazy iz *Stepnoi knigi*' (Stories from the Book of the Steppe), 174; 'Velikaia step' (The Great Steppe), 174; 'V bezbozhnykh pereulkakh' (In the Godless Alleys), 175
Pelevin, Valentin, viii, 12–13, 16, 80, 92–7, 184; *Chapaev i Pustota* (Chapaev and Void), 92; *Generation 'P'*, 94; *Sinii fonar'* (Blue Lamp), 92
perestroika, viii, 3, 11–12, 53, 58, 68, 77, 80, 85–6, 89, 91, 97–8, 106, 111, 116,

124, 126, 135, 137, 193; post-*perestroika*, 110; pre-*perestroika*, 150
Petrushevskaia, Liudmila, 16–17, 116–18; 'Belye doma' (White Houses), 116; 'Bessmertnaia liubov'' (Immortal Love), 116; 'Dva boga' (Two Gods), 117; 'Detskii prazdnik' (Children's Holiday), 117; 'Dom s fontanom' (The House with a Fountain), 117; 'Laila i Mara' (Laila and Mara), 116; 'Mladshii brat' (The Younger Brother), 116; 'Naidi menia, son' (Find Me, Sleep), 117; 'Zapadnia' (A Trap), 117
P'etsukh, Viacheslav, 11–12, 16, 97–8; *Gosudarstvennoe ditia* (The Child of the State), 97; 'Kryzhovnik' (Gooseberries), 98
Platonov, Andrei, 81, 175
pochvenichestvo (native soil movement), 9, 108
Poliakov, Iurii, 7
Polianskaia, Irina, viii, 12, 17, 111, 113–15; *Chitaiushchaia voda* (The Reading Water), 115; 'Predlagaemye obstoiatel'stva' (Proposed Circumstances), 113; *Prokhozhdenie teni* (The Passing of a Shadow), 113–15
Popov, Evgenii, 16, 98–9; *Podlinnaia istoriia 'zelenykh muzykantov'* (The Real Story of the 'Green Musicians'), 98–9
postmodernism, 16, 96, 102, 173; postmodernist, 17, 84, 102; postmodern approaches, 159; postmodern art, 96–7; postmodern devices, 55, 80, postmodern fiction, 92; postmodern innovations,

173; postmodern narratives, 110; postmodern past, 96
Pravda (Truth), 105, 149
Pristavkin, Anatolii, 11, 29
Prokhanov, Aleksandr, 6, 10, 13, 133, 139–48, 183; *Chechenskii bliuz* (The Chechen Blues), 140–2, 144; *Gospodin Geksogen* (Mister Hexogen), 147–8; *Idushchie v nochi* (Those Walking in the Night), 144–6; *Krasno-korichnevyi roman* (The Red-Brown Novel), 142–4, 147–8
Proskurin, Petr, 11
Pushkin, Aleksandr, 41, 166; Pushkin Prize of Alfred Topfer, 73
Putin, President Vladimir, 4, 10, 144, 146–8

Quinn, Anthony, 96

Rasputin, Valentin, 6–9, 11, 13, 23, 56, 133, 148–53, 183; 'Izba' (Peasant House), 152–3; 'Nezhdanno-negadanno' (Unexpected and Unsurmised), 151–2; 'Novaia professiia' (New Profession), 152; 'Pososedski' (Neighbourly), 151; 'Pozhar" (The Fire), 149; 'Proshchanie s Materoi' (Farewell to Matera), 149–50; 'Zhenskii razgovor' (Women Talk), 150–1; 'V tu zhe zemliu ...' (Into the Same Earth), 151
Rein, Evgenii, 22
Remizova, Mariia, 19, 65, 139
Remnick, David, 63
Revich, Aleksandr, 22
Rodnaia Kuban' (Native Kuban'), Krasnodar, 26
Rodnianskaia, Irina, 19, 95

Roman-gazeta (Novel-Newspaper), 8
Rubin, Dina, viii
Rubinshtein, Lev, 167
Russian Nationalist Bolshevik Party, 9, 72
Russian Orthodox Church, 9, 13, 143, 161, 183
Russkoe ekho (Russian Echo), Samara, 26
Rutskoi, Vice-President Aleksandr, 142

Sadur, Ekaterina, 17
Sadur, Nina, 12, 111
Sakharov, Andrei, 45, 63
samizdat, 5, 26
Semenov, Iulian, 154
Serdiuchenko, V., 32
Sergeev, Andrei, 11, 15, 21, 29, 42–4; *Al'bom dlia marok* (Stamp Album), 15, 21, 42
Shalamov, Varlaam, 44
Shcheglova, Evgeniia, 82
Shcherbakova, Galina, 118–19; *Armiia liubovnikov* (An Army of Lovers), 119; 'Radosti zhizni' (The Joys of Life), 118; 'U nog lezhashchikh zhenshchin' (At the Feet of Lying Women), 118
shestidesiatniki (sixty years old), 11
Shishkin, Mikhail, vii, 12, 21, 80, 99–101; *Vsekh ozhidaet odna noch'* (A Single Night Awaits Us All), 99; *Vziatie Izmaila* (The Conquest of Izmail), 21, 99–101
Sholokhov, Mikhail, 22, 41, 63, 82; *Tikhii Don* (The Quiet Don), 41, 82; The Sholokhov Prize, 22
Sibirskie ogni (The Flames of Siberia), 26

Siniavskii, Andrei, 45

skaz (oral narration), 97, 124, 126

Skoropanova, I.S., 16

Slapovskii, Aleksei, 12, 80, 101–2; *Den' deneg* (The Day of Money), 101–2

Slavnikova, Ol'ga, 12, 14, 17, 19, 11, 119–22, 165; 'Bessmertnyi. Povest' o nastoiashchem cheloveke' (The Immortal: A Tale About a Real Man), 121–2; *Odin v zerkale* (Alone in the Mirror), 14, 120–1; *Strekoza, uvelichennaia do razmerov sobaki* (A Dragon-Fly, Enlarged to the Size of a Dog), 120

Slavophilism, 9, 52–4

Smirnova, Rogneda, 17

socialist realism, 173

Solzhenitsyn, Aleksandr, viii, 22–3, 29, 44–8, 53, 56, 63, 175; 'Adlig Shvenkitten' (Adlig Shvenkitten), 46; *Arkhipelag Gulag* (Gulag Archipelago), 23, 44; *Bodalsia telenok s dubom* (The Calf Butted Against the Oak), 45; *Dvesti let vmeste* (Two Hundred Years Together), 46–7; *Kak nam ob'ustroit' Rossiiu* (How to Arrange Things in Russia), 46; *Krasnoe koleso* (The Red Wheel), 46; 'Matrenin dvor' (Matrena's House), 46; 'Na izlomakh. Dvuchastnyi rasskaz' (On the Splinters: A Story of Two Components), 44–5; *Odin' den' Ivana Denisovicha* (One Day in the Life of Ivan Denisovich), 46; *Rakovyi korpus* (Cancer Ward), 44; *Rossiia v obvale* (Russia in Collapse), 46; *Russkii vopros k kontsu dvadtsatogo veka* (The Russian Question: At the End of the Twentieth Century), 46; *V kruge pervom* (The First Circle), 44; 'Zheliabugskie vyselki. Dvuchastnyi rasskaz' (The Zheliabug Settlements: A Story of Two Components), 46

sorokaletnie (forty years old), 11, 64, 68, 72, 137

Sorokin, Vladimir, viii, 12, 16, 80, 102–6; *Goluboe salo* (Blue Lard), 104; 'Nastia' (Nastia), 104–5; *Ochered'* (The Queue), 102; *Pir* (Feast), 104–5; *Tridtsataia liubov' Mariny* (The Thirtieth Love of Marina), 103; *Vladimir Sorokin* (Vladimir Sorokin), 102; 'Zerkalo' (Mirror), 105

Soros Fund (Institute 'Open Society'), 24

Sovetskaia Rossiia (Soviet Russia), 10

Stalin, Iosif, 49, 51, 55, 60, 104, 134; neo-Stalinist, 9; post-Stalin, 11; Stalinist nostalgia, 148; Stalinist rule, 50, 55, 104, 114, 129; Stalinist Russia, 21, 128

Steinbeck, John, 63

Stepanian, Karen, 19, 100

Struve, Nikita, 45

tamizdat, 5

Terekhov, Aleksandr, 12, 106–7; 'Durachok' (The Little Fool), 106; *Krysoboi* (Exterminators), 106–7

Tokareva, Viktoriia, 123; 'Svoia pravda' (One's Own Truth), 123

Tolstaia, Tat'iana, viii, 12, 17, 123–6, 184; *Kys'* (Kys'), 124–6; *Na zolotom kryl'tse sideli* (On the Golden Porch), 123

Tolstoi, Leo, 32, 68, 73

Toporov, Viktor, 78
Trifonov, Iurii, 21, 76, 119, 169–70
Trotskii, Leon, 47
Tsipko, Aleksandr, 147
Tul'gina, Valentina, 111
Turgenev, Ivan, 104
Turupova, Nina, 111

Ulitskaia, Liudmila, viii, 12, 17, 21, 126–30; *Kazus Kukotskogo* (The Kukotskii Case), 21, 127–9; *Medeia i ee deti. Semeinaia khronika* (Medeia and Her Children: A Family Chronicle), 127; 'Sonechka' (Sonechka), 127; 'Tsiu-iurikh' (Tsiu-iurikh – Zurich), 129–30; 'Veselye pokhorony' (The Funeral Party), 127–8; 'Zver'' (The Animal), 127
Ural (Ural), 26, 27, 120
Utkin, Anton, ix, 12, 16–17, 165, 175–7; *Khorovod* (The Round-Dance), 17, 175–6; *Samouchka* (Self-Taught), 176–7; 'Svad'ba za Bugom' (A Wedding on the Other Side of the Bug), 176

Varlamov, Aleksei, 19, 80, 107–10, 161; 'Gora' (Hill), 108; *Kupavna* (Kupavna), 109–10; *Lokh* (Moron), 107–8; 'Rozhdenie' (Birth), 108; *Zdravstvui, Kniaz'!* (Good Day, Prince!), 107; *Zatonuvshii kovcheg* (The Sunken Ark), 109
Vasilenko, Svetlana, 17, 19, 111, 130–1; *Durochka* (The Little Fool), 130–1
Vigor', Iurii, 152
'village prose,' 9, 13, 34, 55, 133–4, 137–8, 150

Vishnevetskaia, Marina, 12, 17, 111, 131–2, 165; 'Arkhitektor zapiataia ne moi' (Architect Comma not Mine), 132; 'Nachalo' (Beginning), 132; 'Uvidet' derevo' (To See a Tree), 131; 'Vyshel mesiats iz tumana' (The Moon Appeared from the Fog), 131–2
Vladimov, Georgii, viii, 20–1, 29, 48–51; 'Bol'shaia ruda' (The Great Ore), 48; *General i ego armiia* (A General and His Army), 21, 48–51; *Tri minuty molchania* (Three Minutes of Silence), 48; *Vernyi Ruslan* (Faithful Ruslan), 48, 50
Vlasov, General Andrei, 49
Voinovich, Vladimir, viii, 22
Volga (Volga), 26–7
Volos, Andrei, ix, 14, 22, 177–81; *Khurramabad* (Khurramabad), 177–80; *Nedvizhimost'* (Real Estate), 14, 180–1; 'Svoi' (Our Own), 178–9; 'Zavrazh'e' (Zavrazh'e), 179

Warhol, Andy, 70
Writers' Unions, 6–8, 52, 58, 98, 111, 133, 135

Yeltsin, President Boris, 3–4, 10, 47, 108, 140–2, 144, 146–8

Zabolotskii, Nikolai, 43
Zalygin, Sergei, 11, 29
Zamiatin, Evgenii, 44
Zavtra (Tomorrow), 10, 140
Zhukov, General Georgii, 49–50
Znamia (Banner), 21, 25, 27, 48, 78, 95, 99, 131, 177